Democracy in
Latin America

DEMOCRACY IN LATIN AMERICA

Visions and Realities

EDITED BY
SUSANNE JONAS *AND* NANCY STEIN

BERGIN & GARVEY PUBLISHERS
New York • Westport, Connecticut • London

Library of Congress Cataloging-in-Publication Data

Democracy in Latin America : visions and realities / edited by Susanne
    Jonas and Nancy Stein.
        p.   cm.
    ISBN 0–89789–165–1 (lib. bdg. : alk. paper). —ISBN 0–89789–164–3
    (pbk. : alk. paper)
        1. Latin America — Politics and government — 1948–
    2. Representative government and representation — Latin America —
    History — 20th century. 3. Latin America — Economic
    conditions — 1945– 4. United States — Relations — Latin America.
    5. Latin America — Relations — United States. I. Jonas, Susanne,
    1941– . II. Stein, Nancy.
    F1414.2.D4316   1990
    327.7308 — dc20   89–27541

Library of Congress Catalog Card Number: 89–27541
ISBN: 0–89789–165–1
ISBN: 0–89789–164–3 (pbk)

First published in 1990

Bergin & Garvey Publishers. One Madison Avenue, New York, NY 10010
A division of Greenwood Press, Inc.

Printed in the United States of America

The paper used in this book complies with the
Permanent Paper Standard issued by the National
Information Standards Organization (Z39.48–1984).

10 9 8 7 6 5 4 3 2 1

Every reasonable effort has been made to trace the owners of copyright materials in this book,
but in some instances this has proven impossible. The publisher will be glad to receive
information leading to more complete acknowledgments in subsequent printings of the book
and in the meantime extends its apologies for any omissions.

CONTENTS

PREFACE

The two years since the initial publication of this volume have seen many new developments, yet remarkably little structural change, in the hemisphere. The contradictions of the "redemocratization" schemes have become clearer, as crises have worsened in "civilian" regimes compromised with (or run by) counterinsurgency armies. Haiti — briefly a Reagan administration "democratic success story" — exemplifies most dramatically the instability of the model. The experiences of Guatemala and El Salvador — and even some of the Southern Cone "democracies" (such as Argentina and Uruguay) — leave few illusions as to the viability of counterinsurgency states in which "democracy" is reduced to a civilian facade. At the popular level, however, there are genuinely new developments; mass-based social movements are growing more rapidly than ever, even in the face of unmanageable economic crises. Increasingly these movements defy control by even the most repressive state apparatus and begin to develop their own models for popular democracy. Although still incipient, these phenomena open up new alternatives for the future.

In a second arena, Reagan policy — specifically the Reagan Doctrine embodied in the "rollback" policy against Nicaragua — has been discredited by Contragate and weakened by its own internal contradictions. U.S. military aid to the Nicaraguan Contras, at its height in the mid-eighties, has now been suspended, as its destabilizing consequences eventually forced even the staunchest of U.S. allies in Latin and Central America to seek an alternative (hence Contadora and the Central American Peace Accords). The development of a new "relative autonomy" on the part of Latin American governments *vis-à-vis* the United States — an incipient restructuring or redefinition in the terms of U.S. hegemony in the hemisphere — was evidenced as well in Latin American initiatives for new economic policies, for a reincorporation of Cuba into the Inter-American system and the rejection of U.S. interventionism in Panama.

Added to the above are indications of a new "political opening" even within the United States itself. Anti-interventionism among two-thirds of the population (the Vietnam Syndrome) held firm, even under the onslaught of Oliver North. The response to Jesse Jackson's campaign indicated a profound change in many sectors of American public opinion.

If these suggest new possibilities, there are also significant new dangers or risks in the post-Reagan era that lies ahead. Chief among them, in relation to U.S. policy in Latin America, is the possibility of a new bipartisan consensus, no longer able to roll back (literally overthrow by military means) the Nicaraguan government, but equally committed to the ruination of the Nicaraguan revolution through other means (primarily economic) and to the military defeat of opposition/insurgent movements in other countries by any means necessary (El Salvador is the most obvious example). The bipartisan commitment to "drawing the line in El Salvador" is increased by the fact that the ideological Right, while no longer as deeply entrenched in the State Department, for example, is likely to be as active as ever in pressuring the new administration not to permit "another Nicaragua" or "lose" another country.

We think it is necessary to address some of these changes and have therefore added new material (particularly on Nicaragua and Guatemala) and new chapters to our original collection of articles, which appeared in *Contemporary Marxism*, journal of The Institute for the Study of Labor and Economic Crisis, San Francisco.

The Editors
May 1989

INTRODUCTION

Susanne Jonas

The triumph of the Nicaraguan Revolution in 1979 was a living example of popular democracy, forged and won through a popular liberation struggle. The Nicaraguan example, the advances of revolutionary movements elsewhere in Central America, the growth of mass-based movements, and the weakening of several military dictatorships pointed to a possible democratic opening in various Latin American countries.

In fact, the apparent democratic opening was already closing by 1980. The Carter administration, determined not to permit "another Nicaragua," moved decisively against the Farabundo Martí National Liberation Front (FMLN) in El Salvador, abandoned any concern for human rights in favor of a strict security/counterinsurgency focus in Latin America, and more generally revived a Cold War foreign policy toward the socialist world and the Third World. Pressures from the Reagan transition team signaled a further rightward shift in U.S. policy.

But the full import of things to come was not yet clear. Even critics of U.S. policy did not comprehend the extent to which a militant New Right would gain influence in both foreign and domestic policy making in the United States under Reagan. We did not know then that Carter's new Cold War thrusts against Iran, the Soviet Union, Cuba, and El Salvador would be hardened by Reagan into a comprehensive strategy of rollback against Third World revolutionary governments. Above all, few imagined the extremes to which the Reagan administration would go in creating and sustaining the monstrosity that is the Contra force today in Nicaragua, and in moving directly to destabilize and overthrow the Sandinista government.

Today the question of democracy remains central in Latin America — but increasingly complex. Popular democracy is pitted against a "redemocratization" process directed by the counterinsurgents in Washington and Latin America. The short-range outcomes of the struggles between popular/revolutionary and counterinsurgency forces are by no means clear. In nearly every country this struggle is taking place against a backdrop of unprecedented economic crisis, resulting in new social dislocations and political redefinitions. Left and progressive movements in Latin America face a challenge to meet changing conditions with new strategies. Progressive North Americans concerned with Latin America must understand these complexities in the context of the consolidation of the New Right as a force shaping both foreign and domestic U.S. policies. In this introduction, we shall try to indicate some of the main factors relevant to such an understanding.

The most apparent manifestation of redemocratization in Latin America today is the replacement of a military dictatorship with a civilian regime in one country after another. Each of the new civilian governments has a dual character, representing the contradictions between popular demands for democracy and the requirements of counterinsurgency. An example is Haiti today, where massive popular uprisings forced the ouster of Duvalier. Yet the United States finally supported this ouster in order to avoid "another Nicaragua" and to establish a controlled transition (with room even for ex-Duvalier officials). The duality is expressed in Eduardo Galeano's question regarding Uruguay in this volume: "Will the country be a fountain of life, or an elephant cemetery?"

As shown by Latin America's recent history and current realities, the struggle for democracy there cannot be reduced to replacing military with civilian regimes. While military dictatorships are overtly more repressive, the underlying goal in achieving democracy is the destruction of the counterinsurgency state itself. That state apparatus was created in the 1960s in order to defeat and eliminate revolutionary movements threatening to create "more Cubas." Since that time, it has been elaborated with increasing sophistication (most recently, through U.S. strategies of "low-intensity warfare"). In essence, however, its structure and goals remain the same as summarized by Ruy Mauro Marini: It is the corporate state of the monopoly bourgeoisie and the armed forces; its objective is not merely to defeat, but to annihilate "the enemy"; it applies a military focus to all political struggle during the counterinsurgency war; and it "explicitly proposes the reestablishment of bourgeois democracy" after the most intensive military phase of the counterinsurgency campaign.

Thus, under certain conditions, civilian regimes are viewed as more effective agents of pacification than military dictatorships — and recent history has shown the former to be more easily controlled by the United States. Indeed, some of the prototypical counterinsurgency states since the 1960s have been shaped under civilian governments (e.g., Betancourt in Venezuela and Méndez Montenegro in Guatemala). It is not the particularities of military *vs.* civilian rule that stamps the counterinsurgency state but its class character, in Marini's interpretation, as a structure for carrying out bourgeois counterrevolution.

Since the 1960s, the dialectic between the counterinsurgency state and democratic projects of one kind or another has dominated the politics of nearly every country in Latin America. In most countries the counterinsurgency forces have been unable to win definitively, that is, to eradicate the resistance movements. However, they have generally been able to keep the insurgencies at bay. The big exception is the Nicaraguan Revolution, which was democratic not simply in ousting Somoza but also in destroying the Nicaraguan counterinsurgency state and, in a larger sense, in calling into question for the first time since the Cuban Revolution the absoluteness and permanence of bourgeois domination through the counterinsurgency state.

Although this dynamic has been repeated in cycles since the 1960s, there are at least two new conditions. One is the deepening economic crisis and skyrocketing foreign debt in nearly every Latin American country. These factors will significantly modify the contours and modalities of the counterinsurgency state, since the International Monetary Fund (IMF) and international banks play an increasingly central role in formulating policy, leaving the Latin American debtor governments (whether military or civilian) with even less control of their economic and social policies.

The second relatively new development is that the Reagan administration has gone beyond counterinsurgency policies of containing the spread of revolution, and now *sponsors* insurgencies against existing revolutionary governments. This is most evident in Nicaragua, where Reagan's redemocratization amounts to overthrowing the Sandinista government and returning the country to control by traditional bourgeois (including Somocista) forces. The instrumentality for achieving that goal is the CIA-created Contra army. Under the circumstances of economic destabilization and sheer terrorism created by the Contra war, the Nicaraguan Revolution faces a struggle against the forces of reaction on a scale and with stakes as high as the Spanish Republican struggle against fascism in the 1930s.

In a cynical distortion of logic and reality, the Reagan administration argues that rollback is justified against Left-leaning or socialist governments, while right-wing dictatorships are "no threat" to the United States, since they are "inevitably displaced by democracy." This presumes a notion of democracy that is intentionally restricted, managed, or, as James Petras writes, controlled and preemptive of the mounting social protest movements.

The U.S.-supported redemocratization is epitomized by elections that systematically exclude serious opposition parties of the Left. It is epitomized by nominally civilian regimes too timid to defy the power of the military counterinsurgents, or even in most cases to bring them to account for their past crimes against the people. It is epitomized by the Argentine official who deplores the human rights atrocities of the previous military regime, while insisting on the need to preserve the armed forces under the civilian regime (and hoping that they will live up to "the best of their tradition"). Since the military remains in charge of the state repressive apparatus, human rights violations are by no means brought under control. The inherently repressive nature and intentions of the redemocratization project are illustrated by the renewed programs of U.S. police aid and training to civilian governments (reviving the Public Safety programs abolished in the mid-1970s).

Viewed from a broader perspective, beyond U.S. intentions, however, redemocratization in contemporary Latin America reflects a dialectic of advances and setbacks on both sides of the struggle. The Reagan administration's cooptation of "democracy" and the replacement of military dictatorships with elected civilian regimes are in part a response to the decline of U.S. political/ideological hegemony in Latin America (in terms of direct political control) and increasing U.S. isolation internationally. With the failure to control erupting social movements in the 1960s and 1970s and with the steady deepening of the economic crisis and the debt explosion more recently, the United States and its allies have been forced to refashion the control mechanisms in Latin America. This is the defensive component of the U.S. abandonment of right-wing military dictators, longstanding U.S. allies who were no longer able to keep the lid on social protest through sheer repression — from Somoza to Duvalier to Marcos, with Pinochet possibly next.

Nevertheless, redemocratization is also an offensive U.S. posture, part of a reassertion of U.S. political hegemony in Latin America. In this regard, the United States hopes to redefine democracy in terms compatible with its interests, to turn to its advantage even situations created by popular Latin American movements — ultimately, to wrest the initiative from those movements and eliminate class struggle and socialism from the agenda.

For the moment the United States and its Latin American allies appear to have seized the initiative. But how long can this last, and how stable can it be? Since it is designed for the purposes of counterinsurgency, Reagan's redemocratization does not even propose to address the underlying social contradictions and unprecedented economic crises that generate militant social movements in Latin America. In nearly every country, for example, stabilization measures imposed by the IMF and the international banks are being forced upon civilian governments as a condition for obtaining new loans and credits to make payments on old loans. These measures, which mean austerity for the majority of the population, are themselves creating popular protest movements.

Compounding these instabilities is another political contradiction which has emerged time and time again in Latin America: the space opened up by the lessening of overt repression (no matter how slight) is inevitably filled by popular demands for real democracy and justice. We are seeing such a process today in strikes, political mobilizations, and a resurgence of left organizations and guerrilla movements throughout the continent. As protest becomes more militant, however, the civilian governments can be expected to resort increasingly to military force. (The prison massacre by the social democratic García government in Peru is an obvious example.) The counterinsurgents may well have to shed their business suits and don their uniforms once again.

A final destabilizing factor is U.S. rollback policy itself. U.S. aggressiveness and possible overt intervention against Nicaragua threaten to engulf the region in a war. This has prompted Latin American governments — bourgeois, generally pro-U.S. governments, acting out of a concern for their own stability — to challenge U.S. Central America policy. This turn of events brings home the irony that the principal threats to Latin American stability come not from Cuba or Nicaragua, but from the International Monetary Fund and the U.S. government.

Within the United States, progressives face a very particular political problem in relation to the above. It is not a question of needing to be convinced that our foreign policy is wrong and destructive. It is a problem of political praxis: the inability to act on the massive public opposition to an interventionist foreign policy and involvement in another Vietnam-type war in Central America, to translate oppositional opinion into an effective political force for changing policy (as happened in France *vis-à-vis* Algeria, in the United States *vis-à-vis* Vietnam).

One key to this problem, we might suggest, is understanding the forms of repressiveness that flow from the New Right's growing power at the level of influencing public opinion (as well as of formulating policy). Overt repression of oppositional views, red-baiting, browbeating, right-wing targeting, and threatening critics in Congress are combined with more subtle practices which are equally dangerous.

One such practice is the use of the Big Lie to sell Reagan policy to the American public. Given the stubborn endurance of the Vietnam Syndrome and the widespread fear of war among Americans, the administration has been forced to clothe its aggressive international posture in a rhetoric of democracy. The Contras are "freedom fighters," sons of America's Founding Fathers, while the Sandinistas are "terrorists." Increasingly, the policy is built upon a foundation of lies. If the lies are repeated often enough, they will permeate the mass media, opinion in Congress and among moderate Democrats — and general public opinion (if not by changing, then by demobilizing, it).

A second aspect of the New Right's attempt to establish ideological dominance in the realm of public opinion is its denial of — in fact, its open attack upon — pluralism. Certain ideas and perspectives are being progressively eliminated from the spectrum of political debate in the United States. There is a literal blotting-out of any perspective that is sympathetic to the Third World, defends the right of popular sovereignty, or even attempts to explain Third World realities in all their complexity.

A further consequence of the New Right's antipluralism, and of the great extension of its power, is a more generalized restrictiveness on the flow of information and ideas. This "chilling effect" — often self-imposed — can be seen, for example, in the dearth of oppositional voices in the major mass media. To take one example: Tom Wicker and Anthony Lewis may continue to voice independent views in their columns, but these views appear to find little echo in *New York Times* editorial policy.

At a time when lies have become the stock-in-trade of public information in the United States and are pervasive enough to overwhelm (or confuse) even some critics of U.S. policy, careful analyses written by committed scholars from both Latin and North America can be vital in combatting the right wing's near-monopoly on ideas. At a time, further, when American foreign policy is racist (in its underlying hatred and fear of the Third World) and truly imperial (in its disdain for Third World sovereignty), it becomes especially important to provide a forum for Latin American perspectives on the problems of Latin America.

Finally, it is our hope that leading Latin American and U.S. scholars can help break through the ideological roadblocks and build a bridge of understanding between the Third World and progressives in the United States — a bridge that is increasingly important to the efficacy of progressive and anti-interventionist efforts in the United States. We are privileged to present such scholars in this volume.

1

THE DICTATORSHIP AND ITS AFTERMATH: THE SECRET WOUNDS

Eduardo Galeano

THE SYMBOLS

A lot of ash has fallen on this purple land. During the twelve years of military dictatorship, Liberty was no more than the name of a plaza and a prison. In that prison, the largest cage for political prisoners, it was against the rules to draw pregnant women, birds, butterflies, and stars; the prisoners could not speak, whistle, laugh, sing, walk quickly, or greet one another without permission. But everyone was imprisoned, except for the jailers and the exiles: three million prisoners, even if the jails seemed to hold only a few thousand. One out of every eighty Uruguayans had a hood pulled over his head, but invisible hoods covered the rest as well, condemned to isolation and incommunication, even if they were spared the torture. Fear and silence became a mandatory way of life. The dictatorship, enemy of all that grows and moves, paved over whatever grass it could trap in the plazas and cut down or painted white any trees within range.

THE MODEL

With slight variations, a similar model of repression and prevention against the forces of social change was applied in several Latin American countries during the 1970s. In enforcing the Pan-American doctrine of national security, the military acted as occupying armies in their own countries, as the armed force of the International Monetary Fund and of the system of privilege which the Fund embodies and perpetuates. The guerrilla threat provided the alibi for state terrorism, which set its wheels in motion to cut workers' salaries in half, crush unions, and suppress critical thought. By spreading massive terror and uncertainty, they hoped to impose a reign of the deaf-mute. The computer at the Joint Chiefs of Staff of the Armed Forces placed all Uruguayan citizens into one of three categories, A, B, or C, according to the degree of danger they presented to the planned military kingdom of the sterile. Without the Certificate of Democratic Faith, provided by that computer and delivered by the police — specialists in Democracy, having taken courses from Dan Mitrione, U.S. Professor of Torture Techniques — one could neither obtain employment nor keep it. Even to have a birthday party, police authorization was required. Every house was a cell; every factory, every office, every school became a concentration camp.

THE AGGRESSION

The dictatorship demolished the system of education and in its place imposed a system of ignorance. By brutally replacing professors and programs, the attempt was made to domesticate students and oblige them to accept both the barracks morality which calls sex *hygienic outlet* or *marital duty* and the mummified culture which considers *natural* the right of property over things and people, as well as the duty of women to obey men, children to obey their parents, the poor to obey the rich, blacks to obey whites, and civilians to obey the military.

The order was given to dismember and detongue the country. All ties of solidarity and creativeness that brought Uruguayans into contact with one another were a crime; a conspiracy, all that brought them into contact with the world; and subversive, any word that did not lie. All who took part were punished — political and union activists and whoever did not denounce them. A simple comment could be considered harmful to the armed forces, and therefore could mean three to six years in prison and sometimes-fatal beatings. They even went to the extreme of censoring news from their neighbors and colleagues, the Argentine and Brazilian dictatorships, because it said too much. To name reality, present or past, was against the law. The wiping out of the country's memory was decreed; for after all, José Artigas and José Pedro Varela, spirited away from the bronze of their very statues, could provide dangerous clues to identity and spaces of discovery to perplexed youth who wondered: *Where does my country come from? Who am I? With whom am I?*

THE RESPONSE

And nevertheless, Uruguayan culture managed to continue breathing, inside and outside the country. In all of its history it had never received higher praise than the ferocious persecution it suffered during those years. Uruguayan culture remained alive and was able to respond with life to the machinery of silence and death. It breathed in those who remained and in those of us who had to leave, in the words which passed from hand to hand, from mouth to mouth, as contraband, hidden or disguised; in the actors who spoke today's truth through Greek theatre and in those who were forced to wander about the world like errant jesters; in the troubadours who sang defiantly in exile and at home; in the scientists and artists who did not sell their souls; in the insolent carnival musicians and in the newspapers that died and were reborn; in the cries scrawled on the streets and in the poems scrawled in the jails on cigarette papers.

But if by culture we mean a way of being and of communicating, if culture is all the symbols of collective identity we express in everyday life, then the resistance was not limited to these outward signs. It was much broader and deeper.

In the final days of the dictatorship, Obdulio Varela, a popular soccer player who knows well the people and the land, offered a bitter summation: "We have grown selfish," Obdulio said at the beginning of 1985. "We no longer see ourselves in others. Democracy is going to be difficult."

And yet, the Uruguayan people knew how to respond with solidarity to the system of dismemberment. There were many ways of finding each other and of sharing — although it be little, although it be nothing — which also formed part, a shining part, of Uruguay's cultural resistance during those years, and which flowered above all among the poorest sectors of the working class. And I am not referring only to the great street demonstrations, but also to less spectacular events like people's kitchens and the housing cooperatives and other works of imagination and anger which have confirmed that solidarity energy is inversely proportional to income level. Or to put it as would Martín Fierro, the fire that really heats is that which comes from below.

THE DAMAGE

There are no statistics of the soul. There is no way to measure the depth of the cultural wound. We know that Uruguay exports shoes to the United States and that nevertheless Uruguayans now buy five times fewer shoes than twenty years ago. But we cannot know to what point they have poisoned our insides, to what point we have been mutilated in our consciousness, our identity, and our memory.

There are a few facts, it's true, that are plain to see — circumstances caused, or at least worsened, by the dictatorship and by the economic policies at whose service the dictatorship turned Uruguay into a vast torture chamber. For example: there are books that can help us to know and to understand ourselves and that could contribute a great deal towards the recuperation of the country's culture. But if the price of just one of those books is equivalent to one-seventh or one-eighth of the monthly salary earned by many Uruguayans, then censorship by price is functioning just as efficiently as censorship by the police did before. The circulation of Uruguayan books has fallen by five or six times; people do not read not because they do not want to, but because they cannot.

The impossibility of return is another fact. There is no damage comparable to the drain of human resources that the country has been suffering for years and which the dictatorship has multiplied. Of those of us who went into exile for having, as one commissary put it, *ideological ideas*, some have been able to return. Some, I say; not all, nor even close to all. In Uruguay there is no work, and when there is, it doesn't pay enough to live. How many can return of the hundreds of thousands whom the system has condemned — and continues condemning — to seek beyond the borders their daily bread? The system, sick with sterility, carries out a curious alchemy: it converts the keys of progress into a national malady. The high cultural level of Uruguayan workers, which could and should be a factor that encourages development, is turned against the country insofar as it facilitates the departure of the population. Now we have democracy, a civilian government instead of a military dictatorship; but the system is the same and the economic policy remains essentially unchanged.

Business freedom — enemy of human freedom — usurpation of wealth, usurpation of life: this economic policy has had cultural consequences that are quite evident. The encouragement of consumption, the consumers' squandering which reached paroxysm during the dictatorship, not only led to an asphyxiating sixfold increase in the foreign debt: it also discouraged creativity. The speculative urge not only empties us of material wealth: it empties us of moral values and, therefore, of cultural values, because it derides productiveness and confirms the old suspicion that he who works is a fool. In addition, the avalanche of foreign merchandise which destroys local industry and pulverizes wages, the readjustment of the economy to adapt to the foreign market, and the abandonment of the domestic market *imply, culturally speaking, self-hate*: the country spits in the mirror and adopts the ideology of impotency as its own.

"Sorry. It's made here," a shopkeeper told me when he sold me a can of meat, the day after my return. After twelve years of exile, I confess that I did not expect this. And when I mentioned it to my friends, they blamed the Process. Neither did I expect the dictatorship to be called Process. The language was, and perhaps still is, sick from fear; they have lost the healthy custom of calling a spade a spade.

THE TASK

Our land of free men is hurt but alive. The military dictatorship that for twelve years forced it to be shut up, to lie, to distrust, was unable to sour its soul: "They weren't able to turn us into them," a friend told me, after the years of terror. And I believe it.

But fear survives disguised as prudence. Be careful, be careful: the fragile democracy will break if you jostle it. From the viewpoint of the owners of an unjust system, one that frightens in order to perpetuate itself, all creative audacity is thought to be a terrorist provocation. A responsible government is an immobilized government; its duty is to keep the *latifundios* and the repressive machinery intact, to forget the dictatorship's crimes and to pay punctually the interest on the foreign debt. The officers left the country in ruins, and in ruins it remains. In the village, the old people water flowers among the tombs.

And the young people? The policy of collective castration was aimed at them above all. The dictatorship tried to drain them of their consciences and of everything else. The system which denies them work and obliges them to leave is directed against them, above all against them. Will they be creative enough, insolent enough, and tough enough to confront the system which denies them? Will they realize in time that for the country to remain democratic it cannot remain paralyzed? Or will the oxygen of liberty make them repent their youth and keep the fear of specters in their hearts? Will they embrace with fatal resignation the destiny of sterility and solitude which those specters offer the country? Or will they act to transform it—even if they do it all wrong—using their capacity for enthusiasm and beautiful madness? Will the country be a fountain of life, or an elephant cemetery?

Translation by Mark Fried.

2

THE CONSTRUCTION OF DEMOCRACY IN NICARAGUA

Susanne Jonas and Nancy Stein

The purpose of this chapter is to analyze the construction of democracy as part of the broader process of carrying out a social revolution in Nicaragua. While noting the effects of U.S. policy, we shall focus primarily on the construction of democracy as an internal process of the Nicaraguan Revolution. In our view, politics there have been shaped first and foremost by Nicaraguan history and by the particular constellation, or alliance, of class forces emerging from that history to make the Revolution.

We shall argue that the Sandinista government has demonstrated, both programatically and in practice, a long-range commitment to developing a revolutionary pluralism, based on the integration of representative and popular/participatory democracy. The Sandinistas have attempted to build pluralism into the structure of the Revolution – as seen particularly in the 1984 election, the 1986 constitutional process, and the ongoing institutionalization and political opening since the signing of the 1987 Central American Peace Accords. In the face of a massive war imposed by the United States, they have had to curtail basic democratic freedoms temporarily, and in some cases they have gone farther than necessary. At the same time, however, even as they responded to the war with specific restrictive measures, they continued to advance the process of institutionalizing basic democratic guarantees, including the right of dissent by organized opposition groups.

Further, we argue, the Sandinistas' commitment to a pluralistic revolution (a subjective factor) has been reinforced by Nicaragua's objective situation. In order to guarantee the survival of the Revolution, especially in the absence of extensive and consistently available external support, the Sandinistas have had to respond to internal demands of various kinds — both from sectors of the working class and peasantry and from minoritarian (primarily bourgeois) opposition forces. On some occasions, they have made serious mistakes, responding too late and consequently paying a political price. Nevertheless, they have been able to learn from and correct those mistakes in time to avoid a serious loss of support and to avoid institutionalizing violations of democratic rights. In short, objective realities have made it necessary to remain accountable and responsive to a broad political base over the long range.

Nicaragua's process of democratic construction remains prolonged, and there are important factors from Nicaraguan history that reappear today as roadblocks. The Sandinistas inherited a centuries-old legacy of the oligarchic state and nearly half a century of Somocista rule. Overcoming that legacy is an extremely uneven process for all parties — both the Sandinistas and the opposition. Whatever the weaknesses of the Sandinistas as a political force, they are institutionalizing a system which permits debate and criticism (and correction) of their errors at a level unprecedented in Central American history.

Skeptics argue that while the Sandinistas speak of building a democracy, they mean something different by that term than North Americans and Europeans. Their conception of democracy does differ in some respects and emphases: it prioritizes the values of serving the interests of the majority, equitable distribution of resources, and popular participation; it also includes leadership by a revolutionary vanguard (the Sandinistas). Nevertheless, the record shows that the Nicaraguan Revolution has come remarkably close to meeting classical Western standards of democracy (even during an externally instigated war), and is moving even further in the direction of pluralism as the Contra war winds down. For this reason, we shall argue, revolutionary Nicaragua has earned legitimacy in Western terms, and has won such legitimacy broadly.

Further, in our view, the Nicaraguan Revolution contributes a unique experience to the struggle for democracy in Third World revolutions. It represents an experiment in combining social revolution with pluralism, an attempt to avoid the choice between those two "incompatible" models of democracy in small, peripheral Third World countries. The outcome will depend on many factors, both internal and external. But if the Nicaraguan experiment is not allowed to work, history may hold the U.S. government responsible for making revolution incompatible with pluralism in the Third World.

METHODOLOGICAL NOTE

Many of us who are engaged in analyzing contemporary Nicaragua and Central America have found ourselves struggling to come up with a reconceptualization of democracy that is adequate to social reality in the region. The very proposal to write about the construction of democracy in Nicaragua requires us to deal with several different political traditions and definitions of democracy. Representative democracy (focusing on competitive elections) as practiced in the United States and other Western capitalist nations is an important component but not the totality of democracy. There is also a tradition, central to Third World revolutions, that stresses direct popular participation in decision making.

These concerns are reflected in the recent work of Central and Latin American and U.S. analysts, including, among others, Torres-Rivas, González Casanova, Nuñez and Burbach, Fagen, Booth, Lobel, Petras and Fitzgerald (see References). Implicit within their writings is a critique of the narrower definition of democracy strictly in electoral and representational terms. A broader concept requires effective popular participation not only in elections but also directly in making the crucial political decisions affecting people's lives. Fagen has offered a useful "working definition" of the "constituent elements" of democracy: "effective participation by individuals and groups in the decisions that most affect their lives," "a system of accountability whereby the behavior of leaders and officials can be monitored, judged, and changed by those who are subject to their authority," and "political equality (before the law, equal opportunity to participate in the political process, etc.)." Within this framework, he continues, the right of dissent should be seen "not as the abstract issue of how much dissent will be allowed, but rather, what forms and channels of dissent are most compatible with the construction of a working consensus supportive of a new political-economic order" (1986: 258).

As González Casanova (1986) put it, democracy is meaningful only if, below the form of representative democracy, lies real popular power. Otherwise, "What democracy are we speaking about, and whom does it serve?" To develop a concept adequate to the social realities of contemporary Central America, it is necessary to link "democracy" to the concepts of social justice (redistribution of wealth), sovereignty and self-determination, and negotiation (versus war) as a means of resolving social conflict.

The following are some of our methodological premises:

1. Our analysis is structural in that it examines political issues in relation to socioeconomic factors, such as underdevelopment, economic crisis, class, and class conflict. More particularly, our starting point is the proposition that representative or political democracy should be analyzed in relation to issues of socioeconomic equality—especially in a region like Central America, where gross inequalities of distribution prevail. Under these circumstances, it makes little sense to speak of democracy without structural change. In this sense, meaningful democratic transitions (as contrasted with temporary liberalization or openings) require a profound social change of one kind or another. Classical representational democracy cannot be achieved on a lasting basis in the polarized countries of Central America today without mass popular movements fighting for structural socioeconomic reforms and a transformation of class relations.[1]

2. The construction of democracy is analyzed here as a historically evolving process. It is neither methodologically sound nor fruitful to apply a democracy checklist, using the most common features of advanced Western democracies to construct a Platonic/universal ideal type against which to measure Central American politics. We agree with Fagen's distinction (1986: 260–2) between "definitional" aspects of

democracy and "instrumental" or "operational" aspects, the latter including such institutions as a free press.

Given the history of long-lasting authoritarian structures and the absence of a populist or social-democratic tradition in Central America, the process of democratic transition is necessarily prolonged. In Torres-Rivas's characterization, Central America's transition period is "like beginning to build a bridge, brick by brick, without yet seeing the other side of the river" (1988: 2).

3. Democracy is examined here both from the perspective of pluralism and representational democracy (the classical Western conception) and from the perspective of participatory or popular revolutionary democracy. Both are to be distinguished from the geopolitical, counterinsurgent conception which in effect equates democracy with anticommunism and which has been the ideological basis for the U.S. war against Nicaragua and other revolutionary nationalist countries. "Counterinsurgent democracy"—or, as others have called it, "death-squad democracy" (Petras and Fitzgerald 1988: 108)—cloaks itself in the forms of representative democracy, while in reality subordinating democratic goals to the necessities of counterinsurgency (see also Torres-Rivas 1988: 10).[2]

4. Following from our premise that political democracy in regions like Central America cannot be divorced from issues of socioeconomic justice for the majority of the population, we also assume that meaningful democracy requires not so much an interelite consensus or "pact" as active involvement by the majority classes. Popular participation should be understood as emerging from a popular base ("from below") and as *autonomous* from control by the state or official parties ("at the top"). This conception implies a concern not only with issues of state power but also with social movements, both organized and spontaneous, not only with the civil and human rights of individuals but also with the construction and functioning of autonomous popular organizations, oriented toward fulfilling collective social goals.

Since one of our primary concerns here is to demonstrate Nicaragua's conformity to Western standards of representative democracy, we give less emphasis to the evolution of mass organizations and their relation to the state. (For detailed studies, see the works by Vilas and Ruchwarger.) Nevertheless, as will become clear in the last section, a concern with these issues is integral to the general framework of our analysis. Furthermore, even as we demonstrate Nicaragua's compliance with Western standards of democracy, we share the conclusion of many Latin Americans and students of Latin America that these standards are not by themselves an adequate measure of democracy in Central America today; and we agree with the Sandinistas that democracy implies a regime and a social order committed to serving the interests of the majority of the population.

NICARAGUAN PLURALISM AND ELECTIONS

"Elections" Under the Somozas, and the FSLN Coalition

A review of twentieth-century Nicaraguan history prior to 1979 reveals that elections have gone hand-in-hand with the oligarchic state, with foreign interventions, and, since the 1930s, with the Somoza dictatorship – which, in its later stages, became the Nicaraguan counterinsurgency state. Such a review reminds us why Nicaraguans and close observers of Nicaragua are unwilling to equate democracy with elections.

The U.S. Marine intervention and occupation that began in 1926 sparked the guerrilla uprising led by Augusto Sandino, an experience which has been called the United States' "first Vietnam." Unable to defeat Sandino definitively, and in the face of great domestic and international opposition to the intervention, the United States had to withdraw its 4,600 Marines in 1933. However, it did so only after having created and trained the Nicaraguan National Guard as a local constabulary force and having hand-picked and installed in power Anastasio Somoza as its head.

After assassinating Sandino in 1934, the Somoza dictatorship, born as an instrument of U.S. counterinsurgency, was "legitimated" in a 1936 election. The subsequent forty-three years of Somoza rule saw regularly staged elections (1946, 1951, 1957, 1963, 1967, and 1974), supported by eight successive U.S. presidents. During this whole period various opposition movements tried to use electoral means to unseat the Somoza dictatorship. Their efforts consistently failed, since Somoza elections were openly fraudulent or rigged, and political movements advocating free elections were repressed. The United States never seriously pressured the Somozas and their cronies to hold a genuine election.

The triumph of the Revolution in 1979 brought to power for the first time in Nicaragua a political coalition under the leadership of the Frente Sandinista de Liberación Nacional (FSLN), committed to the principles of political pluralism (as opposed to a one-party state) and popular participation. The pluralistic orientation stemmed, first, from the desire to overcome the centuries-old legacies of repression and lack of experience in democratic politics. These legacies of emasculated political parties and low political participation were broken for the first time in the mass organizations that developed as part of the popular insurrectionary movement in the late 1970s.

A second source of pluralism came from the evolution of the FSLN itself during the last years of the insurrection, specifically, its development into the coalition of three tendencies which made victory possible. The pluralism growing out of this coalition has remained a cornerstone of FSLN functioning since 1979. A related element has been collective leadership, with decisions being reached by consensus (Gilbert 1988: 46–7). As we shall see, these aspects of FSLN functioning have been important in countering tendencies toward vanguardism, hegemonism, and "verticalism," and in enabling the Frente to admit and correct policy errors.

A third factor has been ideological pluralism. The ideology underlying the Nicaraguan Revolution is a blend of Sandinismo (with its traditions of nationalism, anti-imperialism, and cross-class unity), Marxism, and Liberation Theology (Azicri 1989: 31; Close 1988). More than ideologues, the FSLN is "a party of pragmatists; sometimes stubborn, but finally open to compromise" (Gilbert 1988: 178).

But there is another, more structural basis for pluralism in the Nicaraguan Revolution. Having inherited a nation devastated by civil war and plagued by poverty and underdevelopment, the Sandinistas had to carry out a program of national reconstruction. They recognized that such a goal could not be met without building a sense of national unity among the various movements that had brought down Somoza, that is, without maintaining a broad-based, multi-class coalition.

Hence, the FSLN program committed the new government to political pluralism, as a complement to a mixed economy. In the words of Carlos Fernando Chamorro, editor of the FSLN newspaper *Barricada*, "If we have a mixed economy, we must have a political system that corresponds to that; we want to institutionalize dissent and opposition" (Lobel 1988: 841). As Lobel put it, "Just as the mixed economy has sought to mediate aspects of capitalist development in an economic structure oriented toward the interests of the majority, the new Nicaraguan political structure seeks to combine aspects of representative Western democracy under popular hegemony" (1988: 841).

Nevertheless, this did not imply simply leaving the large property owners a political role commensurate with their continuing economic power. The limits on the political power of the large capitalists stemmed from popular hegemony, that is, the new government's orientation toward the needs of the majority of the population. This orientation was expressed in principle through the emphasis on popular participation in politics by means of mass organizations, and through explicit revolutionary control of the "commanding heights" of politics, including the public educational system and the army (Fagen 1986: 253).

In practice, the revolutionary government had to maintain a balance between conflicting class interests, thus explaining the contradictory politics of the first two years of the Revolution. The FSLN was itself a coalition of political forces (including both Marxists and social democrats) rather than a unified party, and it had come to power through a policy of cross-class alliances. After taking power, the government included non-Sandinistas in Ministerial positions, and in numerous other ways sought to maintain the alliance with democratic elements of the bourgeoisie, rather than establishing a state based solely on the support of workers and peasants. For example, the government prevented popular forces from seizing the property of non-Somocistas. Warren Christopher, U.S. Under-Secretary of State during the Carter administration, noted several months after the Revolution that the government "has been generally moderate and pluralistic" and "has gone out of its way to restrain popular reprisals against capitalists" (1987: 500).

During the Reagan administration, however, the U.S. State Department engaged in rewriting the early years of the Nicaraguan Revolution, deliberately distorting, and quoting out of context, sections of a September 1979 Sandinista document which they called "The Seventy-Two Hour Document," a "communist blueprint." The U.S. objective was to prove that the Sandinista proposition of maintaining a cross-class alliance (political pluralism and a mixed economy) was always a smokescreen for their real intention, which was the creation of a one-party communist state. In fact, the original Sandinista document was a call for restraint and flexibility in dealing with the opposition and for maintaining the cross-class alliance in the face of radicalizing pressures (Central America Historical Institute [CAHI] *Update*, July 29, 1987).

On the other hand, the FSLN was sufficiently concerned with redistributive goals to alienate some sectors of the business community which had initially supported the Revolution (hence, the accusations of "betrayal"). In fact, the Sandinistas never ruptured the cross-class alliance: after businessman Alfonso Robelo quit the government in April 1980 (objecting to the participation of mass organizations in the legislative Council of State), the Junta appointed two new "moderates" (representatives of business interests), and the private sector organizations were included within the Council of State. (Robelo, meanwhile, went on to become a Contra leader.) However, the Sandinistas refused to give in to pressures from sectors of the bourgeoisie that were trying to use their access to political participation to reestablish political dominance – a conception which Robelo, for one, explicitly held (Gilbert 1988: 109).

Within its first year in office, the government promised to hold elections by 1985. For its part, the FSLN has viewed elections "not [as] a concession but rather [as] a way to strengthen the revolution" (Corragio 1986: 97). In preparation for the election, the government sent delegations around the world to study other countries' electoral laws. (The planned delegation was denied entry visas to the United States.) No less important, the government took its first step in institutionalizing the rights of opposition parties, rather than leaving them to depend on the Sandinistas' goodwill, by negotiating with them the Law of Political Parties. For the first time in Nicaragua's history, opposition political parties were guaranteed a role as competitive, not merely cooperative, with the government. Equally as important as the substance of the law was the process through which it was established – a process of negotiations in which the FSLN showed considerable flexibility in relation to the opposition parties (Lobel 1987: 8; *Envío* 1985: 56).

The 1984 Election: A "Model of Probity and Fairness"

In the event, the elections for both president and National Assembly were held a year earlier than originally projected and under the close scrutiny of the entire world. To survey some key aspects:

Participation:

Ninety-three percent of eligible voters registered; although voting is not mandatory, 75.4 percent of registered voters voted; 70.8 percent of registered voters cast valid ballots. (By contrast, the 1985 presidential election in Guatemala saw participation by only 45 percent of the electorate – all this in an environment where voting is compulsory, with penalties or reprisals for not voting.)

Results:

The FSLN received 66.7 percent of the presidential vote and 62.9 percent of the Assembly vote, with 13 percent of the vote going to the Conservatives and 9 percent to the Liberal Independent Party, the two largest opposition parties. These results were significant in countering any hint of a "managed election"; according to members of the Electoral Council, participants on all sides were surprised by the level of support for the non-Contra opposition parties (*Envío* 1985: 59).

Representation:

In principle, no major political tendency was excluded from the electoral process. A total of six opposition parties (ranging from the rightist Democratic Conservative Party and the centrist Popular Social Christian Party and Liberal Independent Party to the Marxist-Leninist Popular Action Movement, MAP) participated, in addition to the Sandinistas. All participants were guaranteed equal resources (campaign funding, supplies, and the like) and equal access to the mass media. A number of emergency restrictions were lifted, so that no party was prevented from carrying out an active campaign or from holding rallies (LASA 1985).

But what about the Coordinadora Democrática Ramiro Sacasa (CD), the coalition supporting Arturo Cruz's candidacy? According to the Reagan administration and advocates of its Nicaragua policy, this was the only real opposition party, and the election was not genuinely contested because the CD did not participate. But the decision to withdraw from the election was made by the CD and its U.S. backers, not by the Sandinistas. Even though the CD used its participation in the early stages of the election to legitimate the political line of the Contras, the FSLN bent over backward and made significant concessions to assure the continued participation of the CD. It was the CD that pulled out, because of its own political weakness and because, according to senior U.S. officials, "the [Reagan] administration never contemplated letting Cruz stay in the race, because then the Sandinistas could justifiably claim that the elections were legitimate" (*New York Times* [*NYT*], October 21, 1984) (see below regarding the U.S. role.) Before even returning to Nicaragua, Cruz told a U.S. reporter, "I'm not really going to run. You know that" (Gutman 1988a).

Much has been made of the charge that the CD's withdrawal was made necessary by harrassment from Sandinista *turbas* or "mobs" — the most noted incident being an August, 1984 rally in Chinandega (see, for example, Leiken 1984, 1985). However, these charges (including the alleged conduct of the *turba* force, of the Sandinista police, and of Cruz himself) have been shown to be factually untrue by foreign journalists who attended the rally (Jenkins, cited in Alexander Cockburn, in *Nation*, December 28, 1985; for further details, see also

Gutman 1988a and 1988b.) Further, Cruz himself has acknowledged that, whatever incidents took place, these did not justify his withdrawal from the election (*NYT*, January 8, 1988).

The lack of good faith on the part of the CD was emphasized by the fact that it withdrew just when the rules of the election had been liberalized, to its benefit. More recently, Cruz himself (who was receiving a monthly salary of $6,000 from the CIA during a twenty-six-month period) has acknowledged that the CD "was dominated by people who never intended to go through with an election campaign," but sought instead "to embarrass the Sandinistas by withdrawing" (*NYT*, January 8, 1988). Finally, as has been pointed out by analyst John Booth (1986: 58), even if the CD had participated and had received all of the abstention votes plus 20 percent of the FSLN votes, the FSLN would still have won the election.

More generally, the openness and fairness of the Nicaraguan election was recognized with a striking degree of unanimity by the participating opposition parties (Reding 1984) and by foreign observers not directly linked to the Reagan administration. Americas Watch (1985) called it "a model of probity and fairness." Based on surveys of the European and international press and inter-views, observers from the Socialist International (which is not consistently or uniformly pro-Sandinista) were overall supportive of the election and critical of the opposition parties that pulled out. Reports on the election in the European press were almost uniformly favorable, as was the report by a delegation from the European Parliament (*Envío* 1985: 20–1, 56; Gleijeses 1986: 435; summaries in the Mexican press of the "Stoltenberg Report" representing the Socialist International). The "Chitnis Report" of the British Liberal Party concluded that Nicaragua's elections were far superior to El Salvador's of the same year (summarized in Mexico's *El Día*, December 7, 1986). Even U.S. observers outside of the U.S. government, such as the ideologically diverse Latin American Studies Association delegation, as well as former American diplomats and Congressmen, judged the elections most favorably (LASA 1985; Smith 1987: 93).

Aside from being honest and procedurally fair, the election was marked by a genuine pluralism, "a high degree of 'open-endedness,' taking the form of continuous bargaining between the FSLN and opposition groups. . . ." (LASA 1985). Although there were incidents of press censorship, a high level of freedom of the press and free speech prevailed overall (Booth 1986: 58), and most of the wartime emergency restrictions were lifted. As reported by the broad spectrum of observers from the LASA delegation, the FSLN could not be charged with abusing its incumbency or its relationship to mass organizations.

Two weeks before the election, the seven participating parties signed a series of accords delineating the major elements of pluralism to be institutionalized in the yet-to-be-written constitution (Reding 1985: 556). The election itself produced an Assembly based on proportional representation. All parties par-ticipating in the elections were guaranteed seats in the National Assembly according to their percentage of the votes won. In addition, all presidential candidates were given seats in the Assembly. As in European parliaments, this system encourages opposition and minority parties to participate, as they are guaranteed representation in the legislature and an ongoing role in the political process.

The new legislature was "exactly the same as any other Western style Assembly," according to the chairman of Nicaragua's Democratic Conservative Party, and generally reflected the great ideological diversity of Nicaraguan political life – a fact that was obscured by the Reagan administration's exclusive focus on the CD (Reding 1985: 557; *Envío* 1985: 56). The results of the election, and particularly the fact that over a third of the vote was won by opposition parties, surprised both the FSLN and the opposition (*Envío* 1985: 59). The wide variation in the level of support for the FSLN also contradicts the charges of a "managed election" (*Envío* 1985: 45). In the words of Mauricio Díaz, leader of the Popular Social Christian Party, one of the opposition parties participating in the election:

An electoral culture cannot be created overnight. I have always maintained that the elections are a tenuous proof that here in Nicaragua the possibility for the consolidation of a pluralist system exists, and that the tendency here is not as the U.S. wants to present it internationally—that we are headed for a totalitarian system—but that here there are social, political and historical conditions for the reaffirmation of democratic principles and values (CAHI *Update*, July 17, 1986).

U.S. Attempts to Sabotage the Election

Since U.S. policy makers see elections as absolutely essential in legitimating and delegitimating governments, it was central to the Reagan policy of gaining support and funds for the Contras to show that the 1984 Nicaraguan election was not valid. For this reason, officials in the Reagan administration had to stick to their preestablished conclusions, even though the evidence (and the opinion of virtually all other observers) demonstrated the opposite.

As became clear in the National Security Council document leaked to the U.S. press and reported in the *Washington Post* on November 6, 1984, there was a deliberate U.S. strategy to denounce the Nicaraguan election as a "Soviet-style sham." This campaign was kicked off by Secretary of State Shultz and the State Department in early 1984, only days after the elections were announced, and the administration continued in this vein before, during, and after the election. Even in 1988, Reagan administration officials (from self-proclaimed "moderates" such as Luigi Einaudi to known hardliners like Elliott Abrams and Robert Pastorino) continued to insist that Nicaragua did not really have an elected government. (To its discredit, the *New York Times* also followed this line as late as March 1988, referring to Nicaragua as "a country that has never yet held a free, contested election," March 25, 1988.)[3]

The United States did not limit itself to denouncing the Nicaraguan election, but sought also to sabotage it and to use it as a justification for further hostilities against Nicaragua. Under U.S. guidance, the Contras carried out numerous activities to sabotage the election militarily (Gutman 1988b; LASA Report 1984: 30). Additionally, as noted above, the United States pressured candidates Arturo Cruz of the Coordinadora Democrática and Virgilio Godoy of the Liberal Independent Party to pull out of the election and "never contemplated letting Cruz stay in the race. . . ." (Similar U.S. tactics with the Democratic Conservative Party failed.) The U.S. goal was "to isolate the Sandinistas and discredit the regime" (John Oakes, *NYT*, November 5, 1984) rather than let Cruz run and accept the result of a free vote. Venezuela's Social Democratic President Carlos Andres Pérez, who was intimately involved in negotiations between Cruz and the Sandinistas, arrived at the conclusion that the CIA manipulated the CD into pulling out, so as "to demonstrate there was no freedom of elections in Nicaragua" (Gutman 1988a: 645).

After the election was over, Washington explicitly threatened Nicaragua, saying that the election constituted a "setback for peace talks" in the region and would "heighten tensions" with the United States, and warned that it intended to pressure Nicaragua to hold a "real election" as a condition for future peace talks (*NYT*, November 5, 1984). The above evidence, then, flatly contradicts assertions that U.S. policy aimed to "democratize" Nicaragua or promoted free elections there.

THE CONSTITUTIONAL PROCESS OF 1986: INSTITUTIONALIZING THE REVOLUTION IN THE MIDST OF WAR

The process of institutionalizing the balance between representative and participatory democracy that began in the 1984 election continued in the writing and ratification of the 1986 Constitution. To be sure, the process was conditioned by its occurrence amidst the Contra war and the fluctuating restrictions of the state of emergency. Nevertheless, the very attempt to "unify and transform" the historically diverging views of democracy under these conditions is notable.

Nicaragua's Constitution is unique in combining the emphasis on political pluralism, separation of powers and individual rights found in Western democracies with the emphasis on social and economic justice found in socialist countries, and notions of equality for women and the rights of ethnic communities. Contrary to statements made by Reagan administration official Elliott Abrams, that the Constitution follows the Soviet-Cuban model, and "is really nothing more than a legal facade" which "codifies the Sandinista party's absolute power" (*Los Angeles Times* [*LAT*], January 26, 1987), it actually incorporated ideas from various social systems, following no one model and imposing no one perspective. It was based on detailed study of the constitutional experience of numerous other countries in both Western and Eastern Europe and Latin America.

The process of developing the Constitution itself represented an important experiment in political participation both by political parties and by citizens directly. There were several stages in drafting the Constitution before its final ratification at the end of 1986 and its official promulgation in Janaury 1987. The National Constituent Assembly elected in 1984 appointed a Constitutional Commission composed of twenty-two members: twelve from the FSLN and ten from the other parties that participated in the elections. Opposition parties constituted 45 percent of the commission, as compared with their 36.5 percent representation in the Assembly. The FSLN occupied fewer seats on the Commission than it was entitled to, in order to assure the participation of all parties.

Between August and October of 1985, the Commission held meetings with twenty-four political parties, religious groups, labor and professional unions, and other organizations to hear their views in preparing the first draft of the Constitution, which was completed in February 1986. Copies were widely distributed; there were twelve televised debates and seventy-three town meetings (*cabildos abiertos*), incorporating 100,000 citizens, held in May and June 1986. As former National Assembly official, Alvaro Arguello, stated, "It is very important that people outside Nicaragua realize how the people here have taken an active role in this process. . . " (cited in CAHI *Update*, April 1986).

The town hall meetings were held throughout the country, with designated days set for various sectors of the population (such as women, unions, professionals, journalists, peasants). The purpose of the meetings was not to ratify what was in the first draft of the Constitution, but to debate the consequences of its provisions and to propose changes. According to one representative in the National Assembly, the *cabildos* had originally been conceived of "to help the people understand the Constitutional issues," but they became "a practical school to help the [Assembly] representatives learn how to legislate according to the people's interests" (*Envío*, August 1986).

More than 2,500 contributions were made in the meetings themselves, with another 1,800 sent in writing. All of these were reviewed and further discussed by the Commission during the redrafting of the Constitution. Most important, the changes resulting from this process of participation were not pro forma, but substantive and significant, some on very sensitive issues.

The level of participation by political parties represented in the National Assembly (not the organizations in the Coordinadora Democrática) varied considerably. At some points they participated wholeheartedly, at other points they pulled back and threatened to boycott the process in order to win concessions from the Sandinistas. They publicized their views through the media and criticized the process from both the Right and the Left. Opposition participants expressed concerns about the potential of the public forums for being manipulated and about the validity of the process taking place during a state of emergency. In the end, however, eighty-seven of the ninety-six members of the National Assembly signed the final version of the Constitution (the nine non-signers coming from three ideologically divergent opposition parties).

The FSLN representatives (some identified with the revolutionary Christian tendency, others with nationalist or Marxist tendencies) did not always vote as a bloc, and were split on some important issues (such as judicial review, the incorporation of international human rights treaties into the Constitution; see Reding, 1987: 262). This contributed to significant input and victories for positions put forward by the opposition parties. In an attempt to achieve consensus, the FSLN went to great lengths to guarantee that the constitutional process was representative of all those who chose to participate, and made significant compromises (earning strong criticism from left opposition parties). Following are some of the issues that were resolved after lengthy debate, often in favor of opposition proposals (with support from some Sandinistas):

1. The mayor of Managua, previously appointed by the President, would subsequently be elected. (The election of local officials was among the issues further elaborated in the Municipalities Law adopted by the Assembly in 1988.)

2. The budget, previously in the hands of the President, would subsequently be submitted to the National Assembly for approval during peacetime.

3. There was strong sentiment both in favor of and in opposition to mentioning God in the Constitution; this was resolved by putting in the preamble a dedication to "the Christians who, from their faith in God, have committed themselves to, and involved themselves in, the struggle for the redemption of the oppressed."

4. There was extensive debate concerning judicial review. The Sandinistas were split over the right of the Supreme Court to rule on the legality of acts of the president or the legislature. This was resolved in favor of judicial review and a clear separation of powers among the branches of government.

5. The independence of the army from the FSLN was one of the most serious issues debated. While the army retains its identification as "Sandinista" and its members are instructed in Sandinista values (nationalism and anti-imperialism for example), the Constitution affirms that its loyalty is to the country and the national constitution, not to one party. Further, the universal draft has opened the army to non-Sandinistas, and it retains a structure separate from that of the FSLN. Since top army officials are Sandinistas, the opposition continues to raise strong objections (see *LAT*, October 17, 1988; Azicri 1989: 24–30); but radical changes are unlikely, given the pervasive consciousness of past experience in Latin America, when "independent" armies deserted or moved against revolutionary nationalist governments (Guatemala in 1954, Chile in 1973).

6. Prior to the 1984 elections, mass organizations as well as political parties had been represented in the Council of State (predecessor of the National Assembly). The opposition resisted any formulation that would give what they perceived as Sandinista-controlled mass organizations a formal role in government decision making or administration. As a result, the Constitution confirmed that the National Assembly would consist only of representatives of political parties.

7. The issue of the reelection of the president was so heated that it was not resolved in these discussions, but was left for future decision by the National Assembly.

Provisions of the Constitution

The Constitution contained eleven titles and 202 provisions. Some of the major ones are described below.

After reaffirming Nicaragua's commitment to pluralism, a mixed economy, and nonalignment, the Constitution guaranteed the same basic rights established in the U.S. Constitution and Bill of Rights, among these: the right not to testify against oneself; the right to be represented by counsel; the right to form and join political parties with the aim of contending for political power; the right to peaceful assembly; protection against unreasonable search and seizure; freedom of religion; freedom of expression, artistic and cultural creation; the right to organize unions and to strike.

In addition, the Constitution included economic, social, and cultural rights— for example, the right to education, health care, agrarian reform, social security, decent housing, and a healthy environment. In the context of Nicaraguan underdevelopment and economic crisis, the guiding principle was that "the basic needs of the poor have a prior claim on scarce resources in relation to the wants of those whose basic needs are already satisfied."

The Constitution guaranteed a mixed economy, including private property, but all forms of property were "subordinated to the higher interests of the nation." For example, any idle or underused land could be expropriated and redistributed to landless peasants as voluntary cooperatives or family farms. Land titles were inheritable, but could not be sold, transferred, or subdivided. Even after adoption of the Constitution, some private sector forces in the opposition did not accept those formulations, and subsequently attempted to reopen these issues (see below).[4]

The Miskito Indians and Regional Autonomy

One of the major issues addressed in the Constitution concerns the ethnic and regional rights of the indigenous population of Nicaragua's Atlantic Coast. Probably the most serious error made by the government shortly after the Revolution was in its treatment of this community. The historical relationship between the Atlantic Coast and the rest of the country was one of distrust and isolation. The new revolutionary government displayed little comprehension of the specific nature of the region or the history and culture of its people, and this was reflected in the government's implementation of national policies such as agrarian reform (Vilas 1988a: 200 ff.).

These troubled relations were compounded by the circumstances of the Contra war. When the Sandinistas forcibly removed the Miskito Indians from the Contra battle zone for military/security reasons, a significant portion of the

Miskito community joined the Contra camp — a situation greatly exacerbated by CIA activities among the Miskitos. Only after this became a major political crisis did the Sandinistas seriously begin to address the situation and the broader problems of the Atlantic Coast; they came to understand that many demands of the coastal peoples were legitimate, and that there would be no peace in the region until these demands had been met politically (Vilas 1988a: 204). The Sandinistas also publicly acknowledged and apologized for the errors in previous policies; they granted amnesty to Miskitos who had participated in Contra forces, and negotiated a ceasefire with the armed indigenous groups, as well as the return of the displaced Miskitos to their homes under conditions acceptable to those communities.

In 1984, the government established a Commission and began negotiations with representatives from the region, to resolve the issue of autonomy for the Atlantic Coast region and to establish a multiethnic national state. As a consequence of this process, several articles of the Constitution guaranteed regional autonomy for the Atlantic Coast and established the right of its inhabitants "to preserve and develop their cultural identity within the framework of national unity, to choose their own forms of social organization, and to administer local affairs in conformity with their traditions." The state guaranteed these communities the use of their natural resources, the right to education in their own languages, as well as the recognitition of those languages for official use, and barred any form of discrimination. The government of Nicaragua was to provide these areas with resources to help achieve an economic balance with the rest of the country.

In order to gain agreement on the new arrangement, community-level forums were held on the Atlantic Coast for several months before the final draft was approved in the National Assembly in Managua. Various specific issues remained to be worked out in subsequent years (codified finally in the Autonomy Statute of 1987).

Although the legacy of serious divisions between Managua and the Coast could not be erased overnight, the new Constitution was internationally recognized as having gone farther than that of any other Latin American country in establishing the rights of indigenous peoples and of an autonomous region. Further, the autonomy process reflected the effort of the government to create a "development strategy responding to the real needs of people and their initiatives of participation" (Vilas 1988a: 207).

When the calamitous Hurricane Joan struck the Atlantic Coast in October 1988, the government earned considerable good-will for its massive evacuation and support of the stricken population — an accomplishment which could be crucial in overcoming the problems of the past.

The Constitution and the State of Emergency

Critics of the Sandinistas have raised concerns that the Constitution was rendered null and void — or, in less extreme versions, significantly weakened —

shortly after its promulgation at the beginning of 1987, by the renewal of the state of emergency that suspended some constitutional provisions. That the state of emergency imposed significant limitations was indisputable: for example, it restricted the rights to strike and to hold public meetings outdoors, and established prior censorship. In particular, as the London-based Catholic Institute for International Relations (CIIR) pointed out, the broad powers given the security forces opened up the potential for arbitrary conduct, making the area of civil liberties "problematic" (CIIR 1987: 36).

However, serious efforts were made to prevent that potential from materializing. There is widespread agreement that the government took measures to hold security officials accountable to human rights standards and to punish those who violated them (see CIIR 1987; Americas Watch 1987.) According to international human rights organizations and representatives of the non-Contra opposition within Nicaragua, the government did not engage in policies that systematically violated international conventions, particularly concerning "non-derogable" rights (see Americas Watch 1987). More debatable were the restrictions of "derogable" rights in particular situations — which many observers regarded as having gone beyond what was necessary, even in time of national emergency (as in some of the instances of closing down *La Prensa*, which even a number of Sandinista leaders view as having been unnecessary and/or arbitrary — despite *La Prensa's* documented record of being supported by covert U.S. funding and of contributing to U.S. destabilization efforts against Nicaragua — see Nichols 1988).

But viewed in terms of its long-range impact, the new Constitution itself limited governmental authority in regard to the state of emergency in two respects. First, by requiring National Assembly approval within forty-five days, it took away the president's right to declare a state of emergency by executive decision. The Assembly debate over reimposing the state of emergency in early 1987 was "lengthy and frank" and made several modifications of the decree (*NYT*, February 25, 1987). Second, the Constitution listed fifty-five Articles that could not be suspended by the president under any circumstances. Further limitations were spelled out in a 1988 law, also with Constitutional standing, setting forth the conditions under which a state of emergency could be declared, and limiting the rights which could be affected by such a declaration.

While the provisions in the Constitution and related laws do not by themselves guarantee the full exercise of democracy in practice, they have gone a long way toward reducing the space for arbitrary restrictions in peacetime and guaranteeing individual rights and liberties. Once codified, they have become fundamental rights of Nicaraguan citizens, to which any future government will be held accountable.

Debates surrounding the Nicaraguan Constitution have by no means subsided; in fact, as of early 1989, they have been revived in new opposition party demands (see below). Nevertheless, its historical significance is indisputable. As assessed by the CIIR:

As a contribution to the literature of human rights, the Nicaraguan Constitution is already something of a landmark. . . .with its unique mix of Latin American, social-democratic and neoradical traditions. It will be—indeed it is already being—studied by drafters of other constitutions. Similarly, the process by which the Nicaraguan Constitution was forged will stand as an example of pluralism within revolutionary leadership. The serious and relatively low-keyed debate in the National Assembly which followed the earlier phases of party political acrimony has also made a positive contribution to the tone of political dialogue in Nicaragua. . . .(1987: 38)

Equally telling was the commentary by a delegation of visiting Congressmen from Guatemala (one of Washington's "model democracies"), which had recently experienced its own process of Constitution-writing and elections, both conducted by a de facto military government. After attending several of the *cabildos abiertos* these centrist Congressmen commented, "Nothing like this could ever have happened in Guatemala."

THE STRUGGLE FOR DEMOCRACY IN A CHANGING CONTEXT

The most remarkable fact about the electoral and constitution-writing processes described above was their occurrence during a full-scale war sponsored by the United States. The objective of the Reagan administration was to overthrow the Sandinista government — and, falling short of that, to cause the maximum possible destruction, to "raise the cost" of having made a revolution, and to turn Nicaragua into a negative example for the Third World. Further, a Pentagon official told the *Los Angeles Times*, "2,000 hard-core guys could keep the pressure on the Nicaraguan government, force them to use their economic resources for the military, and prevent them from solving their economic problems" (cited in *Nation*, May 1, 1989). We shall not trace here the details of that eight-year U.S. military effort via the Contra war — nor of the even more devastating (though less visible) economic war against Nicaragua (see works by Gutman, Kornbluh, Sklar, Robinson and Norsworthy, Conroy, and Walker cited in References).[5]

For our purposes, it is essential to understand the political-ideological complement to the military war, as seen in the U.S. campaign to delegitimize and sabotage both the 1984 election and the entire democratic process in Nicaragua. In the words of Contra chief Enrique Bermúdez in 1986, the aim of Contra military attacks inside Nicaragua was not to foster democratic reforms (which was the Reagan administration's argument at the time) but to "heighten repression" (*Washington Post National Weekly*, March 28, 1987). Similarly, as denounced by House Speaker Jim Wright, in the fall of 1988, the CIA (working with Nicaraguan opposition forces) was engaged in a deliberate policy of provoking a government crackdown during 1988, in order to undermine government-Contra negotiations and national reconciliation in Nicaragua, and to secure Congressional renewal of military aid to the Contras.

In short, the United States under Reagan had a policy of deliberately under-mining the Nicaraguan attempt to incorporate Western-style politics into a revolutionary framework. One could even argue that the United States has viewed the Nicaraguan election, Constitution, and political process in general as a "threat" *not because they were insufficiently democratic, but because they were too democratic,* hence too attractive to other countries. As Reding (1987: 291) commented: "The more Nicaragua becomes a model, even if an imperfect one, for revolutionary change, the more it is perceived to be a threat to its Central American neighbors...," that is, to their counterinsurgent governments. Reding then noted the irony that the American Revolution was destabilizing to the oligarchies of the eighteenth century for precisely the same reason – because of its "reasonableness," hence its moral appeal.

Despite all efforts of the Reagan administration, however, by the late 1980s the massive contradictions of the Contra war had emerged. First and foremost, the campaign to overthrow the Sandinista government had failed. Second, the Reagan policy had contributed to the militarization and destabilization not only of Nicaragua but also of the entire Central American region, and posed the serious threat of a regional war. These contradictions were among the main factors that led neighboring Latin American governments in the mid-1980s to propose the Contadora initiative, in opposition to U.S. policy and for a negotiated settlement of the Contra war. By mid-1987, these same contradic-tions led even the pro-U.S. governments of Nicaragua's Central American neighbors to abandon support for the Contra policy, and to accept peaceful coexistence with Nicaragua. That was the real message of the Arias Plan, as it evolved from a tool of U.S. policy to a challenge of that policy, and of the August 1987 Peace Accords, called Esquipulas II. (For analyses, see various issues of *Envío* 1987–88; Halebsky and Jonas 1988; Robinson 1988.)

The peace process set into motion by the August 1987 agreement signed by the Central American presidents was fundamentally positive for Nicaragua. It recognized the legitimacy and permanence of the revolutionary Nicaraguan government. Conversely, it was a de facto recognition of the illegitimacy of the Contras (as well as their strategic defeat by the Nicaraguan army) and it put the neighboring governments on record as calling for an end to U.S. support for the Contras. This was the "fatal flaw" in the Accords, from the Reagan administration's viewpoint – and the reason why the Nicaraguan government played an active role in advancing the process. The Accords were also crucial in securing the defeat of military aid to the Contras within the U.S. Congress. They afforded new opportunities for Nicaragua to seize the initiative for a regional settlement as well as for negotiations to end the Contra war. Finally, they provided a framework for strengthening democracy within Nicaragua: to be sure, the war was not over; but the possibility of peace and the shift away from the military arena greatly expanded the possibilities for pluralistic politics in Nicaragua.

For these reasons, Nicaragua has viewed the peace process as fundamentally positive, and has gone infinitely farther than any of the other governments in complying with the Accords (even paying the internal political costs of such unpopular measures as freeing ex-National Guard and Contra prisoners). Nicaragua's extensive compliance (and the non-compliance of the neighboring governments) was acknowledged internationally in the Verification Commission Report (CIVS 1988; LASA 1988), and even by observers who were less sympathetic to the Sandinistas (see, for example, editorial in *NYT*, March 11, 1988; Neier 1988). Furthermore, the Nicaraguan government demonstrated a flexibility far beyond what had been expected — in forging the original Accords at the initial meeting in Guatemala, and in saving the second Presidents' meeting (in Costa Rica, January 1988) from complete failure by lifting Nicaragua's state of emergency and announcing other unilateral measures. Most important, in the spring of 1988, the Sandinistas reversed their earlier stance by initiating direct political negotiations with the Contras at Sapoá.

Substantively, in terms of "democratization" within Nicaragua, the Accords provided a context for rescinding measures that the government had been forced to take because of the Contra war — as one Nicaraguan specialist on the subject told us in an interview, "to carry out the program that the Revolution intended in the first place." Most significantly, in terms of moving back to its original goals, the government lifted the state of emergency, restored publishing rights to *La Prensa* and broadcasting rights to Radio Católica, allowed exiled priests to return to the country, and began the release of political prisoners under a broad amnesty program. Also, the government initiated a wide-ranging dialogue with all opposition forces within Nicaragua (including unregistered parties of the pro-Contra Coordinadora as well as parties in the National Assembly) while simultaneously negotiating with the Contras.

But post-Esquipulas realities have been contradictory. Regionally, the other face of coexistence, as defined in the Peace Accords, was containment directed against Nicaragua. (Not surprisingly, even in the last year of the Reagan administration, some post-Reagan strategists in the United States began seeking to define a policy of "positive containment" of Nicaragua — see Vaky 1987; Robinson 1988; Serafino 1988.) Unlike the Contadora proposals, which addressed primarily the issues of security between the United States and Nicaragua, the Peace Accords focused on the internal character of the Nicaraguan Revolution. On paper, the Accords prescribed democratization measures to be taken by all of the Central American governments. But in practice, given the correlation of forces in the region, and the failure of international players to insist on compliance by Nicaragua's neighbors, the onus has been on Nicaragua. Hence, the Accords have put the other Central American governments (and indirectly the United States) in a position to judge Nicaragua's compliance with agreements that these other governments themselves have been violating. Finally, the Accords opened up a process whereby the enemies of the Nicaraguan Revolution, including the Reagan administration, were able to constantly up the demands on Nicaragua.

Internally, beyond the explicit requirements of the Peace Accords, they opened up "space" (and, in some circles, legitimacy) in late 1987 and 1988 for Nicaragua's opposition parties to make new demands for "constitutional reforms" that were not specified in the Accords themselves. Some were designed to limit the power of the government (such as the powers of the president) or of the Sandinistas (such as with respect to the army). Others called into question basic principles of the Nicaraguan Revolution (deleting the reference to Sandinismo as the "fundamental doctrine of the state" in the preamble to the Constitution; limiting the role of mass organizations on the grounds of their being "Sandinista-controlled"; strengthening private property rights, while abolishing the references to agrarian reform). More seriously, some in the opposition took the opportunity to question the legitimacy of the National Assembly as a forum for resolving these issues, thus throwing up for grabs the entire framework of the Nicaraguan government and deliberately attempting to make their dialogue with the government fail (Ortega 1988a: 45).

This process of reopening fundamental questions about the Revolution reached its outside limit in the summer of 1988, with the violent demonstration launched by the right wing of the opposition (the extra-parliamentary Coordinadora Democrática) at Nandaime. The Sandinistas responded by arresting demonstration leaders, temporarily closing down *La Prensa* and Radio Católica, and expelling U.S. Ambassador Richard Melton for being involved in the demonstration (and in the entire process of destabilizing the Nicaraguan government). The Sandinistas' intent was to establish the boundaries of legitimate opposition: they would not tolerate the use of violence or illegal methods or direct involvement by the U.S. Embassy; nor would they accept as "legitimate opposition" the call for a "government of national salvation" (the call to overthrow the new Constitution and its institutions, and to establish a new government). As subsequently revealed by House Speaker Wright, the goal of U.S. covert activities at Nandaime and elsewhere had been to destabilize the Nicaraguan government.

When Costa Rican President Arias and other international figures pressured them to free those arrested at Nandaime, the Sandinistas argued that they would do so (and subsequently did so), but within the framework of their own laws, not in response to international pressures (Arce in *Barricada*, August 16, 1988). Their point was that the Nicaraguan Revolution had established its own institutionality, and this would be the framework for democratization; in this sense, the Peace Accords did not initiate "the democratization of Nicaragua," but provided an opportunity to develop it through the lifting of restrictions made necessary by the Contra war.

There is a final contextual factor that has become decisive in post-Esquipulas Nicaragua, and presents the most serious political challenge to date: the threat of economic collapse. Economic crisis has been part of the Nicaraguan revolution since the early 1980s, particularly after being aggravated by U.S. economic warfare (credit blockade, trade blockade, embargoes), by Contra economic sabotage, and by the diversion of 50 percent of the national budget to defense, to fight the Contra war. However, 1988 was the year in which the economic crisis assumed primacy. The political effects of economic deterioration were compounded by coming at a time when many people had begun to have renewed expectations of improvement, as a consequence of the perceived winding down of the Contra war. These expectations became a lever for the opposition; in fact, the Nandaime demonstration was part of a long-range strategy of organizing around growing economic discontent (as in Chile in the early 1970s). In short, new conditions have shifted the terms of political struggle and have raised new issues of democracy, which we shall touch upon briefly below.

The Electoral Law and the Broadening of Political Pluralism

The fact that the government of Nicaragua derives its legitimacy, in formal terms, from the convincing victory of the FSLN in elections generally recognized as fair and honest does not exhaust the issue of legitimacy. Such a new state also faces the wider and more difficult problem of securing national consensus around itself, its institutions and constitutional priorities. . . .(CIIR 1987: 20)

The construction of such a consensus is an ongoing issue for the Nicaraguan Revolution, one that is very much in process and involves problems as well as advances. Broadly, we shall attempt to show in the following sections that the post-Esquipulas context has led to greater pluralism *vis-à-vis* the opposition political parties; but this by no means exhausts the issues of democratic construction.

As argued above, political pluralism has been expressed in the Nicaraguan Revolution through a multiparty system and competing political forces at various levels. It has also been expressed through the process of negotiations and compromise between the FSLN and opposition groups, both as part of the 1984 elections and as part of the 1986 constitutional process. In essence, opposition forces (minority parties, the Church, private sector organizations) have come to exercise much greater influence than their numbers or social base warrant because of the leverage they enjoy by their very participation in these processes (or, conversely, by their threats to withdraw, which would undermine the legitimacy of these processes). This leverage of the opposition forces has been further increased by the significant international attention given to them (in many cases accompanied by international funding).

To the extent that the opposition parties remain divided and unable to effectively challenge the Sandinistas, critics have tried to blame "FSLN repression." In fact, what left these parties weak was, more than anything else, the legacy of the Somoza era. More recently, their relative weakness stems from their inability to build a social base beyond the small middle class, contrasted with the considerable moral authority of the Sandinistas for winning and leading the revolution. Thus far, the opposition has consisted of numerous, small parties (micro-parties), characterized by disunity, constant splintering and shifting of alliances, and the lack of any coherent program, leadership, or popular support. Although Esquipulas objectively strengthened their hand and should have given them a boost (especially in a context of growing economic discontent), almost all of the opposition parties split at least once during 1988, leaving nearly two dozen opposition "micro-parties" by the end of the year. While retaining an international constituency, they did not manage to develop much legitimacy within Nicaragua (Ortega 1988a: 45; 1988b: 27). Vice President Sergio Ramírez (1988: 11) summarized the Sandinista attitude: "We cannot reduce the political forces of the Sandinista Front artificially in order to say that there is political pluralism in the country."

Nevertheless, the Sandinistas have understood the value of political debate, and many within the FSLN leadership have viewed the opposition as a "healthy correcting force" (Lobel 1987: 15). In the post-Esquipulas political opening, further, they have actually sought to encourage the formation of a serious, credible opposition in order to facilitate policy compromises. As Sandinista officials told us in interviews during the summer of 1988, "The revolutionary process needs a decent opposition — one that is not at the service of foreign interests" and "we are fighting for a society where there is a role for *La Prensa* and Radio Católica" (both of which were temporarily closed down after Nandaime).

Within the context of political upheaval, the National Assembly expended great energy in 1988 to hammer out and pass a new electoral law designed to further institutionalize Nicaragua-style pluralism. The law governed the election of president, vice president, National Assembly representatives and other offices; it regulated the use of media and campaign financing, set all electoral procedures, and established criteria for certifying political parties. To qualify for the ballot, a party would now require a minimum party structure at all levels (national, regional, departmental, and municipal). However, these restrictions applied only to new parties, not to existing ones or those in the process of obtaining certification at the time the legislation was approved. Another major aspect of the law concerned proportional representation: as in Western Europe, in order to gain a seat in the Assembly, a party would now have to obtain at least 5 percent of the vote. Finally, political parties could not receive funds either from Nicaraguan state institutions or from foreign sources — an important restriction for opposition forces that were counting on U.S. funding.

Critics charged that these regulations restricted the development of opposition parties; the counterargument was that in reality they would have the opposite effect. By making the qualifications more stringent for "micro-parties," the law would give opposition forces an incentive to form broader coalitions;

they would be rewarded for developing as a coherent opposition force, rather than for further splintering.

In other respects, the electoral law showed again the flexibility of the Sandinistas *vis-à-vis* the opposition parties. While binding the latter to respect the Constitution and establishing firmly that future electoral reform would come only through the Assembly, the Sandinistas did make important compromises throughout the debate — among these, restoring voting rights to Contras and officers of the National Guard and allowing them to run for office. In addition, they held out the possibility of future amendments to the law in the context of peace talks (*LAT*, August 26, 1988).

In the end, while some members of opposition parties boycotted the debate on the electoral law, only the Communist Party of Nicaragua (as a party) did not join in the final vote. Some opposition figures who had pulled out of the process said they would insist on repeal of the law (*Envío*, December 1988: 30); others commented that "it was better than we expected" (CAHI *Update*, September 21, 1988) and that, while not fully satisfactory, it "guarantees some measure of political pluralism. . . and is much more responsive" than the initial government proposal (*Envío*, December 1988: 30). Even one of the boycotters acknowledged at the end, "This is not a totalitarian law; it does not offer us enough security, but it is a step toward opening up the system for a real challenge to the Sandinistas" (*LAT*, August 26, 1988).

As Nicaragua moved toward the 1990 elections (after the government rescheduled them from November to February), the Sandinistas negotiated further modifications in the electoral regulations with opposition forces (such as the composition of the Electoral Council, the financing of political parties, virtual elimination of press censorship, free time for the opposition on official TV and radio stations, among others) (*Envío*, April 1989). They insisted, however, that the negotiation process take place within the legally established context, the National Assembly. The opposition remained divided over acceptance of these and other concessions as a basis for participating in the elections. Meanwhile, the Bush administration responded along some of the same lines as its predecessor (minus military aid to the Contras): insisting that the Contra force be kept alive in Honduras, renewing the trade embargo against Nicaragua (thereby helping keep the country in economic turmoil), spending several million dollars supporting opposition forces including *La Prensa* (in addition to millions of dollars in "nonlethal" aid to the Contras). President Bush himself, as well as other U.S. officials, began proclaiming that the elections would not be fair, even denouncing the liberalized electoral and press laws as "more restrictive" and repressive than before (*NYT*, April 21, 1989, April 25, 1989, May 3, 1989; *San Francisco Chronicle*, April 25, 1989, May 3, 1989). For the United States, Nicaraguan Vice President Sergio Ramírez commented, "the only way the FSLN can legitimize itself is by losing the elections" (*Barricada Internacional*, April 8, 1989).

Mass Organizations and Participatory Democracy

While the Sandinistas have been willing to negotiate endlessly with the parliamentary opposition, their real constituency is the mass base that made the revolution. At the base, there were many who clamored initially for much harsher treatment of Somocistas, and more recently, who met with stunned disbelief the announcement of direct government negotiations with the Contras (and subsequently amnesty) (*LAT*, October 16, 1988). Here lies the key to the dual identity of the FSLN, the dialectic of its commitment to both representative and participatory democracy.

As we have argued, Nicaraguan democracy cannot be discussed exclusively in terms of Western-style representative democracy. Nicaragua is not the Soviet Union or Cuba—but neither is it the United States or Costa Rica. It represents a particular class project, growing out of Nicaragua's historical experiences of cross-class, anti-imperialist struggle (expressed fifty years earlier in the Sandino uprising). It balances the need to negotiate with the parliamentary opposition (largely middle-class) with broad principles of maintaining popular hegemony.

Hence, beyond competing parties and competitive elections, the other side of Nicaraguan pluralism involves "transform[ing] civil society by creating an autonomous institutional base for the majority from which the State derives its legitimacy and political power is mandated." (Corragio and Irwin 1985: 260). From this perspective, the state derives its legitimacy not only through elections but also through broad popular participation by a mass base independent of the state apparatus (Vilas 1986a and 1986b). This brings us to consider another set of issues related to the implementation of direct popular participation.

Central to these issues are Nicaragua's mass organizations, whose fluctuating strength and autonomy provide a nonelectoral measure of the vitality of Nicaraguan democracy. Since this very complex subject cannot be fully discussed here, as it has been by others (see Ruchwarger 1987; Vilas 1986), we shall briefly use the case of the Sandinista Defense Committees (CDSs) as an illustration. The CDSs, organized initially during the insurrection, came to be the largest of the mass organizations after the Revolution, and became a central part of political life for many Nicaraguans. By the mid-1980s, however, they were playing less and less of a role, and had become defunct in many neighborhoods. In addition, the CDSs and the other mass organizations lost their representation in the National Assembly in the 1984 election (subsequently confirmed by the rejection of the idea of a bicameral legislature in the debate over the Constitution).

Aside from their decline as a vehicle of popular political participation, the CDSs came to be charged with abuses of leadership (such as issuing or withholding ration cards, letters of residence, and other documents for political reasons). As early as 1982, the FSLN restructured the CDSs, in an attempt to deal with these problems. In 1985, the then head of the CDSs, Leticia Herrerra, stated, "We have fallen into a growing bureaucratism and consequently into a nearly total isolation from the masses" (Ruchwarger 1987: 131). In response, the

CDSs held elections for new local leadership. However, support and participation in the CDSs continued to decline.

In 1988, the FSLN appointed Omar Cabezas as the new head of the CDS. He began an investigation, identifying bureaucratism, sectarianism, and a fundamental lack of consultation with the people as major sources of the problems that had caused the committees to lose some of their support. Others identified the problem as opposition to the practice of using the CDSs primarily to *bajar tareas* (assign tasks, top-down) from the Party. In Nicaragua's first independent opinion poll, taken in 1988, respondents were split in their view of the CDSs, with 48 percent in favor of their existence and 47 percent opposed. Even as he cut the CDS bureaucracy by 50 percent, Cabezas stated (1988: 47), as a reflection of his goals, that "The democracy of a movement isn't instilled by decree or imposed from above. It begins at the base" (see also Thayer 1988, and *Washington Post*, August 14, 1988).

In this spirit, major changes were attempted in 1988 in the conception and functioning of the CDSs. In order to change their identification as an arm of the FSLN, an effort was made to transform them into broad-based community organizations, open to all members of the community, and working on issues identified as important by each community. They would no longer carry out policing, military recruitment, or distribution functions that made them open to abuse. At the base level, the Committees for Community Development, as they were renamed, would not be called on to carry out tasks that were the responsibility of either the government or the FSLN as a political party. Thus, the idea was to make them serve the community and organize at the grassroots level, rather than to function as party organizations. The separation of the mass organizations from the party was critical to the FSLN's attempt to revitalize popular participation.

Other mass organizations have also undergone fluctuations and redefinitions, in a long process of "trial and error," compounded by the exigencies of war. Although in practice the mass organizations have always functioned with some degree of autonomy from both the FSLN and the state (see examples in Stahler-Sholk, 1987: 85–6), they were nevertheless very uneven in their functioning, vitality, and independence. The National Union of Farmers and Ranchers (UNAG), representing small and medium agricultural producers, steadily increased its autonomy and influence throughout the 1980s.

By 1988, the women's organization, AMNLAE, was undergoing discussions about separating its identity from the FSLN, in order to provide an independent voice for women. At issue was not only the question of AMNLAE's relation to the FSLN, but the much deeper question of the ongoing struggles for the rights and equality of women. Despite important legal advances, despite statements from top FSLN leadership, despite the positive effects of the Revolution's social advances, despite the incorporation of women into the labor force and into the revolutionary process (in part, through their mobilization for defense purposes), the record by the late 1980s remained very mixed. As Molyneaux (1986) argued, the war, the economic crisis, perhaps even the FSLN's commitment to negotiate with bourgeois opposition forces, including the Catholic Church, limited the state's ability to give priority to feminist demands. This was also part of the context for the debates about autonomous forms of organization for women, the problems of women not incorporated into the formal workforce, the schedule for meeting women's demands (such as access to abortion) (see Molyneaux 1986; Stephens 1988).

On another front, the struggle to redefine the relation of the Sandinista trade unions to the party has been no less complex and difficult. In short, the mass organizations have been undergoing a kind of rebirth, aimed not only at their revitalization in terms of the level of participation, but also at establishing more autonomy in practice (Serra 1988a: 44, 1988b: 29–31). This process of rectification of previous problems in their functioning was reinforced by changing conditions – their exclusion from the formal political arena (the National Assembly) after 1984, and the transition from war to economic crisis as the primary conditioning factor. Taken together, these factors indicated the need for the mass organizations to play a new role, not as part of the government but as part of society, as autonomous representatives of community interests – which, as one close observer pointed out (Serra 1988a: 43), included a role as critics of "deformations" such as bureaucratism or verticalism in the state or party apparatus.

The Economic Crisis: The Greatest Political Challenge of All

The relationship between the government and the people took on even more signficance in the context of the severe economic crisis facing Nicaragua as of 1988–89. In many ways, this became the critical arena for determining the future course of the Revolution, and its class alliances. It was in this arena that political abilities of the Nicaraguan leadership to balance conflicting demands from the capitalist class and from the popular classes would be most severely tested.

The objective situation was staggering. The accumulated effects of eight years of Contra war (which consumed 50 percent of the national budget, 25 percent of economic production, and 10 percent of the labor force; Vilas 1987), U.S. economic embargoes, credit blockades, economic sabotage and destabilization, severe economic crisis affecting the Central American region as a whole (such as falling export prices) and the devastating hurricane of 1988, which caused $800 million in destruction – these factors, compounded by government planning errors, left the country in an unprecedented economic crisis by 1988. Inflation topped 20,000 percent during 1988; by the end of the year, living standards were said to have fallen to pre-World War II levels.

It is beyond the purview of this chapter to go into detail about the economic strategies implicit in the measures taken by the Nicaraguan government since February 1988, in order to regain some level of control over the economy, reduce inflation, and stimulate exports; such analysis has been undertaken by various economists in Nicaragua (see, for example, *Envío* September 1988; Vilas in Cockburn, 1988; Arana 1988; also the Daniel Ortega interview in the *Militant*, July 1, 1988). For our purposes here, the point is that these measures added up to a harsh austerity program (devaluations, cutbacks in government spending and subsidies, wage controls, public sector layoffs), weighing heavily in the short range on the popular sectors as well as other sectors of the population.

At the political level, there was little consultation by the government with the popular sectors about the different options concerning the economic measures before they were instituted (*Envío*, September 1988); subsequently, however, there was a conscious effort to increase the level of information available to the public and to increase popular participation in making decisions affecting them. But, as indicated in the public opinion poll taken in June 1988, nearly three-fourths of those questioned were critical of the government's handling of the economy, declining simply to blame the United States or the Contra war — although they also believed that the Nicaraguan government was seriously trying to solve the problems.

On the positive side, the severity of the situation opened up dynamic discussion and debate throughout the country. The underlying issues included such questions as whether the measures had come too late, whether they should have included compensatory measures to lighten the burden falling upon the popular classes, whether too many concessions were being made to large capitalists, whether the policies should be more oriented toward producers for internal demand as well as export producers.

In a speech in June 1988, President Ortega acknowledged that the measures taken in February of 1988 appeared to be in contradiction with the class interests defended by the Revolution. However, he went on to say, "this must be understood as a necessary step to prevent the economy from collapsing, and to create the conditions so it will recover and become stronger" (*Militant*, July 1, 1988). Clearly, the challenge to the government was to find new ways of dealing with conflicting class interests, of meeting the needs of the workers and peasants, while maintaining an alliance with wealthy producers. (*Barricada* editorial writer Sofía Montenegro captured the political issue in her response to private sector expressions of "lacking confidence" for further investment: "If there is a crisis of confidence here, it is what the workers feel toward the producers" (cited in *Envío*, April 1989).

As in the past, the government's ability to resolve the crisis would depend significantly on listening to popular demands: as one very well-informed analyst put it (Vilas, in Cockburn 1988): "Since the [austerity] policy is going to punish workers and peasants particularly, and since this is a popular government with attention to popular concerns, they'll change the policy."

Taking the Pulse of Public Opinion: The 1988 Opinion Poll

The country's first opinion poll, conducted in 1988, provided a unique glimpse into how Nicaraguans view the government. Carried out under the auspices of an independent organization, ITZTANI, working with the Central American University and the Interamerican Research Center in Los Angeles, California, the poll involved 1,129 people from representative neighborhoods in Managua (see *Envío,* December 1988).

The poll indicated that there was substantial support for the Revolution, but also reflected important areas of questioning and criticism. We have seen above the judgments about the government's handling of the economy. More broadly, 28 percent of the respondents said they identified with the FSLN, while 59 percent stated they had no party identification. (A scant 9 percent identified with opposition parties.) When pressed to answer only "yes" or "no" (with any doubtful responses being classified as "no"), nearly half felt the government was not democratic and 41 percent judged Costa Rica to be the most democratic country in Central America (as opposed to 24 percent for Nicaragua). At the same time, a majority saw the country as moving toward greater democracy, and almost half said the government respected the rights of the opposition parties. While 53 percent opposed the draft, 57 percent supported the relationship between the FSLN, the state, and the armed forces.

Reflecting a strong spirit of national reconciliation, 85 percent believed that dialogue with the opposition was necessary for peace, and 57 percent believed that the Contras should be incorporated into the political life of the country. There was strong support for President Ortega personally, as well as for the government's compliance with the Peace Accords and its commitment to peace. The majority saw U.S. policies as harmful to the region, and 86 percent opposed further U.S. aid to the Contras.

Analyzing the results of the poll by sector, the strongest support for the government came from younger, better educated people from economically better-off neighborhoods. Respondents in poorer neighborhoods, particularly women, were less supportive. The weaker support from the poorer sectors could be because, while sympathizing with the goals of the revolution, they have seen fewer benefits and are bearing the heavy economic burden of the war and the economic measures (*Envío,* December 1988).

Stepping back from the results, the poll itself was encouraging as a measure of the post-Esquipulas political opening, and an indicator of the effervescence and pluralism of Nicaraguan politics. An overwhelming 88 percent of respondents (including 94 percent of those identified with opposition parties) showed no hesitation or fear in answering questions. There is reason to conclude, further, that despite much criticism of the government, the poll was a kind of vote of confidence for the longer-range process of the Revolution.

The poll was also interesting as a barometer of support for the Revolution at another level: while indicating clear areas of criticism of the Sandinista leadership, it showed no pattern of overall disaffection — perhaps a commentary on the ability of that leadership to correct its errors. On the one hand, we have seen indications of a lack of consultation with the base on a number of occasions. These mistakes have been identified by some analysts who are deeply involved in the Revolution as stemming from bureaucratism and a scarcity of trained and educated militants (in addition to lack of strong democratic traditions) (Burbach and Nuñez 1987: 59), and tendencies toward verticalism and centralism (Serra 1988a: 43).

On the other hand, the Sandinistas have shown an ability to self-correct once the consequences of their errors became clear — in a sense, to turn problems into opportunities. The willingness to admit and correct errors has been an important corrective for FSLN tendencies toward vanguardism and "verticalism" — and for inexperience. (In this sense, it is a vanguard, but it is "only one step ahead of the people it leads" — Gilbert 1988: 40.) In the words of Daniel Nuñez, head of the UNAG, "Sandinismo means changing things that are incorrect" (*LAT*, October 17, 1988). In the mid-1980s, the government made sweeping changes to redress the problems on the Atlantic Coast. Likewise, the government restructured its land reform policies that had alienated peasants and created space for the Contras in certain regions (see Vilas 1988). More recently, as seen above, they have undertaken a similar process in regard to reviving and restructuring the CDSs.

In the end, the pressures for correction depend not simply on the good-will of the leadership but also on the level of political development of the population. Nicaraguans are a newly literate and politicized population, seriously concerned about education, actively participating in politics, at times highly critical of the government or the FSLN. As we found in 1987–88 interviews in Nicaragua, "ordinary people" who are members of opposition parties are extremely vocal in expressing their criticisms of the Sandinistas; they have few doubts about their right to speak out, and they do so with great gusto.

At the level of freedom of the press, as well, Nicaragua's *La Prensa* is far more strident a critic than can be found in any other Central American country. Official radio stations carry eight hours a day of open lines for debate and criticism. In addition, over twenty private radio stations have operated more or less freely (with occasional exceptions, such as Radio Católica when it was associated with destabilizing activities), and each of the opposition parties publishes its own newspaper. A 1989 study concluded that there exists, overall, "wide public access to the media" (Artz 1989; see also Nichols 1985). As of early 1989, the Union of Nicaraguan Journalists was waging a campaign to change the media regulations which had served as the basis for censorship during the war, and the National Assembly was preparing to debate the issue. All of this contrasts sharply with Guatemala, for example, where the only progressive opposition newspaper was dynamited off the scene in June 1988 (by government security forces, the evidence indicated), and its editors forced into exile once again.

Nicaraguans are also committed to the democratization of social relations overall (between classes, between women and men). Despite the major continuing problems of sexism and discrimination against women, the attitudes and expectations of young women, for example, are striking in their interactions with their superiors, with men in general, even with international dignitaries: in place of the traditional deference to authority, there is an assertion of equality, a confidence based on being engaged in the attempt to build a new society.

Finally, there is in Nicaragua today an expectation of government accountability to citizens' needs that is inconceivable in other Central American countries. Yet, despite many unmet expectations, despite the realities of war and unmatched economic deprivation, despite the many criticisms of government economic policies, the Nicaraguan people have not turned against the Revolution, or against the Sandinista leadership — indeed, a tribute to the maturity and high level of politicization on all sides. In the aftermath of new cutbacks and austerity measures, one American observer commented to a *New York Times* reporter, "If you tried something like this in most of Latin America there would be riots in the street" (as indeed occurred shortly thereafter in Venezuela). The austerity measures revealed, as the *Times* reporter concluded, "a government that is still deeply confident of its popular support" (Uhlig in *NYT*, February 1, 1989; see also *LAT*, March 6, 1989).

CONCLUSION

The ongoing process of democratic construction raises many unresolved issues of principle and of practice. What are the lasting effects of the U.S.-sponsored Contra war and economic war of the last eight years? What forms will the struggle for democracy take in the new era characterized by political/ideological struggle and unprecedented economic crisis? Given the constrictions of the crisis, how can the needs of the majority be reconciled with the demands of the propertied classes, and what will be the government's policy of alliances in the coming period? How, and with what degree of autonomy, will the mass organizations develop as vehicles of popular participation in decision making? What role will they play in counterbalancing the bourgeois and middle-class opposition parties? What is the changing role of the FSLN as a party in relation to the state? What are the debates within the FSLN about the role of the party as a vanguard, and/or as an engine for mobilizing consensus (see Annunziata 1988)? Reassessing once again the impact of the Central American Peace Accords, will history show them to have paved the way for some form of power sharing in Nicaragua? What balance between the Sandinistas and opposition parties will result from the 1990 election, and how will this affect the social goals of the Revolution? What, in short will be the new blend of political pluralism and social revolution in Nicaragua?

These are among the real issues facing Nicaragua, as opposed to the fantasma image of Nicaragua as a "one-party state." Certainly, these issues will never be understood if they are evaluated from a narrow framework appropriate only to advanced nations, much less from an ideological framework designed to justify the overthrow of the Sandinistas (whether by military force or political/economic measures). Rather, these are, in Fagen's words (1986: 261), issues of "democratic practice associated with socialism in the periphery." They are the political problems and contradictions of Nicaragua's process of democratic construction—a process that moves not in a linear fashion but forward, nonetheless.

In the 1988 opinion poll, as seen above, 41 percent of those polled identified Costa Rica as the region's most democratic country (as contrasted with 24 percent for Nicaragua). Perhaps this statistic contains a broader message than would first appear: no matter how hard Nicaragua may try to democratize under wartime conditions, in the end, war leads to the militarization of civil society, and necessarily becomes a limiting factor on democracy. In this article, we have chronicled the construction of democracy as it proceeded within the logic of war; let us hope that the article to be written a few years hence will trace that process within the logic of peace.

—May 1, 1989

NOTES

The authors would like to thank our colleagues at Global Options and the University of California, Santa Cruz, and others scholars and friends in Nicaragua and the United States, who commented extensively on earlier drafts of this chapter. Their comments and criticisms have been invaluable.

1. This structural perspective is to be contrasted, for example, with one of the major currents in contemporary scholarship regarding democracy in Latin America: the "bureaucratic-authoritarianism" analysis, which has been developed particularly for the Southern Cone (whose experience differs substantially from that of Central America). The main exponents of this analysis (O'Donnell, Schmitter, and Whitehead) deliberately refrain from applying their model to Central America. However, other scholars more particularly concerned with Central America have taken an approach that shares the same basic assumption: that political (representative) democracy can be analyzed apart from a broader conception of democracy which includes socioeconomic equality and popular participation in fighting for such equality (see, for example, Karl 1986). In contrast, we believe that, while the two conceptions can be definitionally separated, in a case like Central America it is necessary from the very outset to examine political democracy in relation to socioeconomic issues and political participation by the majority classes. Therefore, we do not agree with the view that a democracy can be formed primarily by an interelite consensus or pact. Based on Central American historical and current experience, we would argue for a broader view that meaningful "transitions to democracy" there involve more sweeping social change (on the scale of the major bourgeois and socialist revolutions historically).

2. In regard to "counterinsurgency democracy," we refer specifically to the conception of the neoconservative U.S. policy theorists such as Jeane Kirkpatrick, for whom "democratic" is synonymous with "pro-United States" and "anticommunist." Kirkpatrick's famous article, "Dictatorships and Double Standards" (1979), argued that the United States should support the military in countries like Guatemala and El Salvador in their evolution from a (right-wing) "authoritarian dictatorship" into a democracy— while the Sandinista government in Nicaragua must be overthrown, since a (left-wing)

"totalitarian dictatorship" cannot evolve into a democracy. Additionally, the United States must be willing to intervene militarily to reverse the tide of Marxist revolution. Hence, overthrow of revolutionary governments is the specific meaning of the policy of "promoting the democratic revolution," in the words of another proponent of this theory, Michael Ledeen (1985). It is in relation to the counterinsurgent conception of democracy as anticommunism that we can understand the defense made by these policy analysts of the Nicaraguan Contras as model democrats and "freedom fighters." While they speak in the name of representative democracy, their policy recommendations as enshrined in the Reagan Doctrine have proven antithetical, in practice, to democracy in any of its traditional forms.

3. Particularly in the light of the extraordinary amount of criticism directed against the Nicaraguan government for its press censorship laws during the war, a word is in order concerning U.S. press coverage of Nicaragua, specifically that of the *New York Times*. For years the *NYT* (and other major U.S. media) contributed to distortions about Nicaragua, such as the discounting of the 1984 election and the characterization of Nicaragua as a one-party state. In the aftermath of the Central American Peace Plan, the *New York Times* (like other major U.S. media) took the opportunity to put Nicaragua on the hot seat, focusing 80 percent of its Central America coverage on Nicaraguan compliance (or "noncompliance"), raising questions about the Sandinistas' "real motivations" in democratizing (Media Alliance 1988; FAIR 1987). In critical respects, as several analysts have pointed out (e.g., Lewis 1989), the major U.S. media came to adopt or bow to the Reagan adminstration's official line on Nicaragua.

A low point was the *New York Times* editorial, "The Sandinista Road to Stalinism," of July 10, 1986 (a few days after passage of the $100 million in Contra aid, and at the height of the Reagan administration's ideological offensive). The editorial charged Nicaragua with being "totalitarian," suggesting that the Sandinista goal all along had been to establish a police state. Further, the editorial argued that restrictions on civil liberties in Nicaragua could not be attributed to the U.S. Contra war—in spite of the fact that the major opposition parties inside Nicaragua were reported in the *Los Angeles Times* (omitted from *NYT* news articles) to have issued strong statements that the Contra war was precisely the reason for these restrictions, and presaged only "more violence and pain" for Nicaragua. President Reagan subsequently (May 3, 1987) quoted that *NYT* editorial to buttress his pro-Contra argument, in a speech to the American Newspaper Publishers' Association.

4. As pointed out by Andrew Reding (1987: 271), a student of Nicaragua's constitutional process, the commitment to a mixed economy has been very real: in fact, 57 percent of the gross domestic product is from the private sector; 63 percent of manufacturing and 76 percent of agriculture remain in private hands. There is a great increase in the share of land held by small farmers and cooperatives, with over one-third of this increase coming from the dissolution of unprofitable state farms. Hardly a "Soviet-style centrally planned economy!"

5. Verbally, the Reagan administration justified its attacks as pressuring for electoral democracy and "promoting democratic revolution" (see note 2). But in fact, the key to the Reagan policy in Nicaragua—and in Central America generally—has been an obfuscation, promoting anticommunist or counterinsurgent "democracy" under the guise of representative democracy. (We have developed this argument elsewhere: see Jonas 1989). A second obfuscation has been the labeling of independent revolutionary govern-

ments like Nicaragua as "Marxist-Leninist" or "communist," hence justifying an aggressive U.S. policy. So, in the name of "fighting communism" and "restoring democracy," the United States has sought to eliminate the Sandinista government. Falling short of that, the goal has been to cause as much physical, economic, and human destruction as possible, in order to make of Nicaragua a negative rather than a positive example to the Third World.

The other pillar of U.S. policy in Central America has been the fortification of "democratic" (anticommunist, pro-U.S.) governments, either military or civilian, authoritarian or liberal, depending on the circumstances, as bulwarks against nationalist or socialist revolutionary movements—and the military defeat of insurgencies where they have arisen. At the present time there is a preference for elected civilian governments in countries like El Salvador and Guatemala facing such insurgencies. But that is not a commitment of principle. Rather, it is seen as the most effective way (within a counterinsurgency framework) to resolve economic and political crisis and avoid "another Nicaragua." In the present situation, Washington has also used the election of civilian governments in Guatemala and El Salvador to justify action against Nicaragua (the "only unelected government" or "rotten apple" in the region).

REFERENCES

In addition to the references listed below, this chapter is based on interviews in Nicaragua during the summers of 1987 and 1988, with a wide range of participants in and observers of Nicaraguan politics.

Americas Watch
1985 *Human Rights in Nicaragua: Reagan, Rhetoric and Reality.* New York.

———.1987 *Human Rights in Nicaragua, 1986.* New York.

Annunziata, Lucia
1988 "Democracy and the Sandinistas." *Nation* (April 2).

Arana, Mario
1988 "Reforma Económica 1988: Hacia un Nuevo Modelo Económico?" Paper presented at conference on foreign debt.

Artz, Lee
1989 "Public Access and Press Freedom in Nicaragua." Stanford, CA: Mid-Peninsula Peace Center (manuscript).

Azicri, Max
1989 "The 1987 Nicaraguan Constitution: An Analytical Commentary," *Review of Socialist Law* (Netherlands) (summer).

Booth, John
1986 "Election Amid War and Revolution: Toward Evaluating the 1984 Nicaraguan National Elections." In Paul Drake and Eduardo Silva, eds., *Elections and Democratization in Latin America, 1980–1985.* San Diego: University of California.

———.1988 "Toward Reconciliation and Democracy in Central America?" Manuscript prepared for Inter-American Dialogue.

Burbach, Roger, and Orlando Nuñez
1987 *Fire in the Americas.* London: Verso.

Cabezas, Omar
1988 "Organícense como quieran y para lo que quieran." Interview in *Pensamiento Própio* (July–August).

CAHI (Central American Historical Institute)
1986 *Update*, Managua (April).

Carnoy, Martin
1984 *The State and Political Theory.* Princeton: Princeton University Press.

Catholic Institute for International Relations (CIIR)
1987 *Right to Survive: Human Rights in Nicaragua.* Summarized in *Envío*. Oct.

Chitnis, Lord
1984 "Chitnis Report on the 1984 Nicaraguan Election." Summarized by Gregorio Selser, *El Día* (Mexico) Nov. 16, 1986.

Christopher, Warren
1987 "U.S. Policy and the Sandinista Regime" (Sept. 1979). In Robert Leiken and Barry Rubin, eds., *The Central America Crisis Reader.* New York: Summit Books.

CIERA (Centro de Investigaciones y Estudios de la Reforma Agraria)
1984 *Participatory Democracy in Nicaragua*, Managua.

CIVS (Comisión Internacional de Verificación y Seguimiento)
1988 *Informe sobre los Progresos en el Complimiento de los Acuerdos del Prodecimiento para Alcanzar la Paz Firme y Duradera en Centroamérica*, Jan. 14.

Close, David
1988 *Nicaragua.* New York: Pinter Press.

Cockburn, Alexander
1988 "Who Whom? The Sandinistas and the Economy." Interview with Carlos Vilas. *Zeta* (Dec.).

Colburn, Forrest
1986 *Post-Revolutionary Nicaragua.* Berkeley: University of California.

Conroy, Michael
1987 "Economic Aggression as an Instrument of Low-Intensity Warfare." In Thomas Walker, ed., *Reagan vs. the Sandinistas.* Boulder: Westview.

Cornelius, Wayne
1986 "The 1984 Nicaraguan Elections Revisited." LASA *Forum* (Winter).

Corragio, José Luis
1985 "Socialist Movements and Revolution: The Case of Nicaragua." In David Slater, ed., *New Social Movements and the State in Latin America.* Amsterdam: CEDLA.

————.1986 *Nicaragua: Revolution and Democracy.* Boston: Allen & Unwin.

Corragio, José Luis, and George Irvin
1985 "Revolution and Pluralism in Nicaragua." In George Irvin and Xabier Gorostiaga, eds., *Towards an Alternative for Central America and the Caribbean.* London: Allen & Unwin.

Cruz Sequeira, Arturo
1984 "Nicaragua: Revolution in Crisis." *SAIS Review* (Winter–Spring).

Drake, Paul, and Eduardo Silva, eds.
1986 *Elections and Democratization in Latin America.* San Diego: University of California Press.

Envío
1985 "Monografico: The Final Stretch of the Electoral Process, Analysis of Electoral Results (I–II)," and "Interview: An Inside View of the Elections." Managua, Nicaragua: Instituto Histórico Centroamericano.

————.1988 "Central America 1987." Managua: Instituto Histórico Centroamericano (Apr.).

Fals Borda, Orlando
1986 "El Nuevo Despertar de los Movimientos Sociales." *Revista Foro*, Colombia (September).

Fagen, Richard
1986 "The Politics of Transition." In Richard Fagen, Carmen Diana Deere, and José Luis Corragio, eds., *Transition and Development.* New York: Monthly Review.

————.1987 *Forging Peace: The Challenge of Central America.* New York: Basil Blackwell.

Fairness and Accuracy in Reporting (FAIR)
1987 "Nicaragua and the U.S. Media: A History of Lies," *Extra* (October–November).

Gilbert, Dennis
1988 *Sandinistas.* New York: Basil Blackwell.

Gleijeses, Piero
1986 "The Reagan Doctrine and Central America," *Current History* (December).

González Casanova, Pablo
1986 "Cuando Hablamos de Democracia, de qué Hablamos?" (manuscript).

Gorostiaga, Xabier
1982 "Los Dilemas de la Revolución Popular Sandinista" INIES/CRIES, *Cuadernos de Pensamiento Propío* (Nicaragua).

Gutman, Roy
1988a "Nicaraguan Turning Point: How the 1984 Vote Was Sabotaged," *Nation* (May 7).

————.1988b *Banana Diplomacy: The Making of American Policy in Nicaragua, 1981–1987.* New York: Simon & Schuster.

Halebsky, Sandor, and Susanne Jonas
1988 "Obstacles to the Peace Process in Central America." In John Kirk and George Schuyler, eds., *Central America: Democracy, Development and Change.* New York: Praeger.

Hamilton, Nora
1982 *The Limits of State Autonomy: Post-Revolutionary Mexico.* Princeton: Princeton University Press.

Herman, Edward, and Frank Brodhead
1984 *Demonstration Elections.* Boston: South End.

Hinkelammert, Franz
1987 *Democracia y Totalitarismo.* San Jose, Costa Rica: DEI.

Jonas, Susanne
1976 "Nicaragua." *NACLA's Latin America and Empire Report* (February).

————.1982 "The Nicaraguan Revolution and the Reemerging Cold War," in Thomas Walker, ed., *Nicaragua in Revolution.* New York: Praeger.

————.1989 "Elections and Transitions: The Guatemalan and Nicaraguan Cases," in John Booth and Mitchell Seligson, eds., *Elections and Democracy in Central America.* Chapel Hill: University of North Carolina Press.

Karl, Terry
1986 "Imposing Consent: Electoralism vs. Democratization in El Salvador," in Paul Drake and Eduardo Silva, eds., *Elections and Democratization in Latin America, 1980–1985.* San Diego: University of California.

Kirkpatrick, Jeane
1979 "Dictatorships and Double Standards." *Commentary* (November).

————.1982a *Dictatorships and Double Standards: Rationalism and Reason in Politics.* New York: American Enterprise Institute/ Simon & Schuster.

————.1982b Statement before the Conference on Free Elections, November 4, 1982. In *Promoting Free Elections.* Washington: Department of State, Bureau of Public Affairs, Current Policy, no. 433 (November).

Kornbluh, Peter
1987 *Nicaragua: The Price of Intervention.* Washington: Institute for Policy Studies.

Latin American Studies Association (LASA)
1985 Report of the LASA Delegation to Observe the Nicaraguan General Election of November 4, 1984. LASA *Forum* (Winter).

————.1988 Final Report of the LASA Commission on Compliance with the Central America Peace Accords (March 15).

Ledeen, Michael
1985 "How to Support the Democratic Revolution." *Commentary* (March).

Leiken, Robert
1984 "Sins of the Sandinistas: Nicaragua's Untold Stories," *New Republic* (Oct. 8).

————.1985 "Nicaraguan Tangle," *New York Review of Books* (Dec. 5).

Lewis, Anthony
1989 "The Intimidated Press," *New York Review of Books* (Jan. 19).

Lobel, Jules
1987 "The New Nicaraguan Constitution: Uniting Participatory and Representative Democracy," *Monthly Review* (Dec.).

————.1988 "The Meaning of Democracy: Representative and Participatory Democracy in the New Nicaraguan Constitution," *University of Pittsburgh Law Review* 49(3).

Malloy, James M., and Mitchell A. Seligson, eds.
1987 *Authoritarians and Democrats: Regime Transition in Latin America.* Pittsburgh: University of Pittsburgh Press.

Marchetti, Peter
1986 "War, Popular Participation and the Transition to Socialism." In Richard Fagen et al., eds. *Transition and Development.* New York: Monthly Review Press.

Marini, Ruy Mauro
1980 "The Question of the State in the Latin American Struggle." *Contemporary Marxism* 1 (Spring).

Media Alliance
1988 "U.S. Media Coverage of Central America," *Bay Guardian* (Jan. 6 and April 20).

Molyneaux, Maxine
1986 "Mobilization without Emancipation? Women's Interests, State and Revolution." In Richard Fagen et al., eds. *Transition and Development.* New York: Monthly Review Press.

Neier, Aryeh
1988 "Has Arias Made a Difference?" *New York Review of Books* (March 17).

Nichols, John Spicer
1985. "The Media." In Thomas Walker, ed. *Nicaragua: The First Five Years.* New York: Praeger.

————.1988. "La Prensa: The CIA Connection," *Columbia Journalism Review* (July–Aug.).

Nuñez, Orlando
1980 "La Tercera Fuerza Social en los Movimientos de Liberación Nacional." (Nicaragua: unpublished manuscript).

————.1986a "Las Fuerzas Clasistas de la Revolución Popular Sandinista." *Cuadernos de Sociologia* 2 (Managua: UCA).

————.1986b "Agresion Externa, Sobrevivencia, y Democracia Popular en la Revolucion Sandinista" (manuscript).

O'Donnell, Guillermo, Philippe Schmitter, and Laurence Whitehead, eds.
1986 *Transitions from Authoritarian Rule: Latin America.* Baltimore: Johns Hopkins University Press.

Ortega, Marvin
1988a "Notas sobre Proceso Político y Revolución en Nicaragua," *Polémica* 5(2a epoca) (May–August).

1988b "Partidos Políticos y Lucha por el Poder en Nicaragua," *Revista Nicaraguense de Ciencias Sociales* (4).

Pastor, Robert
1987 *Condemned to Repetition: The United States and Nicaragua.* Princeton: Princeton University Press.

Petras, James
1986 "The Redemocratization Process." *Contemporary Marxism* 14 (Fall).

Petras, James, and Frank Fitzgerald
1988 "Authoritarianism and Democracy in the Transition to Socialism." *Latin American Perspectives* (Winter).

Radosh, Ronald
1984 "The Drift toward Repression." In Mark Falcoff and Robert Royal, eds. *Crisis and Opportunity: U.S. Policy in Central America and the Caribbean.* Washington: Ethics and Public Policy Center.

Ramírez, Sergio
1988 "Interview." *Bulletin of the Nicaragua Information Center* (Feb./March).

————.1984 "The Unfinished American Revolution and Nicaragua Today," in Marlene
    Dixon and Susanne Jonas, eds., *Nicaragua Under Siege*. San Francisco: Synthesis.

Reding, Andrew
1984 "What Really Happened on November 4?" *Christianity and Crisis* (Dec. 24).

————.1985 "On Nicaraguan Democracy." *World Policy Journal* (Summer).

————.1986 "'By the People': Constitution Making in Nicaragua." *Christianity and Crisis*
    (Dec. 6).

————.1987 "Nicaragua's New Constitution." *World Policy Journal* (Spring).

Robinson, Linda
1988 "Peace in Central America?" *America and the World, 1987* (*Foreign Affairs* review).

Robinson, William, and Kent Norsworthy
1987 *David and Goliath: The U.S. War against Nicaragua*. New York: Monthly Review
    Press.

Ruccio, David
1988 "State, Class and Transition." *Latin American Perspectives* (Spring).

Ruchwarger, Gary
1987 *People in Power: Forging a Grassroots Democracy in Nicaragua*. South Hadley,
    Mass.: Bergin & Garvey.

Serafino, Nina
1988 "Dateline Managua: Defining Democracy." *Foreign Policy* (Spring).

Serra, Luis
1988a "Organizaciones Populares: Entre las Bases y el Poder." *Pensamiento Própio*
    (Dec.).

————.1988b "Democratización Política y Organizaciones Populares en Nicaragua."
    (manuscript).

Sklar, Holly
1988 *Washington's War on Nicaragua*. Boston: South End.

Slater, David
1987 "Socialismo, Democracia y el Imperativo Teritorial: Elementos para una
    Comparación de las Experiencias Cubana y Nicaragüense." *Estudios Sociales
    Centroamericanos*. (May–August).

Smith, Wayne
1987 "Lies about Nicaragua." *Foreign Policy*, no. 67 (Summer).

Spalding, Rose, ed.
1987 *The Political Economy of Revolutionary Nicaragua*. Boston: Allen & Unwin.

Stahler-Sholk, Richard
1987 "Building Democracy in Nicaragua." In George Lopez and Michael Stohl, eds.
    Liberalization and Redemocratization in Latin America. Westport, Conn.: Green-
    wood.

————.1988 "Stabilization, Destabilization, and the Popular Sector in Nicaragua, 1979–
    87." (manuscript).

Stephens, Beth
1988 "Women in Nicaragua." *Monthly Review* (September).

Thayer, Millie
1988 "Back to the Barrios." *The Guardian* (Aug. 31).

Thomas, Clive
1984 *The Rise of the Authoritarian State in Peripheral Societies.* New York: Monthly Review.

Torres-Rivas, Edelberto
1986 "Centroamérica: guerra, transición y democracia." Paper presented at Congress of the Asociación Centroamericana de Sociología.

———.1987 *Centroamérica: La democracia posible.* San José: EDUCA.

———.1988 "Centroamérica: La Transición Autoritaria hacia la Democracia." *Polémica* #4 (2a epoca) (Jan.–April).

United States Out of Central America (USOCA)
1985 *Democracy in Nicaragua.* San Francisco: USOCA.

Vaky, Viron
1987 "Positive Containment in Nicaragua." *Foreign Policy* (Fall).

Valenta, Jiri, and Esperanza Duran, eds.
1987 *Conflict in Nicaragua.* Boston: Allen & Unwin.

Vilas, Carlos
1986a *The Sandinista Revolution.* New York: Monthly Review.

———.1986b "The Mass Organizations in Nicaragua." *Monthly Review* (November).

———.1987 "El Impacto de la Guerra en la Revolución Sandinista." *Revista Nicaraguense de Ciencias Sociales* #2 (March).

———.1988a "War and Revolution in Nicaragua." In Ralph Miliband, Leo Panitch, and John Saville, eds. *Socialist Register.* (London: Merlin).

———.1988b "Democratización y Autonomía en la Costa Atlántica." *Revista Nicaraguense de Ciencias Sociales* (April).

Vilas, Carlos, and Richard Harris
1985 "National Liberation, Popular Democracy and the Transition to Socialism." In Richard Harris and Carlos Vilas, eds. *Nicaragua: A Revolution under Siege.* London: Zed.

Walker, Thomas, ed.
1982 *Nicaragua in Revolution.* New York: Praeger.

———, ed. 1985 *Nicaragua: The First Five Years.* New York: Praeger.

———, ed. 1987 *Reagan vs. the Sandinistas.* Boulder: Westview.

3

THE ORIGINS OF CRISIS AND INSTABILITY IN CENTRAL AMERICA

Edelberto Torres-Rivas

The years prior to the early seventies were characterized by a series of contradictions in Latin America. The revolutionary storm clouds brewing in the Southern Cone cast a shadow on some societies and paradoxically illuminated others, as illustrated by the return of Perón and the Cámpora period in Argentina, the rise and fall of the Tupamaro guerrillas in Uruguay, the end of the Popular Assembly in Bolivia, and the crisis and eventual downfall of democracy in Chile. Since that period, and clearly many years before, Central American society was generating its own crisis. The region was never affected by that storm to the south, but instead experienced its own cyclone, originating in two factors: those of an internal nature, *strictu sensu*, and those of an international nature.

When exploring the causes of instability in the region (the source of the profound crisis in Central America), it is fitting to speak of *three distinct stages or periods* that feature an unequal combination of economic and political factors. This is a historical process increasingly affected by international events. However, in time this process has taken on a regional dimension. In effect, the crisis is a local phenomenon with respect to its historical roots, the setting it creates, and its individual development. The national character of the crisis, made manifest by its historical subjects and available resources, should be particularly underlined in the first stage, in which Guatemala, El Salvador, and Nicaragua are the countries most openly affected. The crisis today has become *regional* and ends up affecting Honduras and Costa Rica in different ways.

The crisis only took on regional proportions when an external, geopolitical vision confused the deepest roots of discontent and placed the entire issue in the context of a strategic confrontation between two great superpowers. All current attempts to explain the situation in terms of an East-West conflict tend to obscure and thus confuse the historical reasons underlying national conflicts.

STRUCTURAL FACTORS (FIRST STAGE)

The first stage, which can be attributed to different causes in each of the countries, came to an end in the mid-seventies. Ever since the end of the Second World War, the model for economic growth exacerbated the inequalities inherent in an agricultural society: once again, diversification and modernization of export agriculture were based on the gap between the sector based on vast land holdings and capital investments, which responded to international demands, and the internal market sector, which had been reduced to a *minifundio* comprised of impoverished rural masses living below minimum subsistence levels.

Regional policies for economic integration were responsible for the rise of an urban industrial base, resulting in some degree of economic and commercial dynamism. By now it is well known that this industrial growth was based on a labor force with a significant labor surplus that could not be absorbed. The new industry, working within the difficult framework of import substitution, was geared toward producing goods for immediate consumption by middle- and high-income groups. In spite of its modest size, this industrial growth proved to be an important factor which created economic and social inequities, and resulted in an ever-increasing urban population and the growth of poverty belts. The consequent process of social marginalization became visible and permanent, a dramatic testimony to the kind of economic growth promoted by the state, foreign investment, and private national capital.

The foregoing outline is important because the structural factors inherent in this kind of economic growth produced instability and the subsequent crisis in Central America. Some statistics on poverty (defined as the inability to meet basic needs for subsistence and social reproduction) will serve as objective examples (see Table 1).

During the first stage, strictly political factors, which affected each of the five countries differently, were presented as the politics of the masses. Several attempts made to establish political forms and popular participation in the political process or efforts made to insure a state policy of reform capable of altering the status quo in favor of the masses, met with frustration. In this respect it is as important to note Costa Rica's unique experience as an exception to the norm as it is to highlight the predominance of different forms of extreme authoritarian political rule in the other four countries. Of these, Nicaragua was beyond a doubt the most extreme case. The Somoza dynasty was a jarring expression of personal power, of corruption through blurring the difference between what was private and what was public, and of dependence on North American imperialism.

Table 1 — Central America: Estimated Poverty Levels as of 1980

Item	Total	Costa Rica	El Salvador	Guatemala	Honduras	Nicaragua
Total	20,696	2,213	4,747	7,262	3,691	2,733
State of Poverty	13,178	549	3,267	5,166	2,515	1,681
Extreme Poverty	8,647	300	2,427	2,879	2,092	949
Unsatisfied Basic Needs	4,531	249	840	2,287	423	732
Non Poor	7,518	1,664	1,530	2,096	1,176	1,052
Structure Percentage						
Total	100.0	100.0	100.0	100.0	100.0	100.0
State of Poverty	63.7	24.8	68.1	71.1	68.2	61.5
Extreme Poverty	41.8	13.6	50.6	39.6	56.7	34.7
Unsatisfied Basic Needs	21.9	11.2	17.5	31.5	11.5	26.8
Non Poor	36.3	75.2	31.9	28.9	31.8	38.5

Source: CEPAL, Projecto de Necesidades Basicas en el Istmo Centroamericano, based on information provided by the countries and Celade, Boletin Demografico, Año XIV, #28, prepared by the author.

Another very important and increasingly destabilizing factor in the region was the misfortune experienced by the democratic process in several countries. This misfortune became a dead end, or perhaps a road of no return, marked by the slow but inexorable growth of popular discontent.

THE UNFOLDING OF THE CRISIS (SECOND STAGE)

The second stage of the crisis began slowly (it is difficult to specify dates) when various attempts to bring about democracy failed, as did all efforts to introduce reforms in the existing economic system, based on growth without development. The failure is directly attributable to an intolerance for social change and reforms which would ameliorate the worst effects of the extreme concentration of land and wealth and resistance to the opening and sharing of political power, which would provide the masses with real civil liberties.

All efforts to reform the existing economic system and all actions taken to make politics more democratic failed during this second stage. Instead, the result was the creation of special circumstances that abetted the rise of violent forms of popular struggle. These uprisings, which at first seemed to be nonorganic responses to the intolerance for social change, the rejection of all efforts to bring about a more equitable distribution of land and wealth, or the possibility of opening and sharing of political power, were in reality broad-based social movements. These movements with a broad class base were linked with guerrilla organizations, political-military groups whose insurgent activities began setting the stage for the emergence of larger popular movements.

By the early 1970s, the political crises in Guatemala, El Salvador, and Nicaragua had evolved to the point where a new phenomenon emerged: armed resistance with popular support. The resistance defied the traditional forms of authority represented by the state. By challenging the established order, it virtually rejected the past and sought (at times in nonexplicit ways) the creation of a new society to overcome the dark legacy of past dictatorships, political violence, and above all, the extremely difficult conditions of social existence. Slowly, the conditions leading to the formation of autonomous popular movements were set, especially in the rural areas where *campesinos* had been forced into passivity for generations in order to maintain traditional social order.

The social movements were popular and revolutionary and thus constituted a new and original experience. They were new because their predominantly popular nature did not limit participation to a small nucleus of students and members of the urban proletariat. Instead, it was the movement of semi-proletarian urban and rural masses and large sectors of the impoverished middle classes, united by their common status as politically subordinated groups, undergoing the same experiences of arbitrariness and violence as the dominated classes. They were new also because of the diversity of the ideological-cultural currents which came together in the protest — a diversity which combined the Marxism of communist militants or ex-militants, the radicalism of nationalistic sectors of the petty bourgeoisie, and the refreshing presence of Christian sectors which, starting from a religious judgment of the political order, articulated a social criticism and a revolutionary praxis to important sectors of the peasantry.

During the second stage of the crisis, economic disequilibrium was less significant than political events *latu sensu*. It is in this stage that social protest movements acquired a profoundly national, radical dimension which manifested itself ultimately in its most intense form, armed struggle. But well before this level of social protest developed in Guatemala, El Salvador, and Nicaragua, the state and its system of domination had begun to mobilize in response, for a show of *generalized violence* through the strengthening of the state's repressive apparatus and the creation of new forms of institutionalized coercion.

The modernization and equipping of various police forces and of the army were accompanied by two phenomena that are extremely important for understanding the development of the crisis: under the supervision of the army, the state installed new, organic, sophisticated forms of control and repression, generally known as paramilitary squads; and in effect the so-called judicial power was dismantled, to give free rein to the violence and repression that were implemented outside the legal framework which would otherwise guide the state and the population. The resulting disruption of established social norms and the ineffectiveness of the judicial system have given civil life in these countries a tragic sense of social disintegration. The state's inability to provide law and order on a daily basis undermines its legitimacy. State-sponsored violence was a major factor working to break down society even before popular protests took on a more generalized character.

GENERALIZED INSTABILITY (THIRD STAGE)

The third stage of the crisis began in mid-1979, specifically in July of that year, with the fall of the Somoza dictatorship. The well-known events surrounding that extraordinary historical moment are important because they signaled not only the end of a dictatorship, but also the total restructuring of state power, including the defeat of its most important institution for political order—the armed forces. The markedly foreign character of Somoza's power gave the Sandinista victory another equally important characteristic: since Somoza was an important, faithful ally of the United States, his downfall must be seen as Washington, D.C.'s most severe hemispheric political defeat in the last twenty-five years. For these reasons, the North American government immediately began to combat the Sandinistas, even before they had a chance to define their economic, social, diplomatic, or military policies.

The Central American crisis worsened with the triumph of the Sandinistas because the United States decided never to tolerate another such instance. The

U.S. policy of counterinsurgency has now become an open policy of supporting counterrevolution in the region. To achieve its goals, the United States is employing its old political allies and seeking new ones, strengthening at all costs the states' repressive institutions.

From 1979 to the present national instability became regionalized. The U.S. foreign policy of supporting Somoza's former National Guard (operating out of Honduras) was formulated early on, in December of 1981, during a meeting of the National Security Council. As a matter of fact, the Santa Fe Document, written in 1980, before Reagan's election, by the people who would later become his senior advisors on foreign policy had already called for an open policy of intervention. To this one must add the ever-increasing support provided to El Salvador's Armed Forces, which began in 1980 and which, by the first quarter of 1981, had become massive military assistance.

The diplomatic-political and above all, military, involvement also encompassed Honduras, now turned into what is known as the United States's "aircraft carrier" in Central America. Consequently, U.S. policy in the region converted what was once a national social conflict into an open civil war with regional and foreign dimensions. In other words, the counterrevolution regionalized the crisis and increased the level of social and political instability to unforeseen levels. This environment poses a threat to the neutral and peaceful tradition of Costa Rica, whose leaders work to maintain and insure an active, unarmed, permanent state of neutrality.

Counterrevolutionary efforts are confronting popular struggles in a double pincer movement:

1. to attack, with the latest available technology, all forms of legal popular organization (unions, parties, student movements, *campesinos*) in order to keep social protest movements from uniting with armed struggles; and

2. to reduce all forms of rebellion and discontent to purely military action, hoping to destroy them with the superior technical facilities available to the state.

In this manner, beginning in 1980 in Guatemala and in 1981 in El Salvador, the urban popular movement and the most expressly political forms have been brutally attacked and destroyed. Efforts to isolate the guerrilla movement from its social bases have included the conscious isolation of the city through the implementation of White Terror, and the physical destruction of entire populations in rural areas, especially in Guatemala's northern Indian zone and in eastern El Salvador. Guatemala's popular insurrections have been terribly hard-hit.

Obviously, the aforementioned increases regionally instability as follows: in recent years there has been an increasing destruction of productive forces, materials, and equipment resulting from armed conflicts, state-sponsored repression or defensive guerrilla measures. Material losses caused by military activities on the Nicaraguan border, for example, were calculated at $650 million dollars in December of 1984. There is no accurate way to estimate financial losses suffered when over thirty-two Indian peasant villages were destroyed by Guatemala's army during its extermination campaign, in effect from December 1981 to May 1982, or the even greater damage resulting from violent events in El Salvador.

The material destruction is closely linked to the physical annihilation of people (such as murdered and missing *desaparecidos*), be they actively involved in the armed conflict or civilians living in or near the place of conflict. Exact figures are not available for the number of victims — from both parties — in the three countries where the crisis has become militarized. Official estimates published in the *Revista Estudios Centroamericanos* (ECA, No. 429–30, San Salvador, 1985, p. 550) indicated that during 1984 alone 3,108 members of the armed forces and other security services were either killed, wounded, or disappeared and that 8,200 civilians met a similar fate at the hands of the police and the armed forces. No figures are available to determine the number of guerrillas killed. In Guatemala, the situation is very similar, though no reliable figures are available. The Central American Institute for Documentation and Social Research (ICADIS), which operates in Costa Rica, estimates that between 1980 and 1984 approximately 14,500 people were murdered, kidnapped, or disappeared. This figure does not include military casualties from military encounters because the guerrilla forces do not provide statistics on their losses. ICADIS estimates the number of military personnel, police, and other security and army officials killed or fallen in combat to be 4,200.

Presenting a different perspective, Dr. Leonardo Mata, a renowned Costa Rican medical specialist, published an article stating that toward the end of the seventies, according to a United Nations Report, the "*homicide* rate per 100,000 inhabitants was as follows: El Salvador, 60; Guatemala, 50; Honduras, 37; Nicaragua, 28; Costa Rica, 5" (*La Nación*, May 15, 1985, p. 15). But since these are the figures for normal levels of violence, we must add the number of deaths resulting from political violence to get the complete picture. According to the same article, the figure would be 500 per every 100,000 inhabitants in El Salvador, Nicaragua, and Guatemala.

Another important factor adding to the region's instability is the problem of Central America's refugees, internally displaced persons, and migrants. For the purposes of this presentation, we will refer only to refugees and internally displaced persons. Refugees are all those migrants who are obliged by violence and persecution to leave behind all of their material possessions and change their place of residence and employment in order to *save their lives*. These people usually move to a different country, losing most of their material possessions. Most of the figures available on refugees, provided by international organizations such as the United Nations High Commissioner on Refugees (UNHCR) are very different; consequently, we will limit our source to a 1984 study of the University for Peace titled: "Central American Refugees: the Social, Political, and Economic Impact of the Region," pp. 3–4. According to this study, there were 322,354 refugees as of late 1983. Of these, only 91,217 were receiving humanitarian aid. Most of the refugees were from El Salvador, Guatemala, and Nicaragua. The majority of refugees are in Mexico, followed by large numbers of Salvadoreans moving to Honduras and Guatemala, and an increasing number of Nicaraguans living in Costa Rica. (Recent research by the author now estimates the number of refugees to be 360,000 at the beginning of 1985.) The situation for *internally displaced* persons is even worse, since they receive no international aid which, though modest, is helpful. The same source indicates that as of December 1983, nearly one million peasants were forcibly moved from their natural habitat. This figure includes nearly 500,000 Salvadoreans, 400,000 Guatemalans, and more than 200,000 Nicaraguans.

National and international agencies and the governments in the region are not presently equipped to handle a human problem of such immense proportions, where so many lives are at stake. In general, most studies on the Central American crisis choose to ignore the tragic human drama resulting from the violent social conflict. Recent *en situ* studies on the problem at hand revealed that most of the civilian casualties of the repression and the war are women, children, old people, or physically and psychologically impaired adults who are therefore unable to meet the basic needs of social reproduction.

DECISIVE FACTORS AFFECTING THE PRESENT INSTABILITY

In recent years there has been a marked increase in the number of structural, historical causes that add to the imbalance caused by virulent social struggle. It is not an easy task to analytically separate and determine the political from the economic causes, the short- from the long-term causes, or their national or foreign origin. Nevertheless, there are two causes which should be studied. One relates to the present international economic crisis, the other to U.S. foreign policy in Central America.

The economies of the Central American region have, for the most part, gone through a long period of economic growth since the end of World War II. They underwent a few mild crises over the ensuing years, but nothing came close to resembling the crisis that began after 1979 and which intensified dramatically since then. The economic stagnation resulted from the excessive "opening" of the export economies, their dependence on few products and limited markets, the runaway foreign debt (see Tables 2 and 3), and the state and private sector's poor handling of the crisis. In the case of Central America, the problems attributed to the external markets are closely tied to difficulties associated with importation and, consequently, with the serious paralysis of the program for economic integration and intraregional trade. These factors are responsible for the weak economic recovery of 1984 that, when added to the economic trends of the last five years, shows net economic decline.

Table 2 — Central America: Evolution of the Gross Domestic Product (GDP)

Country	Growth of GDP		GDP Per Capita				Rate
	1975-1978[a]	1981-1984[b]	1970	1980	1983	1984	1981-1984[c]
Costa Rica	5.7	-4.5	740	974	834	837	-14.1
El Salvador	5.5	-12.2	422	433	344	339	-21.8
Guatemala	5.5	-5.5	448	589	512	497	-15.5
Honduras	5.8	-0.9	313	356	318	314	-12.0
Nicaragua	1.2	8.8	418	337	331	322	-4.7

Source: CEPAL, notes on economy and development,
#409/410, January 1985, p.12
    a) average yearly rate
    b) accumulated rate
    c) 1970 dollar price

Table 3 — Central America: Total External Debt Disbursed
        (balance at years end in millions of dollars)

Country	1978	1979	1980	1981	1982	1983	1984
Costa Rica	1870	2333	3183	3360	3497	3848	4050
El Salvador	986	939	1176	1471	1683	2000	2300
Guatemala	821	934	1053	1409	1504	1766	1910
Honduras	971	1280	1510	1708	1800	2079	2250
Nicaragua	961	1131	1579	2163	2797	3385	3900

Source: Ibid

The foregoing does not reflect the gravity of the economic crisis, which in turn becomes the major source of social instability, affecting all other orders of life. The economic ills are reflected in high inflation rates previously unknown in these countries, and in increased levels of unemployment, including visible forms of underemployment (which includes people not employed full-time) and invisible forms of the same (which includes people who work irregularly or in low productivity jobs for low wages). Calculations based on data for the whole of Latin America provided by CEPAL (the U.N. Economic Commission for Latin America) reveal the per capita income in 1984 to be the same as it was in 1976. The same calculations, when applied to Central America, push the income figure back to 1969 levels. The general population receives the *same income it received fifteen years ago.* The budgetary deficit, which is also enormous, affects public services, especially basic social services, further reducing the standard of living.

We view U.S. foreign policy in Central America, especially its direct and immediate confrontations with the Soviet Union, as having become a major destabilizing factor in the region. The East-West conflict completely *reclassifies* foreign policy when the region takes on this *unprecedented* strategic importance. In other words, Central America and the Caribbean's geopolitical importance increased during the sixties, when it became an important bastion of the program to redeploy North American troops, as demanded by the new strategy of confrontation with the Soviet Union. Whatever the change has been, from the doctrine of Mutually Assured Destruction to the technical possibility of a prolonged conventional nuclear war, Central America is being perceived as the backyard which must be protected.

Consequently, it is not surprising that no matter who occupies the White House, U.S. foreign policy has become an important domestic issue, and Central America is seen as a political opportunity which cannot be ignored in light of the recent reordering of priorities. From the perspective of national security interests, three objectives have been clearly delineated. All are de-stabilizing from the point-of-view of the national crisis affecting each country in Central America. The first objective is to block, by all possible means, the consolidation of the Sandinista regime. The second is to bolster (militarily, technically, operationally, and financially) the armed forces and the military capacity of the government in El Salvador, which the guerrilla forces came close to defeating. The third is to change Honduras into the major base of operations in the region, including the Caribbean.

These three objectives are intertwined, and all are based on the same need. U.S. policy also includes more modest military assistance for Guatemala and economic support for Costa Rica that is intended to guarantee the regime's stability and limit, as far as possible, Costa Rica's pacifist, neutral position. It is beyond the scope of this chapter to minutely detail overt or covert actions to destabilize the Sandinista regime or the effects of an equally destabilizing U.S. military presence in Honduras. We began this work affirming that the Central

American crisis, which started as national political unrest, and was later compounded by short- and long-term economic problems, ultimately became a profound regional crisis. This larger dimension becomes apparent only when the crisis unfolds on the international level—when the United States plays a major role.

It is probable that we are now in the final phase of the third stage of the Central American crisis. This stage will end when possible solutions to the conflict become more defined, when peace and national sovereignty are guaranteed, and when democracy is the product of a genuinely internal solution, not merely the result of the electoral process. The search for a solution to the crisis is urgent. All of us must work to find it.

4

CONTRADICTIONS OF GUATEMALA'S "POLITICAL OPENING"

Susanne Jonas

The ink was barely dry on the Central American Peace Accords signed in Guatemala City August 7, 1987 when Guatemala's top military officials declared that the Accords "don't apply" to Guatemala. Five days later, in its first-ever public forum on "Twenty-Seven Years of Struggle against Subversion," army officials reiterated their view that "politics is a continuation of war by other means." Both in the forum and in an accompanying multimedia exposition, the army took a pointedly hard "antiterrorist" line, leaving no doubt of its determination to pursue its counterinsurgency war in Guatemala amid the efforts for peace in the Central American region.

As promised, the army launched a major "final offensive" *(Fin de Año)* against the guerrillas, involving aerial bombardments, population displacements, and the leveling of at least one village in the Quiché "zone of conflict" (which left fourteen peasants dead) — all tactics reminiscent of the scorched-earth war of the early 1980s. While failing in its pacification objectives, the intensified war has brought a significant increase in right-wing death squad activity, disappearances, torture, and human rights violations by government security forces generally. Just in the first twelve days of November, there were fifteen kidnappings (some involving torture and assassination), four disappearances, one attempted kidnapping, and twelve political assassinations (*Inforpress Centroamericana*, or *IC*, November 12, 1987).

These events are painfully familiar in Guatemala, but this time the context is the democratic opening initiated by the 1985 election. The civilian government of Christian Democrat Vinicio Cerezo projects itself in international circles as one of democratic transition. U.S. policy makers even refer to it as "posttransitional" and a "consolidated democracy." Realities within the country, however, defy such characterizations and, by late 1987, point to a trend in the opposite direction. Civilian president Cerezo increasingly identifies himself with the army's counterinsurgency campaign, going so far as to visit war zones in military uniform in November (*IC*, December 3, 1987).

It is essential to understand how profoundly the present political opening has been shaped by the scorched-earth war of 1978–1985 and remains limited by the counterinsurgency logic. The full dimensions and horror of that war — a continuation of pacification efforts since the rise of the guerrilla insurgency in the 1960s — are unknown and unimagined in the United States. More than 440 villages were burned to the ground, 100,000 to 150,000 civilians (estimates vary), mainly highlands Indians, were killed or disappeared, leading to charges of genocide. Taken together with severe economic crisis in recent years, the war transformed the structural context for Guatemalan politics in ways that suggest permanent militarization.

Nevertheless, to represent the current period as nothing more than a continuation of the past would oversimplify a complex and contradictory reality. A space has been opened — very limited, but sufficient to modify the terms of the struggle. The new rules of the game permit controlled expressions of popular desires for democratic rights and social justice (through strikes and protests as well as elections). In this respect, the new conjuncture reflects a change from the military rule that prevailed in Guatemala from the mid-1960s until 1985 and a transition (or at least an interlude) of some kind.

But the questions remain: What kind of transition? What is the model toward which Guatemala is evolving in the view of its architects? How central is counterinsurgency to the program of the present and future civilian governments? Can a political opening born of pacification and still controlled by the army really evolve into a democracy?

At a deeper level lie Guatemala's perennial class questions. Can there be a meaningful democratic transition without the elimination of extreme socioeconomic injustices? In the absence of social reforms initiated by the government, what are the options for the four-fifths of Guatemala's population (workers, landless peasants, slum dwellers, refugees, and internally displaced) who live below the official poverty line? And what are the prospects today for a recomposition of the popular and revolutionary movements that represent the interests of that 80 percent majority?

These are among the many questions and debates about recent experience in Guatemala, of which I shall address a few in this article. Beyond Guatemala, these issues are of significance for other transitional countries in Latin America and elsewhere in the Third World (such as the Philippines). The return to civilian rule in many countries has sparked anew the controversies over whether (or under what conditions) any progress is possible without basic structural reform. One focus of debate has been the thesis that a more viable and desirable strategy than social revolution is the nonrevolutionary route of institutionalizing limited political democracy — even recognizing that this entails a trade-off, that is, giving up on the struggle for social and economic equality (see O'Donnell, Schmitter, and Whitehead 1986; MacEwan 1988). O'Donnell et al. do not make this argument for Central America, but others have attempted to do so. By contrast, I shall argue that the recent experience of Guatemala demonstrates once again that, in a country marked by such extreme social inequalities, even limited political democracy cannot be meaningfully attained in the absence of structural reform.

In the Central American context, there is also a more specific issue, because the architects of Guatemala's political opening are consciously attempting to develop a new model for the region, a viable alternative to the Nicaraguan revolutionary model — all the more needed in this era of the Central American Peace Accords. In the words of Guatemalan social scientist and government adviser Miguel Angel Balcarcel:

We must not and cannot fail in this experience of transition to democracy in Guatemala, because its effect goes beyond our borders. The people of Central America have before them now two large mirrors that represent the ideological and geopolitical bipolarization of the world: Guatemala, Nicaragua. Each country represents a different experience in solving its crisis: Nicaragua for its revolution, Guatemala for its return to a state of law and civilian rule after 32 years of military authoritarianism. And each awaits in suspense the success or failure of the other. (*Los Angeles Times*, October 29, 1987)

The comparison with Nicaragua also raises important questions regarding the relationships between representative democracy and participatory or popular democracy and between politicians and popular forces as protagonists of the challenge to counterinsurgency. The Nicaraguan Revolution is based on a broad conception of political pluralism that combines the two forms of democracy (see Fagen 1986; Corragio 1986). By contrast, the present Guatemalan government and the "political class," as some call it (meaning politicians of the Christian Democratic and other parties representing principally the propertied classes) reduce everything to electoral terms and seek to coopt or repress grass-roots popular struggles. Yet, ironically, it is the effort by popular and revolutionary forces to raise broader issues of participation (ultimately, popular power) and socioeconomic justice that has historically created the conditions for political democracy. Conversely, to the extent that the dominant class and the politicians in power restrict the space for popular forces, they generally end by curtailing the exercise of formal democracy and pluralism.

All of these dynamics, I suggest, are being played out in Guatemala today. Even on its own terms, then, Guatemala's political opening and attempt to "solve its crisis" are fraught with contradictions, and the longer Cerezo is in power, the more evident these contradictions become.

THE 1985 ELECTION AND THE "DEMOCRATIC OPENING"

Guatemala provides an exceptional case of the dynamics of counterinsurgency politics over more than thirty years, beginning with the CIA-sponsored overthrow of the nationalist, anti-imperialist democratic revolution of 1944–1954, and followed by decades of revolutionary upheaval and counterinsurgency war. From the mid-1960s until 1985, Guatemala was recognized as the archetypical counterinsurgency state—a concept understood as a combination of the traditional oligarchical state with the institutionalized apparatus created by the United States in the 1960s to defeat and annihilate revolutionary guerrilla movements; other formulations refer to the "militarized state" or the "national security state" (see Marini 1980; Torres-Rivas 1987; Lowy and Sader 1985).

But what about Guatemala today? The 1985 constitutional process and election and the present political opening were initially set into motion by the army as part of its pacification plans of the early 1980s. The Constitution of 1985 reestablished standard political rights on paper and technically returned the country to the rule of law, although at the same time retaining and legalizing basic institutions of counterinsurgency that violate those constitutional rights.

The 1985 presidential election was nonfraudulent and procedurally correct but severely restricted and nonrepresentational of large sectors of the population. Although voting is compulsory, 55.8 percent of Guatemala's eligible voters did not participate (they either did not register, abstained from voting, or cast invalid ballots) (WOLA 1985:76–77). Aside from the small Social Democratic party, no left-of-center parties were eligible to participate; among interest groups, only those representing the propertied classes took part (Trudeau 1989).

The platforms of the participating parties, ranging from the centrist Christian Democrats to the extreme right Movimiento de Liberación Nacional (MLN) differed very little from each other. None of the candidates proposed any serious economic reforms or any restrictions on the military. Although technically civilians, all of the candidates made themselves acceptable to the military by agreeing that "the subversives must be eliminated" (*Inforpress Centroamericana* 1985:38). Several of them had long histories of collaboration with the military and were actively supported by parties or fractions of the army. The campaign was marred by continued illegal executions and disappearances and, more broadly, took place in an environment scarred by thirty years of terror and coercion.

Despite these limits, many Guatemalans hoped that the election would initiate a change and serve as an opportunity to express their rejection of military dictatorship and their desire for democracy and reform. Those who voted gave a 70 percent mandate in the runoff election to Cerezo, who was the most progressive of the major candidates. From this perspective, the election was also an opportunity for some political parties (those acceptable to the army) to reorganize on a more normal basis.

Nevertheless, the dominant reality soon became clear: the election did not involve a real transfer of power from the military to civilians. The election of a civilian had been a project of the army; in fact, it was in many respects the most rational way for the military to retain its power. As reflected in their 1982 "National Plan for Security and Development," important sectors of the Guatemalan military and their U.S. advisers saw elections as a necessary adjustment in their counterinsurgency strategy once the most intensive military phase was completed.

The army and its civilian allies needed the election for several practical reasons:

1. to overcome the international isolation that Guatemala had incurred during its many years as the region's worst human-rights violator—for political reasons, but above all, to attract international aid to alleviate the economic crisis;

2. to regain private-sector confidence and reactivate the economy; and

3. to establish internal stability and legitimacy, which had been seriously challenged by revolutionary and popular movements during the late 1970s and early 1980s.

Politically delegitimated after years of violent dictatorship and corruption, the army had to redefine its relations with the population, in part by taking credit for restoring civilian rule.

From this perspective, the election initiated a liberalization and a recomposition of the counterinsurgency state, but not a negation of it, much less a full-blown democratic transition. More than anything else, it was a necessary restructuring to deal with Guatemala's severe economic and political crises (Jonas 1989).

THE LIMITS OF PLURALISM

On paper, civilian government was supposed to restore Guatemala to the rule of law and a limited form of political pluralism. The reduction in overt state-sponsored violence, the operation of several political parties, and the possibility of exercising constitutionally guaranteed individual rights (or, minimally, the expectation that such rights should be guaranteed) – all these mitigated the purely repressive politics of the past and were thus seen as improvements. Following years of the most brutal repression-*qua*-counterinsurgency in the hemisphere, most Guatemalans appreciated any political opening or *respiro* ("breathing space"), no matter how limited and contradictory.

Nevertheless, all of these advances relative to the past are sharply and definitively limited by the ongoing counterinsurgency war. While formal prohibitions on politics have been relaxed, even moderate and legalized opposition forces practice self-censorship, since they never know whether (or when) they will suffer reprisals for voicing protest. The only oppositional forces that feel secure in voicing their concerns are those of the extreme Right. Many leftist opposition leaders, reformist professionals, and trade union leaders have avoided assassination only by living in exile; a recent delegation of members of the *Foro de Guatemaltecos Democráticos* (exiles living in Mexico) concluded that conditions for return do not exist.

International human rights organizations (including the Inter-American Commission on Human Rights of the Organization of American States, Amnesty International, and Americas Watch), as well as a few public figures within Guatemala, have documented the continuation of systematic human rights violations, indeed a "serious deterioration" of the situation during 1987 (CIDH 1987; *IC*, October 8, 1987, November 12, 1987, December 17, 1987). From January through early October of 1987, according to the Guatemalan Human Rights Commission, there were seventy-eight documented cases of forced or involuntary disappearances and 345 extrajudicial executions, with figures rising even more sharply toward the end of 1987 (GHRC 1987). The number of documented cases is always considerably lower than actual cases — particularly since, with some exceptions, most of the victims have not been leading public figures, but peasants, catechists, trade unionists, and so forth. The total of 1,021 cases of political violence for 1987 represented an increase of 57 percent over the 1986 level, and there were more political assassinations in 1987 than in 1985, before Cerezo took office (*IC*, January 21, 1988).

In addition to these continuing brutalities, there is a psychological war that reproduces the arbitrariness of the past and makes a mockery of the free expression of divergent viewpoints. The summer 1987 army exposition on terrorist subversion included a display of Marxist books; to Guatemalans trained by years of repression, the message was an unmistakable reminder of the boundaries on intellectual freedom. The University of San Carlos, historically a center of political opposition, still bears the marks of the fierce repression unleashed against it. The university's autonomy has been violated time and time again, and its budget has been slashed. Student organizations are having to rebuild from scratch. Generations of student leaders and intellectuals were wiped out. Open attacks are still occurring in the provincial extensions of the university, such as the October assassination by security forces of two ex-student leaders in Quezaltenango.

Despite the continuing pattern of political assassinations, disappearances, and intimidation of human rights activists, in most cases there have been no serious investigations, and no one is held responsible. The president's office has made grandiose claims to have established "a regime of absolute respect for human rights and the fundamental freedoms of all citizens." In practice, however, Cerezo has upheld the "amnesty" self-proclaimed by the army just before he took office. Unlike Raúl Alfonsín in Argentina, he campaigned on a promise *not* to prosecute army officers for past human rights crimes or death squad activities. This impunity with respect to the past implicitly creates a shield of unaccountability in the present. As long as military officials believe that they will never be held accountable for their actions, there is virtually no way to guarantee basic human rights in Guatemala.

Perhaps the clearest example of continuing repression is the massive problem facing Guatemala's refugees – up to 150,000 living in refugee camps in Mexico, according to the *Christian Science Monitor* (September 4, 1987), and hundreds of thousands more internal refugees. The conditions for return from Mexico are insecure, since the army, which remains in control of the program for repatriation of refugees, regards them as "subversives." (The army's exposition in August featured maps showing the Mexican refugee camps as part of the guerrilla infrastructure.)

It is widely recognized that the government repatriation program falls far short of international humanitarian standards and the guidelines in the 1987 Central American Peace Accords. Despite a persistent government campaign, 95 percent of the refugees have refused to return until they are given guarantees of their safety, of liberty to return to their own villages (rather than to camps run by the military), and of an end to the "civilian self-defense patrols" (see below). In 1987, the number of returning refugees was 11 percent of what had been projected by the government (*IC*, November 28, 1987). Top officials of the Catholic Church have also refused to participate in the government program because of insufficient guarantees to returnees.

The chasm that separates Guatemala from any semblance of genuine pluralism and internal peace can be seen in regard to other provisions of the peace accords. While taking minimal steps to appear in compliance, the government has in fact put into practice the army's statements that the "accords don't apply" in Guatemala. "Amnesty" for political prisoners will have a "limited effect" in Guatemala, as the *New York Times* points out, quoting human rights organizations and Guatemalan Government officials, because "the Guatemalan army has killed most people it captured in recent years" (*New York Times*, November 6, 1987; *IC*, December 19, 1987).

To comply technically with the Accords, the government formed a National Reconciliation Commission but gave it no power to act; it was judged by the International Verification Commission not to have fulfilled its functions. In October 1987 the government held one set of conversations with the revolutionary Left (the Unidad Revolucionaria Nacional Guatemalteca, or URNG) in Madrid – the first such talks in twenty-five years. All political parties except the extreme right MLN declared support for continued discussions and for a humanization of the war. Any hope that the Madrid talks might be the beginning of a genuine search for a negotiated settlement was dispelled, however, when government and army officials subsequently declared that there would be no further dialogue. Meanwhile, the army refused to negotiate a cease-fire (as provided in the accords) and began its "final offensive."

Ever since the Central American Peace Process gave added legitimacy to negotiations, the army has been even more insistent that politics is "a continuation of war by other means" and that the revolutionary Left, having been reduced to a mere "annoyance," must be definitively defeated. Indeed, its recent actions suggest that the army has viewed the entire political opening as an opportunity to prepare for a final offensive (in Defense Minister Gramajo's words, "to gain time") and the Madrid talks as an ultimatum to the Left to lay down their arms.

Once it became clear that the army and the government were not serious about peace talks (viewing them as too advantageous to the insurgents) and intended to use this opportunity to wipe them out, the URNG responded with its most vigorous political/military actions since 1984. The last months of 1987 saw occupations and political meetings in *fincas* and towns (one in San Marcos involving 500 guerrillas), takeovers of portions of major highways, ambushes and confrontations with the army, attacks on security installations, and so forth (*IC*, October 29, 1987, November 19, 1987, December 17, 1987). The very increase in army violence and the return to scorched-earth tactics (bombings, destruction of entire villages, population displacements at the rate of ninety families a week, and more) belie the army's thesis that Guatemala has been pacified and the insurgency eliminated as a political force.

THE LOGIC OF COUNTERINSURGENCY IN THE "DEMOCRATIC OPENING"

The continuing counterinsurgency war has left its mark everywhere and has produced major structural transformations of every aspect of Guatemalan life. The effects of the scorched-earth war that destroyed hundreds of villages are visible in vast expanses of land burned in the highlands. Ecological and human devastation continues today in the widespread use of herbicides, supposedly to eradicate marijuana, but widely suspected of being directed against people.

The war caused massive population migrations and relocations. While numerous highlands' cities and towns have been destroyed physically or culturally, well over ten percent of Guatemala's population of eight million (overwhelmingly highlands Indians) were displaced to other parts of the country or abroad, and over 100,000 children were left orphaned (some estimates are much higher). Since the mid-1970s, Guatemala City has at least doubled its population, as a consequence of war and economic crisis.

The logic of the war is also evidenced in the continuing militarization of Guatemalan political life. Even outside the active zones of conflict, large areas of the countryside are kept under tight control. The structures of counterinsurgency and repression were legalized in the 1985 Constitution and remain firmly in place, although in new forms. A clear example is the persistence of the "civilian self-defense patrols" (PACs).

Introduced in 1982 as part of the full-scale counterinsurgency offensive, the patrols were designed to force villagers to participate in the eradication of the guerrilla movement and to eliminate political activity in opposition to the government. Anyone who refused service was fined or, much worse, treated as a subversive. At one point the PACs included one million peasants — one-eighth of Guatemala's population, one-quarter of the adult population!

Two years into the Cerezo government, the PACs seem to have become a permanent feature of rural political life, and there are still an estimated 800,000 members. In fact, they are being expanded; in late 1987 the army announced plans to organize civil patrols in Guatemala City and other urban areas. Cerezo campaigned on a promise to allow villages to vote on whether or not to maintain a PAC, but in the face of army opposition to the idea, he has not implemented it. Today they are called "voluntary," but there is ample evidence to the contrary. Recently, a Quiché agricultural worker who requested a shorter shift in PAC duty was kidnapped by army officers; numerous other cases of reprisals have been reported.

Even the idea of a village plebiscite on the PACs is unrealistic, since it presupposes a model of free men and women making free political choices — a model that is contradicted by thirty years of counterinsurgency politics in Guatemala. It also denies or ignores the realities of pervasive military control and vigilance in towns where many residents are relocated refugees or internally displaced persons, already regarded as subversives by the army. In such a political environment, it will take far more than a village plebiscite to demilitarize.

A clear picture of that environment emerges from interviews with the people directly affected. According to peasant organizers, the army is attempting to coerce highlands villagers into maintaining the PACs even if there is a plebiscite, by telling them: "You asked for civilian government; now we've given it to you. If you want to dissolve the PACs, go ahead; this is a democratic country. But if you do, who will protect you from the subversives?" The implied threat is unmistakable.

The army speaks of the PACs as an instrument of *participación* — by which they mean gaining the active participation of the civilian population, through persuasion or force, in the war against *la subversión*. In interviews and in the 1987 public forum, army leaders boasted, "The PACs were the first contribution of the people to the struggle against terrorism. Even the poorest, most humble peasant could contribute." The PACs are part of the army's monumental battle to "win" the hearts and minds of the Guatemalan people — or, since that battle cannot be won, at least to control their behavior.

The other major institutions of the counterinsurgency war have also persisted in the era of the democratic opening, although in forms more adequate to the conditions and the public relations needs of the moment. The six *polos de desarrollo* (constellations of model villages in the areas of conflict) are advertised by the army as "modern communities for displaced peasants" and the "answer to the problems" of the people. In reality, they remain forced resettlement camps in which every aspect of people's lives is subject to military control. As observers have pointed out, calling them "concentration camps" does not adequately express the sophistication of the control mechanisms in these camps, including psychological manipulation of people's fears, which reduces the need for overt violence.

The Inter-Institutional Coordinating Councils (CIIs) of the early 1980s centralized administrative control of development projects at every level (local, municipal, provincial, national) in the hands of military authorities. Today, such rigid formal military control is less necessary, since civilian institutions have been highly militarized. However, military authorities retain ultimate de facto power in the countryside. In addition, according to top military officials, among others, the concept behind the CIIs has been reintroduced under the Cerezo government in the form of the *consejos de desarrollo* (development councils). Alternative views of the *consejos* place less emphasis on their counterinsurgency function: the government bills them as institutions of "community participation" in development; opposition parties view them as an invention of the Christian Democrats to build their partisan political machine at the grass roots; and the extreme Right even views them as an invitation to leftist organizers. But, as with the PACs, even "participation" has largely military objectives. The *consejos* suggest that development and counterinsurgency have become inseparably intertwined, and it is not clear where one ends and the other begins.

In all of these efforts, the army has drawn heavily upon techniques learned from foreign advisers, most importantly Israeli (see Jamail and Gutiérrez 1987). In addition, the army has been assisted by civilian counterinsurgents, civilians who, in the army's words, "had the vision to get involved" in the pacification wars in the early 1980s and who view the army as the most effective actor in Guatemalan politics. An even more important civilian support base and ideological rationale for counterinsurgency has come from the rapidly spreading right-wing evangelical movement implanted in Guatemala in the early 1980s (see Resource Center 1986).

I stress these points because they are essential to comprehend the sophistication of counterinsurgency in Guatemala's civilian democracy, the depth of military penetration into (integration with) the fabric of normal daily life in rural Guatemala, the army's conscious attempt to overcome the alienation between the state's repressive apparatus and civil society—and the extent to which the line between civilian and military has been blurred. Nevertheless, the ongoing war and the further deterioration in rural living conditions (even in "model villages") indicate the limitations and contradictions of army "developmentalism." They also leave a sobering question of what, under these conditions, demilitarization of Guatemala can mean.

STRUCTURAL IMPOVERISHMENT AND THE CLASS BASE OF THE CEREZO PROJECT

Underlying the war and constantly regenerating it is the extreme (and worsening) concentration of wealth amid pervasive poverty. The largest 2 percent of Guatemala's farms occupy 67 percent of usable land, while 80 percent of farms account for 10 percent of the land. Guatemala is the only Central American country that has not even the semblance of a land distribution law. The 1985 Constitution made a major concession to the landed oligarchy by eliminating the reference in previous constitutions to the "social function of property." Guatemala has one of the world's most regressive tax systems, with less than 20 percent being direct taxes on income and wealth. Meanwhile, according to government statistics, four-fifths of all Guatemalans live below the official poverty line, with 40 to 55 percent (figures vary) living in "extreme poverty" (see Torres-Rivas, this chapter, Table 1). Fully one-half of the economically active population is unemployed or underemployed.

Some of these staggering structural problems (such as land tenure and tax structure) are long-standing in Guatemala, but unemployment, runaway inflation, and a dramatic loss of purchasing power have been severely aggravated by the economic crises and wars of the last ten years. Guatemala City has doubled in size, but there are no real homes, no services, and no jobs for the growing mass of slum dwellers. The human crush is felt everywhere in the capital – on streets and buses, in parks and stores. Downtown streets are packed with vendors of everything imaginable – a sure sign of massive unemployment. Hundreds of thousands of people (a quarter to a half million of them – reliable statistics are not available) are encamped in squatter settlements of cardboard-and-tin shacks (ten across, ten deep) on the outskirts of the city. Epitomizing their precariousness and the potential for renewed social explosion, homes in these settlements slide into the capital's steep ravines during the long rainy season.

Nationally, open unemployment has increased more than 600 percent since 1980. In a country long characterized by financial stability, prices have almost quintupled since the mid-1970s. Economic crisis and economic recovery alike, strikes and increased taxes alike – all have been translated into price increases for items of basic necessity. Real wages and purchasing power have been steadily declining (46 percent from mid-1983 through late 1986 – more than one-third of the decline occurring since Cerezo took office). Yet Cerezo's economic stabilization program is based on holding down wages; in early 1988, minimum wages, which had remained at 1980 levels, were raised only a fraction of what would have been necessary to counteract the sharp deterioration of real wages since 1980.

More generally, the Cerezo government's approach to ameliorating Guatemala's economic crisis reflects a clear orientation toward the needs of the private sector. Inflation is controlled by holding down wages but not prices. The currency is being stabilized; construction is being stimulated; nontraditional exports are being expanded, as well as trade with all possible partners (including socialist countries); and the revival of the Central American Common Market is a priority. But there is no global program for reducing unemployment, and the social service component of public spending has been cut back. In short, "economic recovery" for the private sector is accompanied by austerity for the popular classes.

Cerezo's political response to the problems of increasing impoverishment is *concertación* (social reconciliation) and gradualism, as opposed to "polarization." Seeking to avoid a confrontation with Guatemala's unashamedly violent and intractable landed bourgeoisie, Cerezo has promised *not* to undertake any land reform. (He is thinking, no doubt, of the unhappy fate of progressive, nationalist president Jacobo Arbenz, who was violently overthrown by the CIA and the Guatemalan oligarchy in 1954 for daring to carry out an agrarian reform.) Cerezo proposes to make land available for peasants to rent or buy, but there are no resources for buying, and renting is so exploitative that it is not a reform of any kind.

Quite aside from the questionable viability of this approach in meeting the needs of nearly half a million landless peasants, even Cerezo's one experiment in land distribution is revealing. In response to the peasant *pro-tierra* (for land) movement led by Catholic priest Andrés Girón, the government distributed six farms on the Southern Coast to 6,200 peasant families. But the beneficiaries are living without credit, tools or technical assistance, without health care, nurses, or vaccines to treat rampant diseases, without schools or teachers. As acknowledged even by a government employee visiting Finca San Carlos at the same time I did, the entire project is a monument to lack of governmental concern — and, this time, not directly attributable to the oligarchy.

In other areas as well, judging by Cerezo's recent negotiations with unions and his dealings with the human rights advocacy organization Grupo de Apoyo Mutuo (GAM), and even with the revolutionary left URNG, it becomes clear that *concertación* was never designed for the poor or the Left. In the spring of 1987, over 150,000 state workers went on strike; they did not suffer massive repression, as in the past, but in negotiating the settlement, Cerezo refused to grant the 100 *quetzal* (U.S. $40) monthly wage increase being demanded and made no real concessions to the workers. By sharp contrast, when the private sector held a work stoppage in the fall of 1987 to resist new tax measures, Cerezo went out of his way to protect their interests, promising no land reform, no state interference in private enterprise, and so forth, in this way undermining his one reformist initiative himself.

Cerezo is a remarkably astute and effective politician. Nevertheless, many Guatemalans believe he is making a historic mistake in not giving more to the 80 percent majority of the population. Even within the limits set by his alliances with the propertied class and the army, Cerezo could have found more room to maneuver. There is growing dissension within the ruling coalition (over new taxes, dialogue with the URNG). Even the private sector, which again recently demonstrated its power and intractability, is divided, with modernizing industrialists backing Cerezo. In addition, the army now proclaims that the "breeding ground" of subversion and guerrilla insurgency is social injustice and is itself pressuring the oligarchy to pay more taxes — not out of abstract "reformism," but out of concern for financing the war.

In regard to the army, Cerezo has both less power and more power than is generally recognized: less, because even civilian institutions are militarized; more, because the army deliberately paved the way for Cerezo (or someone like him) to take office and, even today, needs him politically in order to carry out its own objectives.[1] Therefore, the military could have been challenged more than it has been on issues of counterinsurgency, human rights, and demilitarization. Until it is challenged, Cerezo's claims in international circles and among liberals in the Democratic Party in the United States to have democratized Guatemala and resolved the human rights problem will not be credible.

In a 1987 interview with this author, Cerezo stressed the "absolute unity" between his government's agenda and that of the army. His recent actions, from his June 1987 "Army Day" speech thanking the military for bringing democracy to Guatemala to his November visit to the war zone, have reinforced this growing identification. Perhaps it was to be expected, given that he has built his career since the 1970s on the idea of a Christian Democratic partnership with the army. But there is a price to be paid in terms of political legitimacy: many Guatemalans who were initially willing to "give Vinicio a chance" now see him going down a road parallel to that of José Napoleon Duarte in El Salvador.

THE LOGIC OF THE 80 PERCENT MAJORITY

Seen in all its dimensions, Guatemala's opening is a political battleground for competing logics or world views. The alternative to the logic of counterinsurgency is not simply electoral but more comprehensively, popular and mobilizational. Correspondingly, even though, in this political period, elected politicians and the political class appear to occupy the center stage, the major protagonists challenging the oligarchy and military remain the working class and other popular classes, as well as popular and revolutionary organizations.

The incipient revival of protest and popular organizations for the first time since the upsurge in mass organizing in the late 1970s is potentially the most positive aspect of the present political opening. Guatemala's poor have seized upon every opportunity, however restricted, to press their demands, even though in the past — so goes Guatemalan black humor — such openings have served to update the death lists. Despite the risks, the Cerezo opening has seen widespread (often spontaneous) protest movements bubbling up from the base — from the shacks of the El Mexquital shantytown on the outskirts of Guatemala City, from the convent and hospital sheltering internal refugees in Cobán, from the strike lines at the Lunafil factory and various government offices (at the rate of at least one a day in the summer of 1987), from the University in Quezaltenango, from the huts of peasants demanding land on the Southern Coast, from the movements against price increases for basic necessities (most recently, the sharp increase in electricity rates), and for human rights investigations into the fate of the disappeared.

At a deeper level, these movements remind us why it is that Guatemala has been torn apart by internal wars during the last half-century. A central factor leading the United States to overthrow the revolutionary Arbenz government in 1954 was the radicalization of its class base. Class conflicts have been central to Guatemala's wars since then and are reemerging today in popular protest movements. The logic of these embryonic movements is very different from the electoral logic of the political class. Although their struggles are still very restricted today, they may prove difficult for the political class to control, as was the case in the late 1970s, and may eventually coalesce in a challenge to the class basis of power. Implicit within these struggles is the vision underlying the decades of upheaval, past and future, of a Guatemala that belongs to its 80 percent majority.

NATIONALISM, ACTIVE NEUTRALITY, AND RELATIVE AUTONOMY

Internally, the legitimacy of the Cerezo government has been undermined by an inability or unwillingness to take the measures necessary for a genuine transformation. But in this era of democratic transitions and regional peace accords, other factors have bolstered Cerezo's international image — most notably, the development of a nationalist stance and discourse and a policy of active neutrality with regard to the Reagan administration's war against Nicaragua.

Since the early 1980s, the Guatemalan army has developed a nationalistic rhetoric, including claims to have won its war "alone" (without U.S. military aid, which was cut off by Congress in 1977 because of the severity of Guatemala's human rights violations). Army officials have even suggested that they do not need help from a defeated army (the United States in Vietnam) and that the training they had received from the United States since the 1960s was flawed, as it prepared them to be an army of occupation (as in Vietnam) rather than a national army.

Posturing and rhetoric notwithstanding, Guatemala's counterinsurgency campaign was heavily aided and training provided by the United States and its allies/surrogates (Israel and Taiwan). As recently as the spring of 1987, U.S. pilots and helicopters flew Guatemalan troops into a war zone. In 1986 and 1987 the United States used the return of civilian government to step up military aid (U.S. $7.5 million was approved at the end of 1987) — in addition to over U.S. $50 million in Emergency Support Funds, which can be used for military-related projects, and U.S. $2 million in aid for training the Guatemalan police force, which is headed by a top official of army intelligence, the infamous G–2. In fact, the United States has been building up the Guatemalan army since the late

1950s, making it "an ideological and structural creation of U.S. imperialism" (Payeras, 1986: 15) — in its training, techniques, and technology, in its world view and rigid anticommunist ideology. Furthermore, as Defense Minister Gramajo made clear in an interview, the Guatemalan army remains strategically aligned with the United States in the East-West context.

Nevertheless, the nationalistic stance was politically important in beginning to break Guatemala's isolation and establish credibility internationally. With the additional advantage of a civilian government, Cerezo has managed to greatly reduce international human rights monitoring by the United Nations, to make police-training arrangements with Atlanta's Mayor Andrew Young (a liberal Democrat), and to gain additional aid to Guatemalan security forces not only from the United States but also from West Germany, Italy, Spain, Venezuela, and Mexico — all of this despite a generalized recognition that in fact Guatemala's human rights situation remains unacceptable.

The above has acquired new dimensions in the regional context that gave rise to the Central American Peace Accords of August 1987. Beginning in the early 1980s, Guatemala took the lead among the pro-U.S. Central American governments in distancing itself from the Reagan administration's efforts to overthrow the Sandinista government in Nicaragua. Originally a policy of the Guatemalan army, regional neutrality in no way contradicts a strategic alignment with the United States (nor behind-the-scenes aid to the Nicaraguan Contras). Nevertheless, it was very important in altering the correlation of forces in the region and remains a crucial factor in the Peace Process today.

The Guatemalan army and the Cerezo government can afford to take this approach because there is no border with Nicaragua, and the Sandinista revolution does not directly threaten Guatemalan stability. Further, this regional stance is totally consistent with — in fact, reinforces — the army's campaign for the internal pacification of Guatemala, which remains its major priority. (For its part, Washington may disagree with the Guatemalan military about Nicaragua, but the bottom line for the United States remains the latter's ability to pacify Guatemala.) Economically, it is to Guatemala's benefit to normalize relations and renew trade with Nicaragua. Finally, at the diplomatic level, this stance has gained the Guatemalan government the support of Contadora governments (particularly Mexico) and has further reduced human rights criticisms.

More generally, the contradictory relative autonomy being manifested to one degree or another by pro-U.S. governments and military establishments in Central America (most evidently, in the rejection of Reagan's Contra policy since the Central American presidents' meeting of August 1987) is consistent with a continuation of counterinsurgency within these countries. While a contradiction of sorts has developed between the immediate interests of these governments and the Reagan administration, the longer-range counterrevolutionary objectives converge.

CONCLUSION: A MODEL FOR CENTRAL AMERICA?

To return to our original questions: What kind of transition is taking place in Guatemala? And, within this context, what are the prospects for evolution toward meaningful pluralism and for the elimination of extreme injustice?

I would suggest that there has been a transformation (some call it a "recomposition") of the counterinsurgency state that has been in place since the mid-1960s — or, alternatively, the transformation of a national security dictatorship into a national security democracy. This is an attempt to construct a new model, the priorities of which are neither pluralism (as claimed) nor social justice, but order and stability. It assumes a permanent challenge, requiring permanent military mobilization — even when the latter takes forms not recognizable as typically military.

This is, perhaps, a transition, but not a democratic transition. The experience of Guatemala strongly suggests that a democratic transition of any consequence and duration requires more than a nonfraudulent election leading to a civilian regime; it requires very far-reaching and lasting change — change, one could even say, on the scale of the bourgeois-democratic revolutions of the nineteenth century or the socialist revolutions in the twentieth century (or, in Guatemala's own history, the Revolution of 1944–54), which began to change the class basis of state power.

An important lesson suggested by the Guatemalan experience is the unviability under these conditions of the trade-off — accepting the consolidation of a politically democratic regime, while giving up on goals of radically reducing social and economic inequalities. In societies as polarized as Guatemala — and in the absence of structural reforms by the Cerezo government — social protest and unrest will continue to spread. At some point, the government will face the contradiction inherent within the political opening: How far can they allow protest to continue? Can they avoid clamping down? Recent trends suggest that the limits of the opening may be reached sooner rather than later.

A final irony emerges in regard to the stabilizing objective of the Guatemala model. Counterinsurgency has failed, above all in its political objectives of overcoming the alienation of state from civil society, and, specifically, of creating a popular base for antiterrorism. For its part, the Christian Democratic effort to build a popular base has been hampered by an unwillingness to make any real reforms or concessions to the 80 percent majority of the population. Under these conditions, stability and a viable alternative to Nicaragua remain counterrevolutionary dreams. Social revolution in some form or forms remains on the agenda for Guatemala.

The implications of the Guatemala model are broader when that model is projected onto the region. Implicit within the Central American Peace Accords is the unstated question: Could there be a nonrevolutionary alternative for Central America, some analogue to social democracy in Western Europe? This would be a real question if there were a genuinely reformist alternative to

Nicaragua, but the only experiment in making genuine reforms is the Sandinista project itself. In Guatemala (as well as in El Salvador and the other Central American countries), those in power appear to be discarding their opportunities to make genuine reforms.

Meanwhile, the Guatemalan tinderbox could itself become an open threat to peace in Central America, as it has been in the past. Guatemala's oligarchs and generals, along with their U.S. advisers, might once again find themselves in the ironic position of exporting instability, even revolution.

NOTES

The author would like to express her appreciation to Timothy Harding and James Petras, to Margarita Melville, and to colleagues at Global Options, primarily Elizabeth Sutherland Martinez and Nancy Stein, for their editorial comments and suggestions. This chapter was written in December 1987 and was first published in *Latin American Perspectives*, 15 (3): 26–46.

1. I refer here to that fraction of the army headed by General Gramajo, which for the time being remains the dominant fraction—although, as the May 1988 coup attempt reveals, there is another fraction (or there are other fractions) holding a very different view of the desirability of a civilian government. What the coup made clear is that, having made the basic decision to build his principal alliance with a fraction in the armed forces, Cerezo is becoming increasingly dependent on Gramajo, and both are increasingly vulnerable to pressures from the Right.

REFERENCES

This chapter is based primarily on a series of interviews with a broad range of Guatemalans during the summer of 1987—including government and Army officials at all levels, politicians and congressmen (progovernment and opposition), church officials, professionals, journalists, academics, labor union organizers and members, leaders and members of popular organizations, and Guatemalans living abroad.

Aguilera Peralta, Gabriel, et al.
1981 *Dialectica del Terror en Guatemala.* San Jose, Costa Rica: EDUCA.

Barry, Tom
1986 *Guatemala: The Politics of Counterinsurgency.* Albuquerque: Resource Center.

Centro de Estudios de la Realidad Guatemalteca (CERG)
1985 "Contrainsurgencia y Regimen Constitucional." *Temas de la Realidad Guatemalteca* 1 (Mexico).

Comision Interamericana de Derechos Humanos, Organizacion de Estados Americanos (CIDH)
1987 *Informe Anual de la Comision Interamericana de Derechos Humanos, 1986–87.* Washington, D.C.: OEA.

Corragio, Jose Luis
1986 *Nicaragua: Revolution and Democracy.* Boston: Allen & Unwin.

Fagen, Richard
1986 "The Politics of Transition." In R. Fagen et al., eds. *Transition and Development.*
    New York: Monthly Review Press.

Guatemala Human Rights Commission (GHRC)
1987 *Report on the Situation of Human Rights in Guatemala.* Mexico: GHRC (October).

Inforpress Centroamericana (IC)
1985 *Guatemala: Elections, 1985.* Guatemala.

Jamail, Milton, and Margo Gutierrez
1987 *It's No Secret: Israel's Military Involvement in Central America.* Washington, D.C.:
    Association of Arab-American University Graduates.

Jonas, Susanne
1989 "Elections and Transitions: The Guatemalan and Nicaraguan Cases." In J. Booth
    and M. Seligson, eds. *Elections and Democratization in Central America.* Chapel
    Hill: University of North Carolina Press.

Lowy, Michael, and Eder Sader
1985 "The Militarization of the State in Latin America." *Latin American Perspectives* 12
    (Fall): 7–40.

MacEwan, Arthur
1988 "Transitions from Authoritarian Rule: A Review Essay." *Latin American Perspectives* (Summer).

Marini, Ruy Mauro
1980 "The Question of the State in the Latin American Struggle." *Contemporary
    Marxism* 1 (Spring):1–9.

O'Donnell, Guillermo, Philippe Schmitter, and Lawrence Whitehead, eds.
1986 *Transitions from Authoritarian Rule: Latin America.* Baltimore: Johns Hopkins
    University Press.

Painter, James
1987 *Guatemala: False Hope, False Freedom.* London: Catholic Institute for International
    Relations and Latin American Bureau.

Payeras, Mario
1986 "Guatemala's Army and U.S. Policy." *Monthly Review* (March): 14–20.

Resource Center (Albuquerque)
1986 "The Rise of the Religious Right in Central America," *Resource Center Bulletin*
    (Summer–Fall).

Solorzano Martinez, Mario
1987 *Guatemala: Autoritarismo y Democracia.* San Jose: EDUCA.

Torres-Rivas, Edelberto
1987 *Centroamerica: La Democracia Posible.* San Jose: EDUCA.

Trudeau, Robert
1988 "Democracy in Guatemala: Present Status, Future Prospects." In J. Booth and M.
    Seligson, eds. *Elections and Democratization in Central America.* Chapel Hill:
    University of North Carolina Press.

Washington Office on Latin America (WOLA) and International Human Rights Law Group
1985 *The 1985 Guatemalan Elections: Will the Military Relinquish Power?* Washington, D.C.: WOLA.

5

THE REDEMOCRATIZATION PROCESS

James Petras

The redemocratization process involving the withdrawal of the military from positions of government and the subsequent installation of democratically elected civilians can be characterized as: controlled; incremental; segmented; and preemptive.

First, the military regime attempts to control the progression of redemocratization by favoring negotiating partners who emphasize legal-political changes over socioeconomic structural transformations. These favored partners focus on changing institutions of government and not the state. They adopt a style of democratic reform which favors an additive approach (grafting new institutions onto existing ones) rather than a displacement approach (substituting new institutions for old), and they adopt a posture of responsibility for problems inherited from the military regime rather than seeking initiatives dissociating the new regime from the past.

The second feature of the redemocratization process is the effort by the military to encourage incremental changes, to stagger the process of change in discrete stages, thus dispersing the opposition as it discusses, weighs, and debates the significance of each modification. Each timetable, electoral procedure, or constitutional amendment is a potential source of disagreement among the opposition; concessions and agreements strengthen the bargaining relation between the military and its negotiating partners. The sudden and massive intrusion of a democratic package would, on the contrary, have a disruptive effect on the military and foster division between officers favoring a democratic transition and those opposed. The incremental approach allows the military to disaggregate the process of redemocratization and the institutions of the incoming regime, and to bargain and trade off changes for continuities.

The third feature of the redemocratization process is the segmentation of the opposition: the major concern of the military is to be able to differentiate and select those oppositionists who will strike the best deal. In this regard, the military may establish parameters as to who is eligible to participate and who is excluded; the purpose is to divide moderates from radicals, increasing the visibility and organizational capacity of the former while marginalizing and reducing the latter to a secondary force. Successful segmentation is built into the politics of military and civilian groups. Thus, while conservative (moderate) alliances may oppose the legal-political structures of the military, they may be disposed to back similar socioeconomic institutions. On the other hand, while civilian conservatives may agree with civilian radicals in opposing military rule, they reject the radical socioeconomic program. Once the military regime opens up the perspective of a democratic transition, the differences between the military and conservative civilians diminish, and the gap between conservative and radical civilians widens. It is this prior understanding of the political dynamics underlying negotiations that facilitates segmentation, as much as a conscious strategy of the military to divide the opposition.

The fourth feature of the redemocratization process is the preemption of anticipated opposition. The process of redemocratization is not a simple act of volition — an isolated act of will by the military to renounce power either because of internal decay or moral persuasion. Rather, it reflects the military's difficulty in ruling within a context of increasing pressure from below. The fundamental premise underlying the military's decision to accept or initiate negotiations toward redemocratization is its growing sense of political isolation, the disintegration of its initial base of support and, above all, its fear that the alternative is deepening fissures that could destroy the military proper. While the immediate circumstances under which military/civilian negotiations take place may not present an overt and massive challenge to state power, the military realizes that if the process of conflict reaches that stage, no negotiations will be possible. Thus negotiated transitions are preemptive actions taken by the military in anticipation of situations which would completely escape from their control and present totally unacceptable alternatives. The concern of the military negotiators (as opposed to the military hardliners) is less with the particular level of opposition at the given moment and more with the movement and direction of political forces.

As will be seen below, the redemocratization process can be divided into three stages:

1. the predemocratic period of burgeoning social movements,
2. the initiation of negotiations, and
3. the organization of the electoral process and the installation of the electoral civilian regime.

REDEMOCRATIZATION: THE IMPACT OF THE ECONOMIC CRISIS

Basic to understanding the emergence of the social movements and their relative success in recruiting support from other institutions — and within the military — is the dismal economic performance of the military regime. As the Brazilian experience in the later 1960s and early 1970s illustrates (and perhaps the Chilean between 1977–1980), military regimes experiencing growth and providing ample consumer goods and opportunities to middle-class constituents can handle labor and popular discontent: economic success isolates labor and provides a certain kind of legitimacy to its repression (what Barrington Moore once called "terror and progress," in which terror is presented as merely the unavoidable cost of economic progress). The free market economic policies pursued by the Chilean and Argentine military regimes were particularly vulnerable to the multiple blows emanating from the world capitalist economy in the late 1970s and early 1980s. A major hypothesis of this essay is that a continuation of those policies by the newly elected democratic regimes would reproduce that crisis, with detrimental effects.

The economic strategy adopted by the military regimes, and its failure, played a major role in setting in motion the social and political processes toward a return to democratic rule. Essentially, the military regimes opted for a strategy of expansion through exports and external financing, which was accompanied by supply side incentives (subsidies, tax write-offs to investors) and demand side repression (indexing wages below prices, restricting labor organizations). During the expansive period of the world economy — the late 1960s to mid-1970s — this appeared to be a promising approach: bank loans were plentiful and accessible at low interest rates; trade barriers were weakening and free trade was high on most Western countries' agendas; multinational corporations were branching out and establishing productive subsidiaries; and, with the Western banks recycling most of the oil wealth, large sums of financial capital were available to finance borrowers of locally owned enterprises. National enterprises, both state and local, appeared to be gaining at the expense of multinational capital, although the appearance of national autonomy was obscured by the dependence of nationally owned firms on foreign financing.

The world economic crisis — and the accompanying decline in demand in the world market — had a profound impact on the open economies promoted by the military regimes, particularly as no effort had been made to develop contingency plans to cushion its effects. The decline in overseas markets led to a drop in exports; increasing unemployment in the advanced industrial countries led to protectionist pressures and market restrictions; increasing interest rates and subsequent debt payments drained off funds for new investments and imports; and the deepening of the debt problem precipitated new loans to refinance old debts. The economic crisis fed upon itself: multinational corporations were less attracted to investments in crisis areas. The regimes' economic policies resulted in chronic stagnation, declining growth, lowering of the standard of living, and severe austerity programs. The combined effects of the economic crisis, declining commodity prices, and increasing debt were particularly disastrous for the military regimes because of the growth of a largely paper economy: large-scale borrowing during the boom was used to increase imports (particularly luxury items) and to finance real estate and speculative endeavors, as the doctrinaire free marketeers mistakenly assumed that the invisible hand of the market would appropriately order the allocation of investments between productive and nonproductive sectors.

The military regimes which came to power in the 1970s thus borrowed an economic strategy reflecting the dynamics of the 1960s and early 1970s and applied it to a historical context completely antithetical to the one in which it prospered. The collapse of financial houses and banks was accompanied by the demise of numerous industrial enterprises; the austerity measures and restrictions on loans, credits, and imports struck at the civilian middle- and upper-class supporters of the regimes. The deepening of the crisis worsened the barely tolerable economic conditions of wage and salary earners. The decline in commodity prices undercut the position of agrarian/mining exporters. The military regimes which originally legitimated their brutal rule as necessary in order to successfully modernize the economy were now faced with having repressed the people, without having developed the country. The loss of legitimacy—the spiraling socioeconomic problems and the alienation of elite support—created the basis for the emergence of the social movements. Redemocratization was the political outcome of the military regimes' catastrophic economic strategy: the military sought to foist the seemingly insurmountable socioeconomic problems onto the civilian politicians so they could retreat intact back to the barracks.

SOURCES OF REDEMOCRATIZATION

The predemocratic phase is dominated by the growth of social movements which encompass a broad array of social classes and occupational, professional, civic, and human rights associations. The emergence of the social movements and their increasing struggle to create political space becomes the immediate cause for the initiation of the negotiation process. The concern of the military is to shift the problem from the street to the negotiating table: negotiations are seen as a substitute for the street parliaments.

The proliferation of social movements and the increasing intensity of their activity is a signal that the military regime has failed to create an economic model with a substantial social base of support. Consequently, the capacity for long-term rule is seriously called into question. The economic model is based on a restructuring of the economy in which new export-oriented industries, newly established agricultural growth sectors, and increasing access to consumer goods would create a stable coalition of support among industrialists, commercial farmers, labor groups in the dynamic sectors, and middle-class consumers. It is assumed that these social forces would more than compensate for the predictable opposition from workers in traditional industries, declining agricultural and mining sectors, and small agricultural and urban producers. The incapacity of the military to sustain economic development specifically beneficial to its constituents is a key factor in its vulnerability to the new movements. And it is this vulnerability, and desire to recapture ties with its original constituency, which is behind the military's efforts to begin negotiations with middle-class adversaries. While the addition of these conservative upper- and middle-class forces to the opposition is a direct factor setting in motion the initial negotiation process, it is the more militant and dynamic social movements encompassing the trade unions, the slum neighborhoods, the students, and the self-employed business people who pose the most serious strategic threat to the military.

One of the basic concerns of the military regimes of the 1970s was precisely to disarticulate the class-based organizations and, in some cases, to fill the organizational space they occupied with structures associated with the regime. The revival of the social movements and their seeming irrepressible demands is one of the basic failures of the military regimes. More seriously, the absence of a sociopolitical cushion between the military state apparatus and its historic opposition (principally the labor movement) means that the military picks the groups and classes that serve as a bridge between the militarized state apparatus and the social economy. As a sage once noted, bayonets can subdue a population but cannot organize an economy. In summary, the emergence of the social movements is a pivotal event between the period of stable military rule and the beginning of the redemocratization process.

Several features characterize the social movements. First is the *proliferation of social movements*, from rejuvenated labor unions to movements of the self-employed, squatter settlers, neighborhood groups, professional associations, and university and church-associated organizations. The key point about the growth of social movements is that they represent a variety of social classes across the social pyramid. This is both their initial strength and their strategic weakness. While the cumulative impact of combined classes exerts additional pressure on the military regime, it also provides the regime with a variety of potential negotiating partners and political alternatives in exiting from the government. Historical (and future) antagonisms are muted as different social classes create parallel and occasionally converging movements directed at displacing the military regime.

The threshold for entering into negotiations with the military varies among the social movements. The military attempts to enter into negotiation with those sectors whose proposals for redemocratization are most consistent with its orderly retreat toward a position of power sharing. For the military, the displacement from government should not lead to the eclipse of power. Their conception is to retain residual powers in areas of critical concern, such as defense and internal security. In short, the transition to democracy involves power sharing, with the military retaining influence from the barracks. The proliferation of social movements thus catalyzes the redemocratization process but contains within it the seeds restricting its political and social parameters.

Accompanying the proliferation of social movements, and a direct outgrowth of them, are *multiple points of conflict.* Systems of production (factories, mines), distribution (truckers, taxis, buses), services (civil servants, health workers, educators), and sites of habitation (lack of basic services, concentration of unemployment) become points of disruption and confrontation. The potential for violent change increases as the process of mobilization increases. Equally important, the continuation of the military dictatorship serves to radicalize the repoliticized movements. Within a framework in which the choice is democracy or dictatorship, those forces exhibiting the most consequential and successful resistance are more likely to grow. The social movements of the Left, because of their affinity for radical activity, compete with and pressure the moderate forces for hegemony over the movements. In a context of rejuvenated classes and of rising social movements, political groups of the center can be effective only if the military initiates a negotiating framework which promises to inaugurate a transition to democracy within an acceptable time frame. The alternative is for the moderates to adopt a radical mobilizing posture, in order to maintain their presence in the social movements and not to be overtaken by events.

Faced with the new social movements, the desertion of their social base, and the joining together of moderates and militants in common social movements, and fearing violent changes endangering their institutional interests, the military undergoes divisions. Usually three factions appear in the face of the challenge of the social movements:

1. *reradicalizers,* who seek to return to the terror of the initial phase of the military regime and deepen the repression of discontent;
2. *coopters,* who seek to retain military authority but are willing to change personnel and particular economic policies and to incorporate conservative politicians in specific ministries; and
3. *dialoguers,* who are willing to open a dialogue with conservative and centrist civilian groups and to retire from political office while protecting military institutional interests.

The democratic transition becomes possible only when the third group (the dialoguers) is able to gain influence over the second group and to isolate the first group.

There are numerous factors that shape the relative strength of the three groups, the most important being whether the leadership which originally organized the coup was able to retain a collective shared-power system, or whether a single leader emerged who was able to dominate and reshape the officer corps of the dominant military institution (the army). Where the collective shared-power system exists, diverse political currents operate and alternative approaches and responses to the democratic movement are possible. On the other hand, where the single-leader model occurs, the process of political debate and divergent responses is less likely. In the context of the Southern Cone, Argentine and Peruvian military regimes resembled the collective shared-power system; in Chile under Pinochet the single-leader system prevails. The latter has resisted the initiation of a democratic opening, and has adopted the cooptive approach and threatened to reradicalize (introduce the terror of the first period).

The social movements profoundly affect other key institutions in society: the church, mass media, university, health system, and legal profession. These institutions are important in that they confer or withdraw legitimacy and prestige from the regime, and provide international visibility to the resistance. The presence of internal fissures within these institutions and the dissociation of these institutions from the military are key elements in stimulating the emergence of the dialogists in the military. Essentially, the institutional proponents of the democratic transition seek to avoid societal confrontation and actively promote surgical changes in the legal-political system. On this basis, the dialogists in the military perceive an opportunity to recover legitimacy as part of a "third force" between the military regime as it was constituted and the burgeoning social movements. Their hope is that the combined political weight of the institutional forces (including segments of business), the moderate leadership of the social movements, and the dialogist military can secure a pact that ensures a transition to democracy, safeguards military prerogatives (self-regulation, promotions, prerequisites, budgets), and prevents retaliation for crimes committed during their rule.

In summary, the dynamics of social movements create ripple effects throughout the military-dominated society, pressuring institutional divisions, which in turn provoke internal differentiation among the military. The latter becomes most pronounced in the context of a collective shared-power military regime, facilitating the opening of negotiations for a democratic transition.

PATTERN OF RETREATING AUTHORITARIANISM

The retreat of the military from government is basically a decision about choice: to be able to choose among alternatives within the opposition, rather than to have an option imposed by force of arms. The turning point within the negotiating sectors of the military is reached when there is a deep sense of the inevitability of civilian return due to such combined effects as sustained movement, elite defections, political isolation, and unmanageable economic crisis. The decision to withdraw, then, is much more a decision to avoid the totally unattractive choices inherent in a deepening polarization than a conversion to democratic politics. The choices which the military hope to be able to make have to do with the timing and conditions of transfer of government. In both instances, the military seeks, as its minimum program, to protect itself against retaliation for its criminal acts, and to protect its institutional interests (privileges, budgets, hierarchy), the larger social system of which it is part (private property, religion, family), and the alliances with the United States (Western Christian Civilization). In the absence of available opposition groups willing to negotiate from these positions, the military may fight on with an all-or-nothing attitude: the bitter-enders gain ascendancy, the bunker mentality predominates.

The electoral calendar established by the military becomes a testing period to probe the capacity of their civilian negotiating partners to uphold the military's minimum program. It is also a period when the military hopes to put distance between itself and its dirty war against civilians; the transitional period, it is hoped, will induce amnesia and reconciliation. Often a new military figure is selected or emerges to preside over the transitional period: one less obviously associated with the bloody past, one more amenable to dialogue with civilians. The negotiating process and the electoral timetable henceforth become political weapons utilized by the military to keep the opposition within acceptable political boundaries. Militant mass actions are condemned as "endangering the democratic transition," and the military is able to enlist the negotiating civilian sectors in the task of disciplining the unruly opposition. The key card played by the moderate negotiating civilians with regard to the intransigent opposition is the promise that in the aftermath of the elections, political and legal space will be opened for all political parties. This two-step flow of democracy assures the moderates of hegemony and entices (or attempts to entice) the radicals into acquiescence.

NEGOTIATING STRATEGY

The fundamental strategic concern of the military is to protect the military apparatus, even if in the final instance certain high officials are retired as a result of the democratic change. In this context, the terms moderate and radical take on specific meanings. Moderates are willing to respect the military apparatus, its internal organization, its pattern of recruitment and, above all, its monopoly over the instruments of coercion. Radicals are perceived as capable of directly intervening in the military, encouraging structural changes and even organizing new competitive organizations (militias), breaking the military's hold on weaponry.

The immediate concern of the military is to create an agenda of no retaliations, to promote a climate of neither victors or losers, and to guarantee it through an agreement with the civilians providing for military self-regulation. In this regard, to forestall civilian control, the military insists on conducting its own investigation into previous wrongdoing, through a self-selected military tribunal. This constraint on the civilian negotiators, like others to come, is an enormous, double burden on their ability to consolidate power; it alienates a vital human rights constituency (as well as substantial democratic antimilitaristic sectors), and it allows the military to retain power and prerogatives which can return them to political life once again.

The selection process, then, is crucial for the military. The choice of negotiating groups must include those moderates who will preserve the military hierarchy, honor international political and economic ties, and operate within the established institutional channels. There is little space in this negotiating pattern for civilian opposition groups committed to establishing new military-state organizations, sustained popular mobilization, and new forms of mass participation.

SPECIFIC ELECTORAL STRATEGIES

There is a certain irony in the electoral strategy chosen by the military rulers: with their sense of democratic propriety heightened by the threat of the popular social movements, they suddenly express deep concern for protecting the electoral process from totalitarians and ensuring the participation of only democrats. Once again, as in the discussion of negotiating partners, the military is partial to those electoral contestants who will exercise restraint in the area of socioeconomic change, and will mainly confine their innovations to the political-legal sphere. The military's narrow construction of the term democrat thus conveniently excludes those democratic revolutionary socialists and others whose purpose is to utilize the democratic process for a deeper socioeconomic transformation. As in the negotiating phase, the military provides visibility and concessions to electoral participants who favor limited changes (democrats), while creating obstacles to the full exposure of the radicals or Marxists.

The military's timing of the electoral calendar is the second aspect of its electoral strategy: the purpose is to provide time for the possibility of extracting concessions, to demobilize the public, and in the last instance to reverse the process if unfavorable developments appear on the electoral terrain (if a radical electoral outcome is imminent).

From the civilian side, for the moderates, the principal issue is to get on with the elections; agreements with constraints are seen as the realistic compromises needed to replace the military and occupy the highest office. The moderates rationalize the advantages secured at the expense of the radicals in two ways: the radicals are self-destructive, bringing upon themselves the problems they encounter; and the growth of moderate strength reflects the populace's distancing itself from the two extremes (the military Right and the intransigent Left). In this fashion, the moderates bypass a consequential discussion of the programmatic problems raised by their political compromises and, more specifically, of the institutional restraints they will encounter in the postelectoral period when they attempt to cope with the profound socioeconomic problems they inherit from the military.

The ideologues of the center — not a few of them defectors from the Left — bolster the position of the moderate military dialogists through the elaboration of the doctrine of classless democracy: through polemical writings, they attack attempts to examine the socioeconomic forces and institutional arrangements within which redemocratization takes place. With uncanny zeal, the centrist democrats admonish their radical critics to demonstrate greater appreciation for democratic legality, constitutional rights, electoral processes, and the like. The basic fragility of political institutions, especially newly initiated ones, in the context of deep-seated socioeconomic problems eludes these ideologues. This celebration of democracy for its own sake — an understandable reaction to the dark years of dictatorship — is, however, short-lived. The accompanying repressive state institutions and international obligations place a heavy burden on the survival of those democratic institutions — a position occasionally conceded by the moderates, but set aside to be dealt with in the postelectoral period, in pragmatic fashion. However, it is precisely this programmatic style of focusing on immediate issues in a limited context which leads to the strategic weakness of the emerging democracies.

POLITICAL CONSTRAINTS ON ELECTORAL PROCESSES

The military not infrequently attempts to introduce cumbersome electoral procedures to blunt the impact of voters. In Brazil, an indirect electoral process for the highest offices is one such mechanism that provides for voter participation and at the same time controls the outcome. The military frequently centralizes executive powers to override legislative objectives in contexts where the opposition has begun to gain influence in congressional arenas. The centralization of executive powers may also allow the incoming moderate civilian government to observe its agreements with the military, without regard to the objectives of the congress.

The military, in opening electoral space for the civilian groups, usually gains a trade-off: the reserving of powers to the military, outside of electoral controls. The separation of spheres (the competitive electoral sphere, open to civilians, for control of the government, and the military's continued influence within the state apparatus) is a crucial issue determining the limited areas of possible legislative action. This distinction between government and state, rather than the interrelation between the two, is what distinguishes moderates from radicals and is one of the basic reasons why the military will only proceed with the redemocratization process with the moderates. These very distinctions propel the democratic process forward initially but also form the principle obstacles to democratic stabilization.

The military attempts to influence the conditions of electoral competitions in favor of the moderates, extending facilities that increase their visibility while creating obstacles for or selectively banishing disfavored opposition candidates. Moreover, the military takes measures that promote the amalgamation of opposition groups in such a fashion as to allow the moderates to take control over coalitions. In the process of amalgamation, socioeconomic issues are diluted, and politics is reduced to the simple formula of "free elections" versus the military regime, thus maximizing electoral possibilities and minimizing conditions for coherent policy choices.

Finally, the military monitors the electoral campaign to prevent it from exceeding the boundaries of prior negotiation. In the postelectoral period, the military monitors the transfer of government to ensure that the change will not alter the old state apparatus and that the new elective bodies will be grafted onto the past state institutions.

DEMOCRACY AND BEYOND: THE SOCIOECONOMIC PIVOT

The installment of a civilian democratic regime ushers in a new political period. Free speech, press, and assembly are established and restrictions on labor, peasant, and professional organizations are abolished. These basic changes, however, are grafted upon the existing state institutions (civil and military bureaucracy) inherited from the previous regime. The journey toward democracy thus represents both a rupture with past governments and a continuity with previous state structures.

Basic to the transition, however, are the long-term, large-scale economic obligations inherited by the democratic regime, and the constraints these obligations impose on policy. These constraints can be divided into "internal" and "external." Internal constraints include:

1. demands by labor for wage increases to compensate for salaries lost during the military rule;
2. the unemployed, made redundant by economic failures and free market strategies, demanding jobs;
3. locally owned indebted enterprises seeking low interest loans and credits;
4. indebted farmers seeking relief from onerous interest payments; and
5. industrial firms seeking protection, subsidies, and increased state spending.

In the aftermath of the austerity measures of the military, the electorate presses for reactivation of the economy through an active state role, with increased spending and investment.

External constraints include the pressure to maintain debt payments to banks and prior or impending agreements with the International Monetary Fund (IMF), with all of its restrictive prescriptions and pressures, to increase exports to provide hard currency to meet massive service deficits (profit remittances, insurance, freight, and other external payments).

The stability of civilian political institutions is related to their capacity to deal with the political, economic, and human rights issues inherited from the military. Unlike the previous military regime, a democratic government operating in a competitive electoral setting must subject its political decisions to popular consent. Economic and social measures adversely affecting essential constituents alienate electoral support, weaken the incumbent regime, and destabilize civilian institutions.

The international economic credibility of the regime, however, depends upon its capacity to meet its obligations to external creditors. Operating in an international universe of unified banking consortia, refusals to service the debt to major banking groups can precipitate across-the-board rejection of credit by all banking entities. Moreover, the refusal to accept IMF conditions for refinancing of the debt — including IMF dictation in most major economic policy areas — leads to the massive erosion of international financial confidence, and the diminution of access to fresh sources of finance.

The policy choices facing democratic regimes can be analyzed in terms of two periods: the initial period of relatively easy choices and the subsequent period of difficult choices. From the beginning, the new regime's margin of maneuverability is very narrow — although in the initial popular euphoria, delegitimization of the military provides the regime with substantial political capital to make rapid and deep changes with broad popular support, if it possesses the political will. As our previous discussion indicated, however, this is very unlikely given the political compromises and selection processes negotiated prior to the elections. The time frame for universal consensus is quite limited. Popular support in the initial period is sustained (perhaps even increased) through regime measures liberating the press, opening the universities, and legalizing basic freedoms. The easy measures, those that do not evoke any serious resistance and do not have an economic cost may include: the prosecution of corrupt practices of the military and their cohorts (even this measure depends on the nature of the civilian-military compromise); the exposure of illegal embezzlement of funds from state enterprises; the revision of provisions flagrantly favoring speculators, foreign enterprises, and/or family members of the previous regime; an initial pay hike; and the proclamation of intention to reform the old order.

After the initial enthusiasm surrounding these provisions has passed — and given the severity of the socioeconomic problems, it passes quickly — the public turns to the realm of socioeconomic policy. Within six months to a year the legal-political changes have lost their capacity to sustain support and mute criticism. The moment of truth arrives, in which hard choices have to be made — with all of their political and social costs. These are the choices between internal and external constituencies: between allocating resources for socioeconomic improvement of living standards for wage and salary earners, on the one hand, and investment in productive processes, thus ensuring internal political stability, or meeting external debt payments and maintaining international credibility, on the other hand.

The social and economic content of the developing democratic regime plays a major role in determining its future stability. Measures that satisfy external interests but adversely affect substantial electoral supporters can lead to massive disaffection, increased sociopolitical polarization, and political crises.

Radicalization of the political process and the ascent of more populist regimes can trigger a new cycle of military intervention, popular insurgency, and externally directed destabilization campaigns.

Several countries in Latin America are in various stages of the redemocratization process and beyond: Peru and Bolivia have plunged into the phase of hard policy choices (the consequences of their choices are becoming more evident each day); Argentina has completed the electoral phase. Argentine president Alfonsín, in power since December 1983, has recently passed the easy phase and is entering into the period of hard choices; Brazil and Uruguay are entering the electoral phases of the redemocratization process; Chile is in the predemocratic period of burgeoning social movements. The experiences of Peru, Bolivia, and Argentina shed light on the interrelationships between the democratic transition and socioeconomic policy.

In Peru, Belaunde's accession to government brought with it a policy of economic liberalization that was premised on the notion that a free-trade policy would be a stimulus to export-led growth. Large-scale overseas borrowing, incentives to foreign investors, the denationalization of local state enterprises, and the reduction of tariff barriers became the established orthodoxy of the regime. The government agreed to meet its financial obligations to its international creditors, accepted IMF financial and economic prescriptions, and increased military spending, as part of its accommodation with the outgoing military regime. The results have been the worst socioeconomic crises of the century: GDP declined from 3 percent in 1981 to 1 percent in 1982 to minus 12 percent in 1983, and the picture for 1984 was no better. The manufacturing sector declined by almost 20 percent during the first three years of the Belaunde regime, and the debt/GDP ratio increased from 35 percent in 1981 to 50 percent in 1983. On the social side, per capita income declined by at least 10 percent. With unemployment and underemployment reaching 62.8 percent of the economically active population, inflation running to 125 percent (1983), and wages declining by 20 percent in real terms (between 1982 and 1983), the governing center-right Popular Action Party plummeted to third place among the major parties.

Furthermore, deep polarities have been emerging: in the interior, *Sendero Luminoso* (Shining Path), the Maoist guerrilla group, has gained considerable support, particularly in Ayacucho, and appears to be spreading to other provincial areas; on the other hand, the military has taken de facto control of the areas contested with the guerrillas. Military rule has been accompanied by widespread use of terror and human rights abuses (staunchly defended by the Belaunde regime). In the cities, both the Left (the United Left Coalition) and the center left (APRA) increased their support in the municipal elections.

Thus Belaunde's choice to support the bankers, the IMF, and an export-led strategy has created the setting for an increasingly conflictual situation involving guerrilla groups, hardline military officials, and leftist civilian groups. As the economy disintegrates, democratic institutions are emptied of content and the electorate is increasingly disillusioned with the dismal present and future prospects experienced through the democratic regime. The fundamental problem is not the democratic political process, nor can the guerrillas or military be described as the source of democratic decay. Rather, the basic cause for political decay can be traced to the socioeconomic policies adopted by the regime: in devising development policies to satisfy the overseas bankers, the IMF, and Washington, the regime undercut the possibility of stimulating local-based production and effective consumer demand.

In Bolivia, a similar pattern has emerged in the democratic regime of Siles Suazo. The regime honored past debts and abided by IMF formulas prescribing salary freezes, price increases, public sector austerity, and lessening of state controls. (The regime suspended debt payments under massive pressure from the trade unions in the spring of 1984.) The consequences were a minus 8.7 percent GDP in 1982 and a minus 7.6 percent GDP in 1983; price increases of 123 percent and 275 percent in 1982 and 1983, respectively; and a debt service/export percentage of 34 percent in 1983. Value added by manufacturing was 25 percent lower in 1983 than in 1980. On the other hand, Bolivia has paid about $789 million to service the debt — a sum which clearly would have turned the economy around if it had been invested in produc percenttive activities. In addition, Bolivia's export-oriented growth depended on external financing, insurance, and freight costs, which led to deficits in the net balance on service accounts of $2 billion between 1980 and 1983.

The outflow of income and decline in imports and investment capital, accompanied by severe inflation and IMF-encouraged devaluations, led to a severe decline in living standards, provoking widespread popular unrest, including general strikes — which in turn became the pretext for new military conspiracies, plots, and coups. While the regime has proposed to index wages to the consumers' price index, wage increases always lag behind the rapid and steep price increases. While the government proposes an "Economic Plan for 1984–1987," which allocates investment to meet the population's basic needs, the needed resources are channeled to finance the debt, pay external service charges, and provide for the military budget. In all of Latin America, the Bolivian government allocated the lowest percentage of its budget to capital expenditure.

Whatever the good intentions of the democratic regimes in assuming past debts, working within the orthodox policies, and establishing international financial institutions, they have been unable to prevent the deepening economic crises. The result has been that democratic institutions have lost their appeal to large numbers of people, as they are increasingly associated with ineffective and retrograde policies. In Peru, the socioeconomic and human rights situation is decidedly worse under the democratic civilian regime than it was during the previous military regime (particularly its first phase of military rule, 1968–1974, under Velasco Alvarado).

The Alfonsín government in Argentina appears to be heading in the same direction. After much hesitation, and under increasing pressure from both labor and the international banks, Alfonsín chose to ignore labor and knuckle under to the IMF prescriptions: payments to the international bankers took priority over productive investments and exports were increased at the expense of local consumption. Price increases and wage restraints began to dampen the electorate's enthusiasm for the IMF prescriptions. In these circumstances, the continuation of double-digit monthly inflation rates promises to exacerbate political and social antagonisms, with predictable consequences for the political stability of the regime. Social and political pacts at the top, between Alfonsín and the Peronist political and trade union bureaucracy, cannot contain the crises; only a decisive break with the enormous external overhead costs can release the investment resources for development.

Moreover, the unwillingness of Alfonsín even to deal with large-scale criminal offenses of the military has alienated an important sector of Argentine public opinion. His decision to put the offenses before a military tribunal had the predictable result of exonerating the offenders and forcing civilian courts to intervene. The delays and evasions on basic human rights issues reflect the historic institutional compromises that facilitated Alfonsín's ascent to government. The same compromises threaten to erode his public support: most democrats assumed that the radical president would at least bring some of the major torturers and assassins in the military high command to justice. His lack of political will and his orthodox economic policies in the face of the deepening crises have begun to erode the mass euphoria which greeted his electoral victory and his progressive-sounding program. *240663*

CONCLUSION

The process of redemocratization can best be analyzed as a set of interrelated phases in which each period establishes the political boundaries and socioeconomic direction for the subsequent phase. This perspective emphasizes the linkages between the political compromises prior to the return of elected regimes and the choice of socioeconomic policy in the postelectoral period. The critical factor underlying the process of redemocratization is the contrast between the legal-political changes and the socioeconomic and institutional continuities. The critical actors — parties and personalities who lead the return to democracy — are those who have passed the screening process in the previous period of negotiation and electoral competition.

The very commitments that enable these groups to gain political office, however, prevent them from initiating new policies, redefining international obligations, and pursuing profound institutional innovations in the state. The result is a new cycle of democracy, instability, popular disaffection, increasing reliance on the military, and a return to authoritarian rule. The problem is not inherent in Latin American (or any Third World) culture, tradition, or political character or in any other ahistorical/asocial abstraction. Rather, the cycle is rooted in the continuities of class and institutional practice which accept and operate within international and institutional frameworks in contradiction with majoritarian popular inspirations.

EDITORS' POSTSCRIPT

This analysis has been confirmed by subsequent events, most notably in Peru (where James Petras spent the summer of 1986). In Petras's view, the social democratic government of Aprista Alán García has been no more successful than was Belaunde before him in meeting political challenges (particularly that of the *Sendero Luminoso* guerrillas) through military repression. Paradoxically, this reliance upon the military has the effect of weakening García's civilian control *vis-à-vis* the military and, by expanding the authority of the military, ultimately creates a threat to the stability of his own regime. A similar contradiction emerges with regard to the ever larger debt. García's government will be unable to finance even a reactivation of the economy, much less any of the necessary socioeconomic reforms, without withholding payments on Peru's international debt. In this regard, the debt, too, has undermined the possibilities for a stable capitalist democracy in Peru.

Thus, to the extent that it complies with political/military or economic policies dictated by international capital, the U.S. government, and the international agencies under their control, the García government is likely to lay the basis for its own destabilization.

6

FOREIGN DEBT, THE THREAT OF FOREIGN INTERVENTION, AND DEMOCRACY IN LATIN AMERICA

Pablo González Casanova

AN ESSENTIAL ELEMENT IN PREDICTION: THE FOREIGN DEBT

In times of crisis, projections, extrapolations, scenarios, and simulations are in crisis as well. The problem becomes even more acute when it is necessary to generalize about an area as large and heterogeneous as Latin America. If there is a common future from Patagonia to the Río Bravo, each country will experience it in a different way, and the problem is to recognize the specificities of each one, and to discover certain common traits. By limiting the generalization to the immediate future, and beginning with some factors of general influence, it is possible to establish relatively probable profiles.

One factor of general influence is the external debt. The external debt is not a financial problem: it is a political problem. The debt and the policies of payment, which the creditors impose upon the debtors for the management of the national economy, have a long-term social impact. It is not a problem of ideology. No one can deny, as even Henry Kissinger observed, that the demands of the International Monetary Fund (IMF) cripple the economy, increase unemployment, reduce consumption, and threaten "the internal political evolution of various developing countries," which he sees in danger of falling under "anti-Western regimes" (*Newsweek*, January 24, 1983). The problems of ideology appear when the phenomenon of the debt is accepted as a natural fact, or when the dominant or alternative policies are criticized. But the seriousness of the crisis and the importance of the debt are facts recognized by everyone.

In the social sector, according to CEPAL (the U.N. Economic Commission on Latin America), the per capita income of Latin America dropped 2.4 percent in 1981, 4.8 percent in 1982, and 5.9 percent in 1983. The mean rate of inflation rose from 53 percent in 1980 to 61 percent in 1981, 86 percent in 1982, 130 percent in 1983, and 175 percent in 1984. The current value of imports of goods fell 20 percent in 1982 and 29 percent in 1983. The importation of goods dropped from $98 billion to $56 billion, with consequent damage to industrial installations, production, and employment.

Income, consumption, and production all tend to diminish. Latin America is moving backwards. There are studies indicating that some countries today have the standard of living they had ten, fifteen, twenty years ago. Some countries have been harder hit than others. For example, the rates of inflation for 1984 — 175 percent for the region — are only 106 percent in Peru, but they rise to 195 percent in Brazil, to 175 percent in Argentina, and to 2,300 percent in Bolivia. This has more or less acute effects in each country resulting from the unequal distribution of income, the loss of confidence in local currency, the flight of capital, the decapitalization of the country, and the underselling of goods, products, and services in foreign currencies.

The debt is an essential indicator of the crisis, of its significance and of its alternatives. "The global amount of the debt has come to represent more than half of the internal product generated in one year, and more than triples the annual value of all exports of goods and services from the region; just the payment of the interest represents a rent paid to the exterior equal to a third of current exports," writes Pedro Vuskovic (1984).

The maelstrom of the crisis, the central factor in the deepening of the crisis in all its aspects, is the foreign debt. It is the basis for the policies imposed by the creditors, organized collectively in the International Monetary Fund. Many governments sign the "letters of intent" agreeing to austerity policies imposed by the IMF and only complain of the "social costs of payment" as a misfortune. But no government — constitutional, republican, or more or less democratic — can reach point zero of investments and spending. It is not possible to impoverish the people indefinitely. It is not possible for these governments to constantly sink deeper into debt. The crisis, more than a statistical aberration, would be political.

Nevertheless, the debt and its consequences, other factors being equal, tend to grow indefinitely. The Inter-American Development Bank (IDB) has sketched out two scenarios which show an "irrefutable" growth in the dimensions of the debt for 1990; it could be $76 billion more in the best of circumstances or $264 billion more in the worst of circumstances, on top of an estimated $353 billion today. According to the Economic Commission on Latin America (ECLA), the debt will reach $450 billion in 1990, twice what it was in 1980. Debt service will be almost 100 percent of the value of exports. As the economist Vuskovic has observed: "No interest rate above 6 percent would allow a gradual reduction of the debt, whatever the time for repayment, even 99 years. . ."

(Vuskovic 1984). The problem is that the average rate of interest is 10 percent and has even reached 12 percent at times.

Thus the debt has grown in an uncontrollable manner and has become politically, economically, and socially *unpayable*. This fact has been pointed out not only by economists such as Vuskovic and heads of state such as Fidel Castro.* "Many creditors have realized," says the Chilean economist Orlando Caputo Leiva (1984), "that Latin America is not in a position to pay the debt under present circumstances." The Swiss Bank, the International Bank of Payments, and various central banks of Europe, as well as various European governments, "have requested the initiation of global negotiations between creditors and debtors." What is more, the World Bank has criticized the gravity of the measures of the IMF imposed upon the debtor nations in relation to interest rates and conditions.

The problem is that, on the one hand, the governments of Latin America are not prepared to demand a global moratorium which would permit a long-term renegotiation from the position of strength which they would gain from acting in concert; on the other hand, the IMF and the private banks are not ready to change their policies. Worse yet, the present administration of the United States has proven to be even more inflexible than the IMF in handling the problem.

Other alternatives seem to be closed. In order for the countries of the Third World to be in a position to pay without continuing to sink deeper into debt, it would be necessary to reduce the interest rates and the administrative commissions. The loans would have to be converted into fixed assets, and in effect the repayment period would be lengthened; prices and/or amounts of exports from Latin America would have to be raised, and imports would have to be cut back. Protectionist measures taken by the United States and other industrialized countries would have to be attenuated, and the United States would have to lower the fiscal deficit caused by military spending.

As these and many other measures appear unlikely, one may ask: What is going to happen? The first alternative for the creditors is an indefinite renegotiation; the second one appears to be violence. The first alternative for the debtors appears to be paying and paying, renegotiating and restructuring the debt; the second, to lead or fall prey to internal movements of protest—popular or authoritarian—by forces which in sporadic and isolated ways will refuse to pay the debt, or by forces which in dictatorial and repressive ways will oblige continued payment. The renegotiation and restructuring of debt payment would appear to be the first conservative alternative for avoiding a crisis within the crisis. But the impossibility of guaranteeing the indefinite reproduction of a society and a state which keep going further into debt makes it very difficult to think of this first alternative as a very probable solution. Under these circumstances, the second best for the vested interests is violence in the form of military intervention—internal or international, covert or overt.

The obligation to pay could end up by "imposing the denationalization of the debtor economies," of enterprises, resources, and even territories. The creditor states (and it is necessary to test the hypothesis empirically) can demand that the debtors pay "with the transfer of national properties what they cannot pay with current export income." Where the economic policy of the IMF ends, a certain type of war — military as well as economic — may begin. This is not highly probable, but it is possible. It is not probable because the people's capacity to resist is increasing, but it is possible because of the interventionist and arrogant mythology which prevails in the dominant circles of the creditor countries. And even if it is only a possibility, it should be given attention.

A POSSIBILITY: THE INTERVENTIONIST SOLUTION

The danger of a military solution is one of a history which repeats itself. Intervention is a reflex act from past history. The danger exists not only to the extent that the Latin American governments might feel obliged to declare unilaterally a suspension of debt payments, but especially in that they may do so individually and too late, when they are even weaker and more beaten down. The danger is accentuated by the crisis of U.S. hegemony in Latin America.

The crisis of hegemonic power on the continent is a fact of major importance. Its manifestations are many and constant. They can be seen in the fall of Batista in Cuba (1959), of Trujillo in the Dominican Republic (1961), and of Somoza in Nicaragua (1979). All these were military men and dictators trained to serve the inter-American system between the two World Wars.

The hegemonic crisis is manifested as well in the democratic, nationalistic, and popular movement which developed in 1965 in the Dominican Republic, in the popular rebellion of Curaçao (1969), in the national democratic movement of Surinam (1980), in the Black Power movement in Trinidad, and in the revolutionary experience of the New Jewel Movement in Grenada (1976–1983).

U.S. military and political triumphs in the Caribbean are particularly unstable: the allies or subordinates of the U.S. government have suffered severe military and political defeats. More of the same is going on in Central America. Nicaragua, as Cuba before her, is beginning to acquire the characteristics of an invincible country, from a political point of view, and even from a military one — this, in spite of all the pressures and blockades. The crisis exists in Guatemala and El Salvador as well, two countries living in a state of permanent civil war since the 1960s, where the hegemony of the allies and subordinates of the United States is constantly called into question. Honduras is an occupied country showing an unstable equilibrium since the end of the period of military reform (1972–1978); the country having been converted into a new military base of the United States, large areas remain under the direct control of the U.S. Army and of the Nicaraguan Contras. Costa Rica has faced a growing social mobilization since the beginning of the 1980s, with increasing contradictions of a weak government which, for better or for worse, cannot control its own territory. Behind its back, or with the consent of only one sector of public officials, the Nicaraguan Contras move around at will on Costa Rican territory.

In South America, the hegemonic crisis of the United States is revealed through the fall of the dictatorial governments imposed in the 1960s and early 1970s. The second generation of dictators of the inter-American system, the generation of the internal war, has begun to lose its footing. The resignation of Hugo Banzer from the Bolivian government (1979), the electoral defeat of the military regime in Brazil in 1974 (and more recently in 1985), the need to call elections and turn over the government to a civilian in Argentina (1983), the process which ended in elections in 1984 in Uruguay: all these are "proof of the bankruptcy of the military regimes" which arose in the inter-American system as a response to the Cuban Revolution and to the revolutionary tide which was subsequently unleashed in Latin America.

The fall of these governments and the precarious stability of many of those remaining indicate the loss of U.S. hegemony in the region. The problem is that U.S. ideologues confuse U.S. hegemony with U.S. national security: they see in the loss of hegemony a loss of national security. There is no other way to explain the statements and behavior of U.S. government officials and military chiefs. Accustomed as they are to dominating the Caribbean, Central America, and even South America, they see any hegemonic defeat as a threat to U.S. interests and national security, (sometimes only to the latter). When Reagan said about Grenada: "It is not nutmeg that is at stake in the Caribbean and Central America; it is U.S. national security," he meant just that: the problem was not one of economic interests, but one of national security. And U.S. national security was not seen as threatened by an island inhabited by 20,000 families, which would have been ridiculous — an island where private investments represented 70 percent of the total, and where the airport under construction (supposedly a Cuban-Russian military base) was being built by two private firms for purely tourist purposes, as has been proven. But Reagan's argument followed a clear hegemonic logic: Grenada was a bad example; it needed to be punished. Without that, the potential instability of islands like Saint Lucia, Saint Vincent, Dominica, Antigua, and others could become threatening, and involve them in a tendency to challenge U.S. hegemony even more — something the president tried to prevent in the purest interventionist style, with the most advanced counterrevolutionary techniques, and with the most sophisticated technology — all of these being characteristic of U.S. hegemonic ideology.

The tendency to repeat measures which have succeeded makes interventionist culture, counterrevolutionary techniques, and technological superiority into veritable articles of faith. The interventionist ideology has a varied conceptual and practical tradition. It has served to resolve problems from the expansion to the West and Mexico to the expansion into Central America and the Caribbean, not to mention other continents. This makes it very difficult to think of resolving problems of hegemony without using military intervention in the first or last instance, as needed. It seems even more difficult to apply noninterventionist concepts. The historical tendency is intervention, and breaking with the tradition would constitute an act of historical creation.

Some of the most successful interventions have been the ousting of president Jacobo Arbenz in Guatemala (1954); the intervention in the Dominican Republic, where the U.S. sent 23,000 soldiers to prevent the elected government of Juan Bosch from returning to power (1965); the ousting of President Allende in Chile with the help of $8 million to the Chilean Contras (1973); and the most recent intervention, in Grenada, where the U.S. sent 1,900 Rangers and Marines. If the interventions directed against Cuba in 1961 and 1962 did not meet with success, nor the more recent, indirect ones against Nicaragua and El Salvador, this is thought to be "because they were not undertaken in time," with "sufficient energy and tenacity." It is "because the advice of the experts on internal warfare was not followed": recommendations for "maximum harshness in the shortest possible time," "without moral repugnance at violence," "without attention to international laws," with clear statements about the use of "discriminate terror," without fear that "repressive dictators" might emerge — old hypotheses renovated in the 1960s and 1970s, enriched by neoconservative thinking, now on the ascendancy. To this one must add the myth and motor of the West: technological supremacy.

The loss of hegemony by the United States has provoked a voluntaristic reaction that, without supporting the idea of a superior race, does maintain that of "our technical genius" and "our industrial prowess," to quote Secretary of Defense Caspar Weinberger in his address to Congress, and it summons the United States to take up "the formidable technical tasks" presented by Reagan in his speech of March 23, 1983 on Star Wars.

The ideology of technological supremacy is confirmed by truly impressive arms which attack and outwit the enemy, "think" with precision, act with great speed and have a high probability of hitting their targets with a single shot. There is equipment that can give intelligent orders, devices which wait and attack. Information is excellent. There is equipment which analyzes and plans: the machine discovers and pursues the enemy. There are "electronic vision devices" (visionics) which bring on mirages in the enemy, and North American robots (robotics) which fight for and instead of the North Americans.

How can Latin Americans face a technology so much superior to their own? According to the myth, Latin America's only recourse is the Soviet Union. Every time Latin Americans are successful it is because the Soviets are aiding them. A relative reality becomes a false generalization and is converted into an ontological truth. The technological contempt for Latin America is mixed with a racist contempt of colonial origins, and is complemented by an entrepreneurial contempt for inefficiency, and a moral contempt for corruption. Half-truths confirm myths and dogmas. All of this increases the tendency towards military, interventionist solutions and combines well with the mentality of the inter-American advocates of military coups or *golpes* and their ideologies.

The *golpista* military types have at least four ideologies: national security, internal war, neoclassical Friedmanian economic theories, and "Catholic uprightness" (see Maira 1984). The theory of national security affirms that there is a planetwide clash in which it is indispensable to defend the ideological frontiers (more than the geographical ones) within each country and on the American continent: we are talking about defending Western and Christian civilization against the threat of totalitarianism and communism. Therefore it maintains, with a military logic, that it is necessary to eliminate constitutional guarantees and human rights, political parties, trade unions, and popular organizations. All of this in defense of democracy, a regime which will be imposed when the military or its successors have defeated and controlled the totalitarian forces. This theory of using authoritarianism against totalitarianism is supplemented by the theory and practice of internal war, in which the enemy is "the people." In economics, the Friedman neoclassical theories are sustained with stringent orthodoxy. These theories correspond to the ideologies of the present U.S. administration, the IMF, and the General Agreement on Tariffs and Trade (GATT): privatization of enterprises and public services, denationalization, elimination of customs duties and of measures protecting national industry, reduction of public spending, and increase in indirect taxes.

In addition to these lay ideologies there is a religious one, presented in its most conservative versions, such as Action Française, the neo-Francoist defense of limited democracy, and the ministerial teachings of Jerry Falwell regarding the Moral Majority.

How can one think about the future perspectives of Latin America without reference to these phenomena? And if one thinks about them, how is it possible not to fear a solution of extreme violence? When Fidel Castro says that "an invasion of Nicaragua is really impossible," that "there are no dangers of right-wing military coups," that "the staying capacity of the revolutionaries in El Salvador is such that they can fight indefinitely," that "the Sandinista revolution is irreversible," and that "the United States would need millions of soldiers to occupy Cuba," he seems to assume a certain level of rationality which does not necessarily include the logic of genocide, nor interventionist mythologies, nor those of technological, racist, and colonialist superiority, nor the theoretical servility of the *golpista* inter-American military. Although all the phenomena referred to by Castro are improbable, they are not impossible, especially when one considers the strengths and weaknesses of the new popular and democratic movements of Latin America. What is unquestionably valid in his observations is that from neither a military nor a moral point-of-view will the Latin American people allow themselves to be intimidated by interventionist threats. If some political leaders allow this intimidation to dictate their policy, they will no longer represent their peoples.

A UNIVERSAL DEMAND: DEMOCRACY

Throughout our America, there is a struggle for democracy as politics and as power. The common utopia of democracy shows a concrete path which today is rapidly becoming associated with a struggle for power. In 1979, General

Figueiredo, president of Brazil, said, "I have to make a democracy out of this country." As Francisco Weffort observed, "It is not the people who make a democracy, but the leading representative of dictatorship" (Weffort 1984:32). "Today," adds Weffort, "the political struggle in Brazil is as much a fight for democracy as it is one for hegemony within democracy" (Ibid.:59). The same can be said of the rest of Latin America.

In the most diverse conditions, in all of Latin America, the struggle for democracy is also a struggle for power. This fact is not strange, for two reasons: first, the struggle for democracy is sufficiently general or abstract for the battle to be fought by many different forces; second, the struggle for democracy is sufficiently old to indicate that it is not enough to fight for democratic forms without also fighting for the power beyond the forms. Both of these considerations have provoked an extensive historical accumulation or tradition, with the result that today, both struggles are taking place everywhere: for democracy and for power.

The double struggle varies from country to country, according to the weight of various factors: nation, people, citizen, social class, the corporations and workers, consumers, and various types of leadership and ideology (see O'-Donnell 1978; González Casanova 1984). It is possible to distinguish some very significant variations:

1. There is a serious problem when the democratic and populist forces have a history of profound divisions that they cannot overcome or that they overcome only precariously. An example is today's Argentina, where the forces which defeated the dictatorship are finding enormous ideological, political, and existential difficulties in building an organization that is both united and respectful of the various autonomous positions. The problem appears in a different form in Panama, where there is conflict between the pro-Torrijos military and civilian forces and those forces which come from other branches of the democratic nationalist and socialist tradition.

2. The struggle for hegemony as a class question appears in very different forms when there is a democratic opening, when there is a simulation of democracy and when all political activity is forbidden. Take the cases of Brazil, Paraguay, and Chile: in Brazil, much more than in Argentina (see Viola and Mainwaring 1984), there is greater control of the democratization process: the army and the bourgeoisie hold the reins of power. In Paraguay, one of the most sophisticated dictatorships in terms of its combined use of repression and consensus, the dictator has been reelected for the fifth time, after thirty years of power. Since this last election, everyone thinks that at his death, democracy will prevail, and the Paraguayan bourgeoisie is preparing to inherit the state and control democracy in its own way.
   While in Brazil the democratic forces are quite powerful, and in Paraguay they have the weakness of a civil society systematically undermined by the state, in Chile, however, they are potentially strong as heirs to a very powerful civil society. Their current weakness is the result not only of the dictator's hard line, but also of the bourgeoisie's efforts to control an imaginary process of democratization which would not include the left-wing parties. This results in the existence of two democratic alliances—the oligarchic and the popular—fighting with each other, not to mention

the existence of many other forces emerging as a result of twelve years of dictatorship, with a perspective of struggle as a vital heroic act, even of martyrdom.

3. In other countries, it is relevant to note the problem of struggles which tend to become partial or corporatist (in the sense of worker-peasant or popular corporatism) and thereafter seek only to defend their own members and their immediate interests. This is the case in Bolivia, where the great mass movements on the one hand and the government on the other have not succeeded in imposing a minimal social and economic policy to support the democratic project. After the great mass mobilizations and the frustrated demands for co-government presented by the worker and peasant organizations, there has been a retreat by the main actors, a lowering of their demands. Regressions of the same type—although based on different circumstances—can be observed in Ecuador.

4. Mexico, Venezuela, and Peru show another significant element in the struggle for democracy: the search—with varying degrees of success—for centrist positions. In Mexico, the old centrist tactic of the PRI (the party of a state that attempts to group the maximum number of forces and goals and to combine social negotiation with political and electoral negotiation) leads to a rare situation in which all the parties seem to reduce their demands and coalesce towards the center. The crisis of the state is now visible because a liberal-conservative party, the PAN, is exerting pressure in ways that do not always indicate a desire to reach an agreement. Furthermore, the state itself fears the transformation of a one-party political system into a more pluralistic system, in which the left-wing organizations would have a minimum of real power. The old, popular coalition that formed the state maintains its nationalism and its support for the principles of nonintervention and self-determination of peoples. The government is playing an important role in Contadora, yet at the same time it persists in a more or less orthodox application of the policies of the IMF. Its conciliatory and centrist spirit is entering into a crisis that increasingly weakens its foreign policy and threatens its own stability.

In Venezuela, the race of the majority of political forces towards the center is generating a situation of conformism which manifests itself at the most varied levels, from party politics to labor union politics to international policy. In Peru, on the other hand, the triumph of the center represented by the APRA, with 25 percent of votes for the Left and the near annihilation of the Right in electoral terms, gives the dominant political force a remarkable position of strength, which it combines with a particularly energetic position *vis-à-vis* the external debt. Recently elected president Alán García proposes a reorganization of the foreign debt payments in the light of economic development (rather than economic development being determined by the debt, as has been the case up to now). Pressured by the Left, which he respects and from which he receives support, the president of Peru nevertheless has to face insurrectionist movements like *Sendero Luminoso* that are much less amenable to negotiation. But even with them he is engaged in the search for social and conciliatory solutions.

5. In Uruguay there is a dominant civil society without a state. The democratic forces, being organized with enormous weight from the left-wing parties and the trade unions, demonstrate possibilities of formulating long-range demands. Conciliatory measures and certain structural tendencies to impose something like a populist policy constitute brakes on and possible deviations from this otherwise great strength. The principal

brake, of course, is having to govern without a state, and with the prodictatorship military.

6. In other nations such as Colombia and, on a much larger scale, El Salvador, guerrillas dominate large areas of the country. They are rebel movements disposed to negotiate from a position of strength. Given the impossibility of dominating the entire national territory from either a military or a political point-of-view, after several decades of armed struggle the rebels have become convinced of the necessity of maintaining their strength and negotiating capacity. They are trying to impose a negotiation in which they would not lose the power they have gained, and they are defending this power by military means. Their struggle for democracy has acquired the characteristics of a national and popular struggle, and tends to join all the struggles—those of working people, the nation, citizens, and militias—into one. Within their ranks and among their leaders, a revolutionary perspective predominates, but the resistance in its totality proposes particularly conciliatory goals and negotiations, so long as it does not lose the power so painfully gained. As this power is not sufficient to give them national hegemony, they propose to gain it through negotiations and through the strength they already have.

7. Nicaragua presents the most advanced case of the union of the people, the nation, and the citizenry around a democratic project. The struggle against the dictator joined all the struggles, which were then deepened by the imperial onslaught. In the midst of an extremely harsh economic, political, ideological, and military offensive, the government maintains a broad ideological, religious, cultural, and political pluralism. It has a mixed economy, and holds elections with firm guarantees to the opposition parties. All of the propaganda against Nicaragua cannot obscure these facts. Internationally, Nicaragua has received oil from the Soviet Union at a moment when Mexico stopped sending oil, but in foreign policy Nicaragua has succeeded in maintaining independence from the two major power blocs. Its disposition to negotiate is very great; the only thing it will not accept is the rebuilding of the colonial pact. To compromise with the Contras—most of them former soldiers of the dictator rearmed by the empire—would mean undoing all that has been accomplished and recreating the neocolonialism against which Nicaragua has fought so hard. But in everything else, Nicaragua shows an incredible flexibility.

When one looks at the variations in the struggle for democracy and power in Latin America, there is no doubt that at a certain point the national question and the popular question are definitive. If the struggle against military dictatorship and for political democracy is the starting point, a struggle against the various forms of foreign intervention is inevitable, and occurs sooner rather than later when a serious program of economic and social development is under way. The only problem is that such a program tends to unleash an offensive from the propertied classes and the hegemonic powers, which see themselves threatened by necessary reforms. The offensive is so persistent and violent that the defense of the nation and of the people, and the organizing of popular and national power, acquire not only representative forms of democracy but also participatory ones—as well as forms of articulation between government and civil society which preserve the independence of the nation and popular hegemony in the process of democratization. The drive to strengthen the government through the people, and vice versa, increases the importance of participatory democracy, the phenomena of co-government, and the centralization of power.

Thus, previous experience serves as a means to avoid falling into patterns of patronage, *caudillismo*, and corporativism, and to maintain an ideological and political pluralism that has disappeared in other cases of civil society's articulation with the state. The past limitations of populism and corporativism are being overcome. To confront populism, a universal expansion of the participation process occurs: to confront *caudillismo*, collective leadership emerges; and to confront centralism, decentralized authority expands, dispersed yet coordinated throughout the whole country. In Nicaragua they are even learning from some of Cuba's experiences in order to reach a higher level of pluralism and strength amidst varieties of religious and ethnic minority groups that did not exist there.

The history of power and democracy in Cuba established Cuba's need not only to survive but also to raise its national and popular goals to the level of socialization of the means of production and the election of representatives in villages, factories, trade unions, and government within a single-party system that linked civil society and the state not only through representatives, but also through co-managers. This phenomenon is difficult to understand unless one takes into consideration the long history of an organized society and a state threatened by military blockades. The struggle for democracy and power first drew Cuba nearer to the socialist countries headed by the Soviet Union, and later associated Cuba with the socialist bloc. The process of democratic movements in other Latin American countries will not necessarily be the same: their struggles for democracy and power could consolidate broader internal alliances which make nonalignment an international reality where a mixed economy and ideological and political pluralism are more than transitory phenomena — true historical innovations corresponding to various situations and values.

The principal struggle for democracy in Latin America will depend, internally, on the manner in which the peoples win hegemony of the process, and externally, on how democratic forces from other parts of the world help them solve the problems which emerge from the international context — for example, those problems manifested today through the external debt and the constant threat of foreign intervention. Today, the struggle for democracy in Latin America appears as an impossible goal if the governments there continue to suffer the effects of the external debt, which is becoming technically and politically impossible to pay, and if some of the internal and external causes of increasing indebtedness are not altered.

The democratic and popular forces in Latin America do not seem to have the necessary weight to declare a moratorium, or to force a renegotiation corresponding to the interests of the indebted countries. If some governments succeeded in declaring a moratorium on the basis of popular and national demands they would be less vulnerable to foreign intervention, as long as they undertook the action jointly with other governments; but for the moment there are no signs that any such thing will happen. It is most probable that suspension of payments will occur in isolated ways and in situations of extreme weakness.

Under these conditions, a worldwide democratic movement becomes the primary necessity: a movement which would demand that the governments of the creditor nations and the General Assembly of the United Nations reduce military spending by a sufficient amount to cancel the debt, and at the same time, that they take complementary measures toward not only a new world economic order, but a new world political order. To this effect, the priority struggle for the popular and democratic forces must be, on the one hand, for a collective and immediate decision to declare a unilateral moratorium or suspension of debt payments, which would allow the debtor nations to negotiate from a position of strength. On the other hand, it would mean the creation of a new culture of deterrence, based not on technological superiority but on political seriousness and a recognition of the new correlation of forces in the world today. In this sense, the fate of Latin America will be closely linked to that of the world.

THE YEAR AFTER: THE UNPAYABLE DEBT

The unpayable nature of the debt is increasingly recognized in financial circles and in the imperial countries. It is seen as a danger to the international banking system and particularly to the United States. But the calls for coming to agreement on lower interest payments, moratoria, or even cancellations or absorptions of debts, have been met in practice by appropriations of assets, privatization and denationalization of enterprises, and new concessions of resources and markets.

There is an acceleration in the transnationalization of national and state-owned enterprises and of formerly internal markets—a process in which the most notorious members and politicians of local private enterprise are enthusiastically collaborating. Foreign debts become foreign investments; what was formerly public and national becomes private and transnational. The imperial ambassadors—the North American managers and the Latin American entrepreneurs—are destroying the state's commitment to the people; they weaken it and convert it into a "minimal state" of spruced-up, ever-prudent functionaries who are frightened and put in their place every time they have an idea of their own or create a problem, no matter how insignificant. The tactic is to make the functionaries of the debtor countries weaker and weaker—and more and more prudent.

In general, the governments submit to the objectives of the IMF. Their supposed shows of collective resistance are illusory, symbolic, pure wishful thinking; in practice, they act alone, isolated, as the IMF demands of them. And on their own, they present resistance that is only partial and ephemeral (Bolivia, Argentina, Peru) or that obeys the goals of paying interest and principal and applying regressive economic policies (Chile, Venezuela, Mexico).

When, as a consequence of inability to pay, desperation because of popular pressures or imprudence in taking populism or democracy seriously, some government suspends payments, it immediately appears on the list of delinquent debtors, and is threatened with multiple reprisals. When any such government shows a degree of independence in its foreign diplomacy (as the Contadora countries and their nearby sympathizers have done), they are pressured to redraft the text of any agreement in a manner requiring Nicaragua to promise to disarm itself and sign the agreement – without the United States signing or promising anything.

The debtor governments are weakened economically, politically, diplomatically, and they pressure the popular and revolutionary governments to go one step farther. With them, Reagan is reconstructing the hegemony of *America* (without any accent, because the word is in English). The debtor governments pass from nationalism as a policy (contradictory though it may be) to nationalism as demobilizing rhetoric. They use nationalism in order to prevent the people from becoming aroused, in order to keep them tranquil, or in order to mobilize the people on their side.

Something similar is happening with social justice, development, and the discrete limited democracy. It is true that structural reforms are being made, but when these are discussed something very significant is obscured: the structural reforms of the indebted governments feed the process of transnationalization. It is true that they take some "modernizing" measures, but always on the basis of transnational technological development, of the development of North American know-how, and of the capitalization and growth of efficient monopolistic enterprises. They are thus increasing unequal development, accentuating dependency, and combining the rates of differential exploitation – thereby impoverishing (without facing protests) not only the marginalized sectors of the population, but also unionized workers and the middle strata of the poor country (inefficient and corrupted).

In the United States a chauvinistic phobia regarding Latin Americans is growing: they are the source of drugs and terrorism. Mexicans are the source of drugs, and Nicaraguans of terrorism. Latin Americans, with their ills – poverty, unemployment, population growth – threaten a country like the United States that, without them, would be tranquil, prosperous, and healthy.

The phobia extends to all of the underdeveloped peoples. What the Jew represented to Hitler the Libyan represented to Reagan. The flunkies talk like parrots: a Nicaraguan child is worthless because she is Nicaraguan; a leftist congressperson is a terrorist because he or she is a leftist. But the attack is more sophisticated than was the Nazi. Neoconservative Yankee thought attacks the Latin American bourgeoisies, simultaneously flattering and scorning them. It includes among the objects of scorn (which it laughs at, bribes, sniffs at, isolates, attacks, and subordinates) civilian politicians, military personnel, and businessmen. How can the Latin American peoples avoid catching fire (it says, in the Yankee language) with such ineffective, corrupted, authoritarian, antidemocratic rulers, or with cowardly entrepreneurs who export their capital to the United States itself and who even send abroad the money that the United States lends them? Among the military rulers, not even Stroessner or Pinochet can be saved, nor de la Madrid nor Costa Rica's Monge among the civilians. And as for those who still oppose Washington with some popular measures, they never stop calling them irresponsible, demagogic, and terrorist.

The United States is forging something more than a colonial fascist policy. It is monopolistic, and based on fear and hatred, with nothing but scorn for the underdeveloped. It is monopolistic and transnational, combining colonialism, chauvinism, certain remnants of racism and imperialist interventionism in the economy, television, politics and war with a savage liberalism, a fundamentalist democratism and state terrorism—all of which are legitimized by the state and the dogma of the North American people's superiority in technology and efficiency. Racism doesn't appear as racism, but as development in the face of underdeveloped Africans, Arabs, and Latin Americans. Superiority doesn't appear as racially based, but as North American democracy or efficiency.

The danger, that upon the explosion of the foreign debt bomb there could be a war of conquest, would be growing if U.S. government policy were not really proposing to guarantee that the debt will be perpetual and that popular protests will be limited to terrorism—since in questions of the debt the banks prevail and in questions of terrorism, the CIA.

In the face of this reality, the popular resistance which exists today is nothing compared to what it could be. Still, the majority of the peoples and national leaders continue thinking in terms of prudence, of conformism, without even mentioning when they will return to the Natural Order of Things, which Reagan has declared in order to regain U.S. hegemony and in which he appears to be predominant and to be regaining it.

Today, only in a few points of America does the resistance of the peoples appear uncontainable, as in Nicaragua or El Salvador. A harsher imperialist attack against those peoples might be the drop which would overflow the glass of our Vietnam. Perhaps then even the offended bourgeoisies and the scorned debtor governments—or at least some of their members—would begin the struggle. Revolutionary nationalism would then be something more than rhetoric.

NOTE

Part of this chapter was originally presented at the United Nations University Symposium held July 11, 1985. The opinions expressed herein are solely those of Dr. González Casanova.

* Editor's note: On May 20–21, 1985, the March 1985 interview with Fidel Castro on "the unpayable debt" appeared in the Mexican newspaper *Excelsior* and appears as Chapter 7 in this book.

REFERENCES

Ballon, Eduardo
1985 "Los movimientos sociales en la crisis: el caso peruano," PAL/UNU, mimeo.

Camacho, Daniel, and Rafael Menjívar
1983 "El movimiento popular en Centroamérica: 1970–1983," PAL/UNU, mimeo.

Campero, Guillermo
1985 "Luchas y movilizaciones sociales en la crisis: ¿se constituyen movimientos sociales en Chile?" PAL/UNU, mimeo.

Caputo Leiva, Orlando
1984 "Deuda externa y moratoria." UNAM, Cuadernos de la DEP.

Castro, Fidel
1985 "Entrevista." *Excelsior*, May 20 and 21.

Dos Santos, Theotonio
1985 "A crise e os movimientos sociais no Brasil." PAL/UNU, mimeo.

Filguiera, Carlos H.
1985 "Movimientos sociales en la restauración del orden democrático: Uruguay 1985." PAL/UNU, mimeo.

Gomez Calcaño, Luis
1985 "Los movimientos sociales ante la crisis." PAL/UNU, mimeo.

González Casanova, Pablo
1984 *La hegemonía del pueblo y la lucha centroamericana* (San José, Costa Rica: Editorial Universitaria).

————.1985 "El nuevo pensamiento latinoamericano." UNU, mimeo. Research paper prepared within the framework of the UNU's Project: "New Social Thought," coordinated by Dr. Anouar Abdel-Malek.

Hoag, Paul
1984 "Space militarization, Peace and the Third World." mimeo.

Kissinger, Henry
1983 In *Newsweek*, January 24.

Laserna, Roberto
1985 "La acción social en la coyuntura democrática." PAL/UNU, mimeo.

Leites, Nathan, and Charles Wolf, Jr.
1971 *Rebellion and Authority: An Analytic Essay on Insurgent Conflicts* (Chicago: Marham).

Maira, Luis
1984 "El Estado de Seguridad Nacional en América Latina." PAL/UNU, mimeo.

O'Donnell, Guillermo
1978 "Apuntes para una teoría del Estado," *Revista Mexicana de Sociología*, October–December, 1157–1200.

Pierre-Charles, Gérard
1983 "Movimientos socio-políticos en El Caribe," PAL/UNU, mimeo.

Rivarola, Domingo
1985 "Los movimientos sociales en el Paraguay," PAL/UNU, mimeo.

Rojas, Fernando
1985 "Los movimientos sociales frente a la crisis en Colombia," PAL/UNU, mimeo.

Salomon, Leticia
1982 *Militarismo y reformismo en Honduras* (Tegucigalpa: Guaymuras).

Sol, Ricardo, ed.
1983 *El reto democrático en Centroamérica* (San José, Costa Rica: Departamento Ecuménico de Investigaciones).

Vega, José Luis
1982 *Poder político y democracia en Costa Rica* (San José, Costa Rica: Porvenir).

Verdesoto, Luis
1985 "Los movimientos sociales, la crisis y la democracia en el Ecuador," PAL/UNU, mimeo.

Viola, Eduardo, and Scott Mainwaring
1984 "Transition to democracy: Brazil and Argentina in the 1980s," Kellogg Institute, mimeo.

Vuskovic, Pedro
1984 "La aritmética de la deuda externa," mimeo.

———.1985 "El desarrollo latinoamericano, la crisis y sus perspectivas." mimeo.

Weffort, Francisco C.
1984 *¿Por qué democracia?* (São Paulo: Brasiliense).

Wolfe, Alan, et al.
1980 *A questao da democracia* (São Paulo: Paz e Terra).

7

THE UNPAYABLE DEBT: AN INTERVIEW WITH FIDEL CASTRO

Regino Díaz

Interview granted by Fidel Castro Ruz, first secretary of the Central Committee of the Communist Party of Cuba and president of the Council of State and of the Council of Ministers, to Regino Díaz, editor of the Mexican daily newspaper, *Excelsior*, concerning Latin America's foreign debt, March 21, 1985.

DÍAZ: *Can there be unity among such dissimilar governments in Latin America?*
CASTRO: I think so. The economic crisis and the debt will unite the Latin American countries, much more than the War of the Malvinas did. In that case, the Latin American peoples were united by a problem which we might call one of family relations — sentiment, morals, and politics; it was a struggle against a sister people caused by colonial pretensions, historic plunder, an act of injustice dating back to the period when England was the most powerful empire in the world. The War of the Malvinas was a war waged by a European country against a Latin American nation, but it wasn't something that affected the Latin American countries' vital economic interests. Except for the Latin American patriotic aspect and the political aspect of the matter, they had nothing to win or lose economically. That solidarity was truly selfless. In the case of Latin America's economic crisis and foreign debt, however, the solution of that problem is a matter of survival for the Latin American countries.

There is talk of the crisis of the 1930s. The present crisis is worse than the one in the 1930s. Except for oil, Latin America's export products have less purchasing power than they had during the crisis of the 1930s. Even if we don't go so far back, referring to the prices our products had twenty-four years ago, the purchasing power of our main traditional export products, including sugar, is in many cases only a third or a fourth of what it was at that time.

Let me give you an example. Twenty-four years ago, it took 200 tons of sugar to buy a 180-HP bulldozer. Now, it takes 800 tons of sugar at the world market price to buy that same bulldozer. And, if you analyze coffee, cocoa, bananas, and the minerals Latin America exports, the amount of products needed to buy a bulldozer or other piece of construction, transportation, agricultural, or industrial equipment imported from the developed countries is three to four times as great now as it was then. Compared to 1950, the deterioration in trade relations is much greater.

What is the difference between the 1930s and the present situation? At that time, Latin America's population was less than a third of what it is now; today's social problems are incomparably greater than the social problems in the 1930s; these problems have been accumulating. That is, we now have three or four times as many people, and social problems have multiplied since the 1930s.

The most important thing, though, is that, at the time of the crisis of the 1930s, Latin America had practically no foreign debt. Now, we have a bigger crisis, incomparably greater accumulated social problems, and a debt of $360 billion. A mathematical analysis of this situation shows that this debt cannot be paid, and this is so whether you analyze the situation as a whole or whether you consider the individual situations of the countries; in some cases, it's more serious than in others, but it is serious in all, without exception.

According to the latest official data gathered by the United Nations Economic Commission for Latin America and the Caribbean, Brazil owes $101.8 billion; Mexico, $95.9 billion; Argentina, $48 billion; Venezuela, $34 billion; Chile, according to calculations that, in my opinion, are very conservative, $18.4 billion; Peru, $13.5 billion; Colombia, $10.8 billion; Costa Rica, a small country with a population of around 2 million, $4.0 billion; Panama, with a similar population, $3.5 billion; and Uruguay, $4.7 billion. And these are conservative figures, since, according to reports by distinguished Uruguayan and Chilean friends, Uruguay's real debt is $5.5 billion, and Chile's is $23 billion. That is, the official figures are lower than the real level of debt. In many cases, it isn't easy for the international agencies — or the governments of the countries themselves — to know the real amount of their debts because, in addition to the controlled debts, there are other ones, to private bodies, that aren't reported.

DÍAZ: *Are the debts of the countries with the most indebtedness, such as Brazil, Mexico, and Venezuela, really greater than is said?*

CASTRO: I'm not sure. A figure of $105 billion is mentioned for Brazil, around $100 billion for Mexico, and $35 billion for Venezuela, but none of the figures that are mentioned frequently are lower than the ones given in the official data of the international economic agencies. Some countries, such as Argentina, are using 52 percent of their exports to pay the interest on their debts. Bolivia is using 57 percent of its exports for this purpose; Mexico, 36.5 percent; Peru, 35.5 percent; Brazil, 36.5 percent; and Chile, 45.5 percent — and this when it is considered practically impossible to keep going when 20 percent of exports are absorbed by payments on foreign debts.

What do these figures mean? That it is impossible for any country to develop under these conditions. This has been expressed in the fact that the gross domestic product (GDP) of the Latin American countries as a whole dropped between 1981 and 1984. In Uruguay, for example, it dropped by 13.9 percent; in Argentina, by 6 percent; in Chile, by 5.4 percent; and in Venezuela — in spite of that country's enormous economic resources — by 6.1 percent.

Since the population has grown during these years, the per capita GDP has dropped even more — in Bolivia, by 24.6 percent; in Costa Rica, by 14.1 percent; in Chile, by 11.2 percent; in Mexico, by 6.3 percent; in Argentina, by 11.8 percent; in Venezuela, by 16.2 percent; and in Uruguay, by 16.2 percent. In the case of Venezuela, the per capita GDP dropped not only between 1981 and 1984 but also in the last seven consecutive years, plummeting by 24 percent. The incidence of the economic crisis and of the foreign debt, especially in the last few years, may be seen in the fact that each country's production has not only stopped developing but has even declined. Some countries are making truly impressive efforts to confront the situation. Here, I will cite three of the largest, most important ones:

In 1982, Brazil exported $20.2 billion worth of goods; in 1984, it exported $27.0 billion worth. In 1982, it imported $19.4 billion worth of goods; in 1984, its imports were reduced to $14.4 billion worth.

In 1982, Mexico exported $22.1 billion worth of goods; in 1984, it increased its exports to $23.5 billion worth. It reduced its imports from $14.4 billion worth of goods in 1982 to $10 billion worth in 1984.

Argentina increased its exports from $7.6 billion worth of goods in 1982 to $8.7 billion worth in 1984 and reduced its imports from $4.9 billion worth in 1982 to $4.3 billion worth in 1984.

By making great efforts to increase their exports and by cutting their imports drastically, to levels that are nearly untenable for their economies, these countries obtained favorable balances of trade. Brazil obtained a positive balance of $12.6 billion; Mexico, one of $13.5 billion; and Argentina, one of $4.4 billion. All of these balances — the results of tremendous efforts, using and practically exhausting their stocks of raw materials and possibly adversely affecting the maintenance and replacement of productive installations — have been used exclusively in all three countries to pay the interest on their debts.

As a whole, the Latin American countries paid $37.3 billion for interest and profits in 1984 — nearly $3 billion more than in 1983 — and they received $10.6 billion in loans and investments.

In 1984, Latin America's net transfers of financial resources abroad for interest and profits rose to $26.7 billion. In just two years, 1983 and 1984, the net flow of financial resources from Latin America amounted to $56.7 billion. That is, the Latin American underdeveloped countries are financing the economies and development of the richest industrialized countries of the world with impressive sums of money. These are the facts. And that money has gone forever; there is no possible way of getting it back.

The growth rate of the debt has declined and fallen far below the record 24 percent reached in 1981. This is only logical: now, nobody dares to lend those countries any more money. Even so, for one reason or another, their debt grew by 5.5 percent. It is expected that, in the next ten years, the interest on it — even if it is held at more or less the same level — will average $40 billion a year.

Twenty-four years ago, when the Alliance for Progress was created, Kennedy proposed a program of economic cooperation for meeting Latin America's social problems and development needs, calling for $20 billion to be invested over a period of ten to fifteen years. That idea arose during the period of obsessive trauma over the Cuban Revolution and sought to avoid the creation of objective conditions that would be propitious for new revolutions. Now, the economically underdeveloped countries of this hemisphere, with twice the population and triple the social problems, will be giving the industrialized countries $40 billion a year as interest on their debts. In ten years, they will have to pay $400 billion — twenty times as much as Kennedy suggested investing over ten to fifteen years as economic cooperation for solving Latin America's economic and social problems, when there were half as many people and incomparably fewer accumulated social problems, the international economy was advancing full speed ahead, there were no crises, and the prices of their basic export products had much greater purchasing power.

The political, economic, and social situation of Latin America is such that it can't hold up under any more restrictions and sacrifices.

In recent months, when the International Monetary Fund's measures began to be applied, there were repercussions in the Dominican Republic, a country that had a relatively stable political situation, with a constitutional regime. Rising prices, triggered by the devaluation of the Dominican peso, which had been at par with the U.S. dollar but was reduced to a rate of three pesos per dollar applied to the foreign currency that was invested to import medicines and other articles of popular consumption, caused an uprising. The government's reply was to order the army and the police into the streets to put down the protest demonstrations. The result, according to the official figures, was fifty dead and 300 wounded. Many people say that the real number of victims was larger. A few weeks ago, new demands by the IMF led to the application of a rate of exchange of three pesos per dollar on all import products, including fuel. The government, acting before the people did, once again ordered the army and the police to occupy the cities and try to crush the people's protests. This has created a situation of great desperation and tension in the Dominican Republic.

Another recent example of this occurred in Panama, after the new government was inaugurated. A 7 percent tax on certain services and the postponement of wage increases for doctors and teachers that had been agreed on previously caused a similar situation. Hundreds of thousands of people took to the streets, but there was no repression and no victims, due to the attitude of the National Guard, which has played a progressive role, has struggled for the recovery of sovereignty over the Canal, and has close ties with the people. It doesn't want to fire on the people. As a result, the measures had to be annulled. And these weren't measures for solving Panama's serious economic difficulties, which are similar to those of the rest of the Latin American countries; rather, they were simply attempts to balance the budget to a certain extent and thus create the minimum conditions that the International Monetary Fund requires for beginning to renegotiate the debt.

In Bolivia—where the preliminary report of ECLAC had predicted that inflation would be 1,682 percent in 1984 and where it really, according to the latest figures, rose to 2,300 percent in one year—an economic situation has been created that has completely paralyzed the country, with tens of thousands of miners armed with sticks of dynamite, workers, students, and other people in the streets, and farmers mobilized in the countryside blocking highways and demanding wage increases, price controls, supplies of provisions, and other measures in a real state of desperation, making the situation almost unmanageable. Nobody knows how the country can emerge from the serious economic crisis that is afflicting it.

The curious thing is that these things that I've mentioned have come about practically spontaneously, in response to the objective situation.

DÍAZ: *Why hasn't there been a coup d'état?*

CASTRO: I should talk about this later on, when I go into how I think events in the various countries will develop as a result of this situation. I am simply pointing out things that have taken place spontaneously as a result of the economic crisis and the debt.

The economic situation has the most serious characteristics in Bolivia. There, as I've already said, the GDP dropped by 16.1 percent between 1981 and 1984, and the per capita GDP dropped by 24.6 percent in just three years. The value of Bolivia's exports dropped from $828 million to $730 million between 1982 and 1984. Its modest imports increased from $429 million in 1982 to $460 million in 1984—very meager figures. It is practically impossible for a country with Bolivia's population, problems, and needs to keep going with just $460 million worth of imports.

The $270 million in its favorable balance of trade for the last year had to be used to pay the interest on its debt. That is, in the three countries mentioned, the International Monetary Fund's measures or attempts to apply those measures have caused serious political and social conflicts, based on a situation in which people are totally opposed to the imposition of new measures to lower the standard of living and to making new sacrifices.

A democratic opening has been created in the South American countries, and this has awakened enormous interest and great support in Latin America and the rest of the world. Almost simultaneously, democratic openings have appeared in three important countries: Argentina, Uruguay, and Brazil. With regard to Uruguay, this is important not so much because of the country's size or resources as because of the symbolism involved in its return, after long years of military oppression, to a constitutional regime, since this is a country that had been a model of democratic institutions for a long time. Uruguay, like Chile, used to be called the Switzerland of the Americas. The U.S. administration declares—almost presenting it as a result of its policy—that democracy is making advances in Latin America. What is really making advances is the crisis.

These democratic openings have come about, of course, partly because of the people's struggles and resistance to military dictatorships but the fact that the economic crisis is so serious that the military men—who are demoralized and bewildered—don't feel capable of handling the situation has contributed a great deal.

The military men are withdrawing from public administration. If the economic situation had been less serious, they would have resisted, would have tried to remain in government longer. Now, they have turned state administration over to the civilians and have left them a terrible inheritance, to be sure. If the economic problems stemming from the debt aren't solved, those democratic processes, too, will inevitably enter into crisis.

In Uruguay, as people close to the new government have said, the foreign debt amounts to $5.5 billion; exports amount to only $1 billion. Such important markets as the textile market in the United States have just been hit by protectionist measures, and important meat markets have been seized by the European Economic Community, whose meat production is subsidized. The standard of living dropped by 50 percent during the years the military government was in power. How can the government of a country in those conditions—where civilians have just taken control, thanks to the people's support, after years of savage repression—apply the International Monetary Fund's measures and demand new sacrifices by the people? The democratic processes in Argentina and Brazil are confronted with similar situations.

It is impossible to conceive of the new leaders of those countries, who headed the democratic processes during the long years of military dictatorship, ordering the army and the police into the streets to fire on the people in order to apply the International Monetary Fund's measures and pay every last cent of their debts. These leaders have stated three things perfectly clearly: that they aren't about to burden the people with the consequences of the debt, that they aren't about to apply recessive policies, and that they aren't about to sacrifice their countries' development. That is, they have stated these three basic premises. What hasn't yet been said is how these premises can be applied if no solution is found for the problem of the debt.

The first thing the IMF demands is a reduction in the rate of inflation, a reduction in the budgetary deficit and restrictive measures of a social nature that increase unemployment and aggravate the problems that have been accumulating and multiplying for long years. Consumer prices in Latin America as a whole rose by 130.8 percent in 1983 and by 175.4 percent in 1984. With these levels of inflation, it is practically impossible to manage the economy.

I wonder how it is possible, in these circumstances, to demand that this group of Latin American countries—whose economies have not only stagnated but regressed in the last few years, while the population has continued to grow at a high rate — extract $40 billion from their economies each year and, in ten years, turn over $400 billion just for the interest on their foreign debts. What new sacrifices would these countries have to demand and what restrictions would they have to apply in order to pay that fabulous amount of interest, plus reduce inflation and promote development? What prospects and hopes do they have with which to stimulate this epic, costly effort? What arguments can they use to move the people and obtain the consensus, unity, support, and spirit of sacrifice required by such an enterprise? It is a practically impossible task. In some cases, the levels of inflation are truly astounding — as in Bolivia, where it was 2,300 percent; Argentina, where it was 675 percent; Brazil, 194.7 percent; and Peru, 105.8 percent. How can anyone ask that, in a single year, those countries reduce their inflation, balance their budgets, and also pay astronomical amounts as interest on their debts?

Moreover, the figures on the transfers of resources to the industrialized world which I've already mentioned refer exclusively to what has left those countries officially, as interest payments and profits. The flight of capital should be added to this — a figure that, because of the way this capital leaves, is practically impossible to estimate. It is known, however, that tens of billions of dollars were sent from Venezuela to the United States in the last few years and that the same thing happened in Argentina. The Mexicans know that when economic difficulties arose and a devaluation was seen to be inevitable — there are always many indicators that make it possible to guess when a devaluation has become inevitable — tens of billions of dollars were also sent from Mexico to the United States.

I have referred to just three countries, but this has happened throughout Latin America, because of a very logical, very simple, and perfectly understandable mechanism: when the money of a Latin American country — any Latin American country — begins to be devaluated at an accelerated rate, people lose confidence in it.

DÍAZ: *And in the government.*

CASTRO: People usually lose confidence in the government, but it isn't always right to do so; sometimes new governments come along and inherit this situation. It could be said that not even men can be blamed for this crisis; it is the result of a crisis of a system of domination and exploitation that has been imposed on the underdeveloped world. Later, I will go into this idea further; I have tried to be orderly in setting forth my points-of-view.

The economic crisis has hit, and the brunt of it has been passed on to, the economies of the least developed countries. It may be said that this is a process that has been developing for some time and has had more or less serious consequences, depending on each country's economic resources and also on the greater or lesser efficiency with which it has defended itself against or tried to overcome the crisis; there is a wide range of cases. Doubtless, the policies followed in Chile, Argentina, and Uruguay — the official policies of the military regimes — have had terrible consequences.

I remember that, in the last few months of Allende's administration, for example, Chile was importing $100 million worth of meat a year. Nevertheless, a few months after the coup, Chile began to export meat. How? On the basis of the dead, the people who were made to disappear, the thousands of victims of torture and other horrible means of repression, the massive firing of civil servants, the drastic cutting back of social services, massive layoffs of factory workers, wage cuts, and the drastic lowering of the people's standard of living. Logically, many people who used to eat meat stopped eating it, and, in a few months, Pinochet was able to begin exporting it.

That wasn't the only thing Pinochet did. He presented himself as a champion of Western principles, Western values, capitalism, and free enterprise. As a result, economic advisors, economic specialists, and professors of the "Chicago School" immediately appeared to show him how Western interests and the interests of capitalism really had to be defended. They expounded the theory that if he wanted to have efficient industry, he would have to open the doors to foreign competition and place Chilean national industries in competition with European, U.S., and Japanese industries and those of such countries as South Korea, Taiwan, and Singapore, where the big transnationals had taken their technologies and imposed their discipline — for which, of course, they also needed authoritarian regimes based on force. The principle that is axiomatic for any developing country and has been accepted for a long time — that the nascent industries of the developing countries have to be protected against the competition of countries with more resources, more technology, and more development — was abandoned. As a result, industry was ruined, the number of the unemployed increased, and the debt shot up.

In Chile, where the most sophisticated economic principles of the Chicago School were applied rigorously, the foreign debt, which had been only $4 billion when Allende was president, rose to $23 billion — of all the figures that have been mentioned, this is the one that seems most realistic to me — and unemployment reached a record high for the Latin American countries: 18.6 percent of the work force. You know that, in addition to the unemployed, there is always a large number of the underemployed, who work only a few hours in various activities trying to subsist.

The same economic policy that was applied by the military dictatorship in Chile was also applied in Argentina and Uruguay. You can imagine what it meant to place Argentina's automobile, truck, and tractor industries, which produce high-quality vehicles — as we know, because we have Argentine trucks, cars, and other equipment here — that meet the Argentines' needs perfectly well and that meet our needs for transporting sugarcane and providing taxi service, in competition with the Japanese truck and automobile industries, which have highly automated plants that employ robots in many operations and use Japanese steel made with high-technology, high-productivity industrial processes. In short, they were placing Argentine skilled workers in competition with the robots of Japanese industry.

I asked an emissary of the party that won the election in Uruguay, who visited us recently, if the military men in Uruguay had done exactly what the military had done in Chile and Argentina. He said, "Yes, exactly the same thing." He even mentioned the case of an industry that produced hair curlers or something like that: when the same—but cheaper—South Korean articles appeared, the Uruguayan industry was ruined. That is, the same economic formula was applied in the three countries, through the political formula of a military coup, the overt use of force against the people and the most ruthless methods of oppression was applied first in Chile, Argentina, and Uruguay. You can appreciate the disastrous consequences of those political methods and economic measures.

The paradox of all this is that the United States, the most industrialized country in the world, uses all kinds of tariff and other formulas to jealously protect not only its industries, which are far from competitive in many branches, but also its agricultural products, such as beet sugar and even corn syrup for sweetening soft drinks. Yet its professors come to teach us how to tear down our tariff barriers and make our industries competitive.

I don't have enough information about Brazil, about what the military men did there in the economic field and how they did it—which formula they may have used and what gave rise to its enormous debt. Rather, I have the impression that Brazil didn't follow the exact same policy as Chile, Argentina, and Uruguay, that it may have protected its national industries more against foreign competition, and that what it did was fling open its doors to the transnationals so they could make big investments there and set up plants, attracted by cheap labor, offering them all the advantages, guarantees, and securities that a strong-arm regime could. But I have the impression that the Brazilian military men were more concerned about protecting their national industries than the Chileans, the Argentines, and the Uruguayans were.

DÍAZ: *Weren't some corrupt public officials to blame for the creation of this foreign debt?*

CASTRO: I'll tell you. That is an element to take into account, because it was a factor, and I've tried to explain how the policies of the governments of those three countries that I've mentioned aggravated the crisis in each of them. It's an example of how the governments' actions can be better or worse and, of course, have an influence on the situation. Several factors had a bearing on the creation of that debt. They included the policies mentioned: if you open your doors to foreign competition and ruin your national industry, you will have to pay fabulous amounts each year for imports and, as a result, will be forced to ask for loans.

DÍAZ: *Or if the money is misdirected.*

CASTRO: I'm trying to explain things in a more orderly way. Those countries' foreign debts—which are a result of their increased imports—are one of the factors. Also, much of that money went for weapons and other military expenditures. Another part served to make a lot of people rich—that is, much of the money was stolen—and a lot of it was sent abroad in various ways. The money lenders didn't care what was done with it. That period coincided with an enormous accumulation of funds, much of which came from the surpluses that were created in several big oil-exporting countries and deposited in banks in the United States and Europe. There was so much money that the money lenders, the banks, went running after debtors, offering them loans. The usual situation was reversed: generally, it's the debtors who go to the banks to ask for loans, but, in many countries in Latin America, the bankers went around looking for debtors in order to lend them money at interest rates that were much lower than they are now—that is, money was lent at lower interest rates, and much higher interest is charged now. I can say more: a dollar that is overvalued by nearly 40 percent, according to some experts, is collected. It's as if I lent you a kilogram of gold and then asked you to return 1.4 kilograms of gold, apart from the higher interest charged for those 1.4 kilograms of gold.

In short, a part of that money may have been invested in a more or less useful way; another part was squandered on various things, apart from arms—it served to support absurd, antinational policies that were ruinous for local industries, or was stolen, or was sent abroad, or was misspent on arms, or squandered on other things—and some of it, in theory, may have been invested in something useful.

DÍAZ: *Such as?*

CASTRO: Well, some industrial equipment may have been purchased and installed somewhere, or perhaps it was used to pay for an infrastructure project or a road or a hydroelectric power plant was built—investments of that sort. But, in fact, that enormous debt didn't result in development for Latin America.

When I was talking about inflation associated with the flight of capital, I tried to explain that the 175.4 percent rate of inflation for the group of countries in 1984—which is quite generalized inflation that affects all of Latin America, to a greater or lesser degree—resulted in loss of confidence in national currencies. The natural tendency of everybody who has an amount of money and wants to protect it is to change it for dollars and deposit them in U.S. banks. Even though various measures have been taken in different countries to protect their foreign currency income and keep it from being sent abroad, there are always many ways of getting dollars. In nearly all countries, in addition to the official exchange rate, there is a parallel exchange rate. I talked with some Dominicans, and they said that anybody who has money in national currency could obtain dollars without any great difficulty, either through the banks or in the street, though you always get a little more in the street.

Anyway, when confidence is lost in a national currency—which is the case in the Latin American countries—many people who want to make their money secure—usually they belong to higher-income sectors and have the equivalent of $50,000, $100,000, $500,000, or a million dollars in national currency—exchange it, deposit it in the United States at a high interest rate and have their money and interest guaranteed.

Even though, in this situation of inflation, countries tend to pay higher domestic interest rates, precisely in order to attract money and prevent the flight of capital, the present high levels of inflation in several Latin American countries practically make it necessary to use a computer to get weekly estimates (daily estimates in the case of Bolivia) of how much the national currency has been devalued, so you can know what the interest paid by the local banks really means and what is happening to your money. On the other hand, people have the alternative of exchanging their money for the foreign currency of a country that pays high interest rates so that, far from being devalued, it will rise in value, and they exchange it and deposit it in a safe place. Latin American countries with underdeveloped economies don't have an easy time of it, and they are beset by traps on all hands.

I am pointing this out because, as I told you, to the figures given on interest payments and profits – to all those figures – we must add the money that leaves those countries every year, because all countries are affected, to a greater or lesser degree, by the flight of capital, mainly to the United States.

You are Mexican. Just today, I read an international wire service report that contained information issued by the National Bank of Mexico, stating that the Mexican economy had lost more that $7.6 billion through the negative flow of foreign currency in the first nine months of 1984, not only for interest on its debt (which amounted to 67 percent of the nearly $13 billion that left the country), but also because, between January and September, the flight of foreign currency rose to more than $2 billion. In contrast, income from loans amounted to only $5 billion or so, with $192 million coming in as foreign investments. At least the Central Bank of Mexico has a clear view of the foreign currency that is leaving the country.

Well, I was talking about the flight of capital. This has occurred not only in Latin America but in Europe and Japan, as well. In 1983, $40 billion flowed to the United States, partly in response to the policy of high interest rates paid there. I understand that between $4 and $5 billion were transferred from the Federal Republic of Germany (BRD), which is a great industrial power, to the United States last year because interest rates there are 4.5 points higher than in the BRD. With that kind of monetary policy, money flows toward the United States from all quarters. During that same year, 1983, $170 billion in foreign capital was invested in stocks and bonds in the United States. In order to be able to support a budgetary deficit of nearly $200 billion and a trade deficit of another $123 billion, you have to drain money away from the rest of the world.

And, if there is a flight of capital from such highly industrialized countries as Japan and the BRD (not to mention Spain, Italy, France, and England, all of which unquestionably have industrial development – some more, some less – but which fall short of the levels achieved by the BRD and Japan), what can you expect to happen in countries with weak economies that are struggling for development and have a lot of economic and social problems, such as the countries of Latin America? What could happen? How could the Latin American countries defend themselves more successfully against a policy that is adversely affecting the rest of the more developed industrial powers?

Other factors have also contributed to this crisis and to this debt, and I'm going to mention them to you. One of them — a really decisive one — is unequal terms of trade. This phenomenon has existed throughout history and can be traced precisely during the last four decades. I believe that economists should study and analyze this phenomenon more deeply in order to understand its essence and mechanisms better. It is a kind of law that operates in trade between the developing and the industrialized countries. I've already mentioned this: the constantly rising prices for the equipment, machinery, and other finished products we import from the industrialized countries, together with the declining purchasing power of the developing countries' basis exports.

The purchasing power of those products as a whole, including oil, dropped 21.9 percent between 1980 and 1984. This means that, if you take these products as a whole, some of whose prices dropped more than others, if, with a given amount of those products you could buy one hundred units of something in 1980, in 1984 you could buy only seventy-eight with the same amount. This is a very important element. If Latin America's exports in 1984 were worth $95.0 billion, the near 22 percent drop in their purchasing power, in itself, meant a loss of nearly $20 billion just because of the deterioration in the terms of trade.

To this must be added what we have lost through high interest rates — rates that are higher than the ones that were in effect when the debt, or a large part of it, was contracted and which remain artificially, arbitrarily high. Because of this, we have already lost more than $10 billion — in the interest that is superimposed each year. To this, we must add the loss consisting of the real increase in the debt and its corresponding interest caused by the overvaluation of the dollar. If you received $100 billion, and dollars are now overvalued by 30 percent — I'm going to say 30 percent not 40 percent here — your debt objectively increased by $30 billion plus the interest on that $30 billion.

Then, in just these four ways — because of our being charged extra for their products and being paid less for ours, compared to the situation in 1980; because of the artificially high interest rates, a consequence of the United States monetary policy; because of the flight of capital; and because of the fact that we are paying with more expensive dollars, inflated ones, that have been over-valued — the Latin American countries' economies were illegitimately stripped of more than $45 billion in 1984: $20 billion for the deterioration in trade relations, $10 billion for excessive interest, $10 billion for the flight of capital and $5 billion (a conservative estimate) for the overvaluation of the dollar. Adding it all up, including what can be considered normal interest on the debt, in just one year the Latin American countries have turned values equal to around $70 billion over to the rich, developed world. And $50 billion of that was in cash.

Can the Latin American countries' economies withstand that drain? Can they continue to withstand it? Can anyone think about political and social stability in the Latin American countries, when they are subjected to such unheard of, ruthless extortion? Can such demands be upheld from the moral point of view? Is this policy — of overvalued dollars; of exorbitant interest rates; of the unfair trade relations that are imposed on all of us; of the promotion of and support for repressive, bloody governments, which has happened in several states; of the economic theories and formulas and the monetaristic formulas that advisors recommended be applied in those countries; and of the irresponsible lending of fabulous sums without any concern about what that money was invested in or what it was used for — is this policy fair or defensible?

If you consider and analyze the fact that this phenomenon of the deterioration in the terms of trade has occurred, historically, for decades and that it is a problem that has been discussed in the Third World, in the Movement of Non-Aligned Countries, and in the United Nations when the need for the New International Economic Order or a new world economic order was expressed, and if, to this and to everything else I have already pointed out, you add the protectionist policies of the richest industrialized countries, plus the dumping and unfair competition with subsidized products which those same industrialized countries habitually engage in, how can you fail to understand the difficulties and the terrible crisis to which Latin America is now subjected?

Alfonsín isn't to blame for those problems, nor are Sanguinetti, Tancredo Neves, the leaders who will be chosen in the upcoming election in Peru, Belisario Betancur, Febres Cordero, and Siles Suazo, because they simply inherited those problems. Pinochet can be blamed for the large part of them, because of his fratricidal coup and his enthusiastic contributions to and cooperation with that policy for nearly twelve years. The Government of Panama and the Government of Costa Rica aren't to blame, nor is the Government of Mexico or the Government of Venezuela. In short, as a rule, I should honestly say that all these aspects make for a situation that escapes the control, the desires, and the wishes of governments.

I believe that it is of decisive importance and absolutely necessary to solve the problem of the debt — and to do so without delay. If this isn't done, none of the democratic processes that have been initiated can be consolidated, because the same economic crisis that made the military withdraw from public administration, practically in flight, in such countries as Argentina, Uruguay, and Brazil will drag the democratic processes that have been inaugurated in those countries into the whirlwind of insoluble difficulties, social tensions, and economic problems.

Pinochet's methods and even the Dominican Republic's methods for imposing the International Monetary Fund's draconian measures cannot be applied in the political, economic, and social conditions in many Latin American nations — nor are their new leaders about to accept them.

The crisis is advancing and will continue to do so. It is nothing but an illusion to believe that it can be solved with mere palliatives, debt renegotiations, and traditional formulas. I can see that many Latin American politicians of all kinds have changed their attitude. I would even say that there are fewer and fewer conservatives in this hemisphere, because many who have traditionally been considered on the Right, and organizations and parties that have been called conservative, are aware of how deep and serious these problems are. Who can talk to them now of the Chicago School, of tearing down tariff barriers, of letting those countries' nascent industries compete with the industries of the most developed countries, with high productivity and high technology? Who can persuade them to promote free competition in their own domestic markets between their countries' industries and those of the United States, Japan, and Europe? They feel very bitter and defrauded. I am speaking now of conservative politicians and individuals, not of the many intellectuals, filmmakers, artists, writers, other professionals, and representatives of a broad range of political parties, running from the center to the Left, or of the workers, women, students, doctors, and teachers.

Therefore, I have maintained — and I have said this to U.S. citizens; visitors from Japan, Europe, and many other capitalist and socialist countries; and to many journalists who have visited us — that the problem of the debt must be solved and the economic crisis overcome, or there will be a social upheaval in Latin America. And, if you ask me what kind it will be, I would say that there will be quite generalized revolutionary social outbreaks.

DÍAZ: *Not right-wing ones?*

CASTRO: I think not. I'm convinced that the processes of democratic openings won't be threatened by right-wing military coups, and I'll tell you why. That has already happened; it was the last resource employed to confront earlier crises that were only a pale reflection of the present situation. That was the resource first used in Brazil, more than twenty years ago; then in Chile; then in Uruguay; and still later in Argentina: strong-arm military regimes that made tens of thousands of people disappear — if you add up all the people who have disappeared, all over, they come to tens of thousands. And tens of thousands more were murdered, tortured, or forced into exile. Never before, anywhere, had such horrible repressive methods been used.

DÍAZ: *What if the people vote for the right wingers?*

CASTRO: The people in several of those countries are now emerging from a veritable inferno. Their main concern is to leave that inferno behind, and they often choose formulas that make it most probable, feasible, and rapid for them to emerge from the inferno. We shouldn't be deceived about the development of events.

The formulas of repressive fascist military coups have already been used, and the military themselves are getting out of public administration in those countries, because they can't handle the situation. The only one left is Pinochet, and he's ever more isolated, both at home and abroad — a kind of Somoza in the

Southern Cone, building up the pressure in the boiler. If he does this too long, Chile may explode with such force that it will cause more damage than has been known anywhere else. Don't you think that, in normal situations, in countries such as Bolivia, with a tenth of the problems that have occurred in the last few weeks, there would have already been enough pretexts for ten military coups?

DÍAZ: *But there might be a vote for the right wing, a democratic vote for the right wing, protesting without knowing why against the progressive governments.*

CASTRO: Well, I know what you're thinking about. As a rule, in any crisis situation the party in power loses support rapidly, and the people move to the opposition parties. Wherever you have a government – if you like we'll use the classical definitions – of the Left or of the Right, conservative or liberal (though these words no longer imply any great differences), in stable societies, the people move to the opposition party because they tend to blame the one in power for their serious problems and difficulties. This is a general rule, as may be seen in Europe, even though those societies are more stable.

Apart from the exceptions, if the present economic and social situation in Latin America continues to deteriorate, I don't believe that future developments are going to take place through idyllic electoral, constitutional, and political processes. This may happen in some countries; not all countries have the same situation. The situation in Venezuela and Ecuador isn't as serious as in Bolivia. This isn't a principle that can lead you to deduce that the same thing is going to happen in all countries. No. But there is no doubt that this crisis is already affecting all governments, to a greater or lesser extent. None can be excluded from this reality.

How do I view the situation in general, particularly in South America? I'm not speaking about Central America; these problems have been causing outbreaks in Central America for some time now. I believe that, if a solution isn't found for the economic crisis – and above all for the crisis of the debt – South America is going to explode. I am deeply convinced of this. The old formulas for avoiding those outbreaks have already been applied; the instruments used throughout history have already been exhausted. The present crisis is more serious, deeper, and more generalized than ever before: the military are withdrawing from their positions in state administration; they cannot manage the countries; and they have left the civilian governments a fearsome legacy. Now the civilians have the responsibility of finding solutions.

I'm not making inflammatory, subversive statements – far from it. That isn't my intention. I'm simply analyzing what is happening and what is going to happen, as serenely as possible.

If you ask me, as one journalist already did, "As a revolutionary, aren't you glad that this is so?" I'm going to tell you what I think. Right now, there is something more important than social change, and that is our countries' independence. This situation has brought the Third World countries to such a state of dependence, exploitation, extortion, and abuse that independence and the struggle for the New International Economic Order have become the main issue for the Latin American and other underdeveloped countries. Social changes alone are not the solution. Social changes may bring greater justice, speed development, and make the efforts and sacrifices of all more equitable and more humane. We have effected these changes and are satisfied that we have done so, but the considerable progress that our country has made in economic and social development wasn't exclusively due to them. It is also due to the fact that, within our sphere, we have — to some extent — achieved a new international economic order in our relations with the other socialist countries. Eighty-five percent of our trade is with countries of the socialist community, and, while the terms aren't the same with all of them because they have different levels of development and availabilities of resources, our relations are based on truly fair principles of cooperation and trade.

For example, in our economic relations with the U.S.S.R. and other developed socialist countries, we have overcome the tragic law of unequal terms of trade that has historically governed the relations between the Third World and the developed capitalist powers. We receive fair prices for the products we export, satisfactory prices that are protected by agreements against deterioration in the terms of trade — the phenomenon through which the Third World's exports (except in unusual market conditions) have ever-decreasing purchasing power, while its imports grow ever more expensive.

We aren't affected by protectionist measures in our trade with the other socialist countries. We don't suffer from dumping or unfair competition by socialist countries. Our financial problems, which stem from our need for development credits, have been solved without delay or difficulty. We have been able to postpone payment of our debt for ten, fifteen, and even twenty years without interest. If the industrialized capitalist countries employed the same forms of trade and economic and financial relations that we have with the socialist community, the problems I have mentioned would be solved and the Third World countries' development would be guaranteed.

I believe that this is of enormous importance, because, I repeat, we have solved our problems not only through social changes but also because, as a Third World, developing socialist country, Cuba has established a form of new international economic order with the rest of the socialist community. Without these foundations, our great economic and social successes — our tremendous achievements in public health, education, physical education, and sports, the elimination of unemployment and malnutrition, and the raising of our people's material and cultural standard of living wouldn't have been possible. Nor would we be able to offer the technical cooperation we do to dozens of other Third World countries. That requires resources, large investments and credits, technology, and a great deal of international cooperation over a long period of time. Many poor countries with scanty resources couldn't make those advances without the New International Economic Order and without a lot of international cooperation.

Social changes can bring about a better distribution of social wealth, more justice, and more concern for the poorest, neediest classes in the country, but social change alone is not enough. Therefore, we consider that the fundamental premise for the Third World countries' independence, sovereignty, and development — and even for their right to make social changes — is the disappearance of the iniquitous system of exploitation through which the Third World countries are victimized. That is, we consider the struggle for the new world economic order — that economic order that was talked about and agreed to at the United Nations ten years ago, largely thanks to Mexico's initiatives, support, and participation — to be the most essential thing in the short term. Marx himself always considered economic development to be a premise for socialism. Experience forced a number of countries, Cuba among them, to take the socialist road of development. Each people should decide for itself what it wants to do. I am absolutely convinced that for the peoples of the Third World, who have a great variety of systems and forms of government, different degrees of development of their productive forces, and the most diverse forms of political and religious beliefs, development is their most important current task and a vital priority for all, without exception, in which they can unite in a common struggle.

We must get to the bottom of the problems that have created underdevelopment, that adversely affect our countries' development, and that are widening the gap between the industrialized countries and the countries of the Third World. It has often been said that the gap should and must be closed but, far from being closed, it continues to widen. Now, it is wider than ever. Some industrial countries already have production figures equal to $15,000 per person. Compare them with Africa's per capita production figures of barely a few hundred dollars a year and with the figures for Latin America. The ratio was 10 to 1 some time ago, but now it is 15, 20, 30, and in some cases 40 or 50 to 1. That is, the gap between the industrialized world and the underdeveloped world is widening.

The per capita income gap is also widening. Far from making progress, we are regressing; instead of developing, we are growing more underdeveloped. We have been going through a process of underdevelopment, not development. When the differences between you and the industrialized countries are increasing and you are farther and farther away from them, you are growing more underdeveloped — even if a mathematical index says that you have grown 2 percent or 3 percent, for the gap has grown even more and your world is becoming poorer in comparison with the developed world. The situation is even worse because, while the population in the industrialized countries is growing by 0.6 percent, 0.7 percent, or 0.8 percent, the population in the Third World is growing by 2 percent to 3 percent, which means that, within the next fifteen years, 80 percent of the world's population will be living in the Third World. This is why I say that a new system of international economic relations which will really make development possible is of paramount importance.

It is understandable, then, why I think that if the new world economic order isn't achieved, the terrible problems affecting our countries won't be solved just through social changes. I repeat: even in a poor country, social changes can bring about better distribution and solve important problems (among other things, by promoting respect for human life by ending the horrible injustices and inequalities that may exist, in both very rich and very poor countries), but I consider the struggle for the new world economic order to be the most important thing the Latin American and Third World countries can do now, because it can lead to the creation of the conditions needed for real independence, real sovereignty, and even the right to carry out social changes — and not only the right but the objective possibility of doing so.

There is one essential thing: the cancellation of Latin America's foreign debt in itself won't solve our problems; it would only offer a few years' respite.

There are several countries in Latin America in which, if you canceled their debts tomorrow, you'd have solved practically nothing. Problems have become so serious in some countries — Bolivia, for example — that cancelling their debts wouldn't have any impact. They might be able to count on an additional $200 million, or $250 million, or $270 million, which was their favorable balance of trade last year, but the problems that have accumulated in those countries are so serious that $270 million wouldn't even give them a "breather." I've been told about installations at which it costs $16 to produce a pound of tin, while the present world market price is $5 a pound.

There are some countries where cancelling the debt would undoubtedly provide a respite; it would give a respite to Argentina, Uruguay, Brazil, Venezuela, Colombia, Ecuador, Peru, and — yes — Mexico. Mexico isn't one of the countries with the most difficult situations, but it would surely provide a respite for Mexico, too.

Now, then, we should be aware of the fact that there can be no final solution for our problems as long as the ominous law of sustained deterioration of the terms of trade remains in effect; as long as the industrialized capitalist powers continue to impose the protectionist policies; as long as the practice of dumping subsidized products in order to grab markets and depress the prices of the exports on which many Third World countries depend continues; as long as monetary policies are imposed by means of which a powerful industrial country determines the interest to be paid and we are lent money at one value and expected to repay it at a higher value; as long as the capital we need for development is drained away; and as long as models and methods such as the ones recommended by the Chicago School are imposed.

Just yesterday, in a note to the Government of the United States, the Andean Pact countries expressed their deep concern over the drastic reductions that are being made in their sugar quotas on the U.S. market. The United States — which in 1981 was still importing 5 million tons of sugar — reduced its sugar imports to 2.7 million tons in 1984, and, in the future, its imports won't go over 1.7 million tons. The countries involved described the situation as terrible. These protectionist measures by the United States will reduce Latin America's revenues by hundreds of millions of dollars and will create surpluses that will further depress the world market price.

A little over twenty years ago, Cuba had a quota of over 3 million tons on that market. One day it was taken away and parcelled out among other countries in this hemisphere. The pretext then was the Cuban Revolution, which had to be crushed without mercy. Now, when the debt amounts to $360 billion, what pretext will the United States give for eliminating the Latin American countries' sugar quotas? If we don't overcome these problems, we will obtain only a respite ... but the real causes of our difficulties won't be solved. I believe that this is the time to wage this struggle. Such a serious crisis situation has been created that the Third World countries are being forced to think, to unite, and to seek solutions, regardless of their political stands and ideologies, as an elementary matter of survival.

I believe that the Latin American countries need to wage that struggle and that, fortunately, they have excellent conditions for waging it. The struggle to solve the problem of the debt will benefit all the Third World countries — not just the Latin American countries but all the developing countries in Asia and Africa, as well. I feel that the debt should be cancelled. Mathematically, it can be shown that it is unpayable.

The problem no longer involves the amount of the debt, but the interest that is paid on it. I base my view on four hypotheses, all based on the assumption that the debt won't grow. First hypothesis: that the ten-year grace period is granted for paying the capital; that, during that period, the interest will continue to be paid, as it has been thus far; and that ten years will then be given for its amortization at an interest rate not exceeding 10 percent. Latin America would have to pay $400 billion in the first ten years and an additional $558 billion the next ten years. In twenty years, Latin America would have transferred $958 billion — nearly $1 trillion in U.S. terms, or $1 billion in English terms — to its creditors. That is, nearly a trillion dollars would leave these countries, in spite of their enormous accumulated social problems, their enormous economic problems, and the development they will have had to forego. In twenty years, they would have to extract nearly $1 trillion from their modest economies and send it to the industrialized capitalist countries. Is this possible? Is it conceivable? And this, I repeat, is assuming that the debt won't grow and that the interest rate doesn't go over 10 percent during the amortization period. Is this conceivable, especially if the other problems I have mentioned — unequal exchange, protectionism, dumping, and so on — are taken into account? No.

Second hypothesis: that the formula of paying a maximum of 20 percent of the value of each country's exports each year is applied and that interest rates don't go over 10 percent. The exports of Latin America as a whole are already close to but haven't reached $100 billion. Let us even assume that, even if those exports surpass that figure, no more than $20 billion will be paid each year. In that case, we would pay $400 billion in twenty years, and, at the end, we would have a debt of $1.2 trillion—that is, after we had paid $400 billion, our debt would be triple what it is now.

Third hypothesis: that a ten-year grace period is granted, including interest; an additional ten years is granted for its amortization; and the interest doesn't go over 10 percent in any given year. This would undoubtedly mean a ten-year respite. In twenty years, $1.5 trillion would have been paid.

Fourth hypothesis: that the interest rate is lowered to 6 percent, a ten-year grace period is granted, including the interest; and an additional ten years is given in which to pay. This would certainly be the kindest of the four formulas, but in twenty years $857.5 billion would still have to be paid.

I have put forward four hypotheses. In all, I have assumed that the debt wouldn't grow and that the interest rates would never exceed 10 percent, and all of them show that the debt and its interest cannot be paid. Based on reality, on all the problems I've mentioned, it is simply impossible to pay the debt. It can't be done from a practical standpoint—our economies couldn't survive it—and it could never solve the problem of development. The debt is an economic and political impossibility. It is also a moral impossibility. The immense sacrifice that would have to be demanded of the people and the blood that would have to be shed to force them to pay that immense sum of money—that, to a large extent, was drained away, misspent, or embezzled—would be unjustifiable. Any attempt to pay the debt under the present social, economic, and political circumstances in Latin America would cost our suffering and impoverished nations rivers of blood, and it could never be done. Our peoples are not to blame for underdevelopment or for the debt. Our countries are not to blame for having been colonies, neocolonies, banana republics, or coffee, mining, or oil republics whose role was to produce raw materials, exotic products, and fuel at low cost and with cheap labor.

Economic specialist and historians tell us that the fabulous amounts of gold and silver that were extracted from the entrails of our nations and amassed over the centuries thanks to our peoples' sweat and blood financed the development of the industrialized world that is now the creditor demanding payment of the debt. The amount wrenched away from our peoples in just the last few decades through unequal terms of trade, high interest rates, protectionism, dumping, monetary manipulations, and the flight of capital is much greater than the total amount of the debt. The riches and well-being of which we have been deprived through the imposition of economic dependence and underdevelopment cannot even be estimated, let alone measured. It is our peoples who, by right, are the creditors of the rich and industrialized Western world, both morally and materially. The BRD has been paying Israel cash compensation for the Nazis' genocide against the Jews. Who is paying compensation for the deliberate destruction of our peoples' lives and riches throughout the centuries?

As a result of all these mathematical calculations and moral, historical, political, and economic reflections, I have come to the conclusion that the Latin American debt is unpayable and should be cancelled. It has been said that failure to pay the debt would destabilize and sink the international financial system. This isn't necessarily so. I suggest that the industrialized creditor countries can and should make themselves responsible for the debts to their own banks. As a rule, the public debts of the industrialized countries increase; it is a historic fact that they tend to increase. All that the industrialized states make themselves responsible for is the interest on their increasing public debts.

In 205 years the public debt of the United States has reached $1 trillion – when I say "trillion," I'm referring to the U.S. trillion, which is equal to the English billion – a million million. The U.S. public debt reached that figure in 1981, but from 1981 to 1984, in just three years, it increased by another $650 billion, and it is estimated that it will reach or surpass $2 trillion by 1986. This is almost never mentioned in the United States, however. It doesn't seem to be much cause for concern. Rather, it stresses the growth of the economy – and, as a matter of fact, the economy was reported to have grown by 6.8 percent in 1984. So, if we follow the theories and concepts of official economics, we see that the increase in the public debt hasn't ruined the economy or impeded its growth; nor has it hampered the optimism with which some U.S. economists talk about future economic growth and development. If the federal government of the United States, plus the governments of other industrialized powers, were to make themselves responsible to their private banks for the debts of Latin America and other Third World countries, this would imply added increases in their public debt.

Where could they find the resources with which to pay the interest on the increases in their debts without affecting their countries' economies? That's easy: from military expenditures – and not all military expenditures, just a small percentage of them: 10 percent or, if interest rates remain as high as they are now, a maximum of 12 percent.

With this modest percentage of their military expenditures, the industrialized powers could make themselves responsible to their own banks for the foreign debts of the Latin American and other Third World countries – and military spending would still be fabulously high and cause for concern.

Military spending throughout the world now amounts to a million million dollars (a trillion, according to U.S. nomenclature, or a billion in English). And if the arms race (which world public opinion considers absurd and unacceptable in a world in which there are more than 100 underdeveloped countries and billions of people who lack food, health care, housing, and education) isn't ended, that spending will continue increasing until it unleashes a nuclear catastrophe, which would be more dangerous than the economic catastrophe from which a large part of mankind is suffering. If the former were to take place, talking about the latter would make no sense at all.

It would be very sensible and wise if the reduction in military spending were associated with the beginning of a solution for international economic problems. All economists have stated that with a fraction of the money now spent for military purposes, the problems of underdevelopment and poverty that beset the world could be solved. This problem of increased military spending and the danger it poses to mankind was the subject of a meeting held in New Delhi, in which individuals of such international prestige and authority as Rajiv Gandhi, Julius Nyerere, Raúl Alfonsín, Miguel de la Madrid, Andreas Papandreu, and Olof Palme participated.

By issuing ten-year treasury notes and treasury bonds, the United States could make itself responsible to its own creditor banks for all the credits given to the Latin American and other Third World countries. This wouldn't affect U.S. citizens' current contributions to the budget. The banks would recover the capital they had invested, U.S. export companies would increase their exports, and U.S. investors abroad would increase their profits. More important, such a solution would create jobs in all the industrialized countries; their industries would use a large percentage of their installed capacities, and international trade would increase.

It should be kept in mind that the main problem confronting the industrialized countries isn't their domestic public debts or foreign debts. It is rather the scourge of unemployment, which is steadily increasing in most of the Western countries, with figures in the order of 3 million in Britain, despite its new oil resources; 2.6 million in the BRD, a postwar record; 3 million in France; 2.8 million in Spain; and so on. Solving the problem of the underdeveloped countries' foreign debts could be an important step toward emerging from the prolonged international economic crisis — which is far from over, despite the optimistic forecasts that some would make. The economy of the European Economic Community grew by a mere 2.4 percent of 1984, and better results aren't expected this year. What is growing — constantly — is unemployment. According to very recent data, the U.S. economy had growth difficulties during the first quarter of this year.

Even though solving the Third World's foreign debt problem would doubtless provide relief for many countries, it would fall far short of solving the problems of development. Within a few years, if unequal terms of trade, protectionist measures, dumping, monetary policies based on the economic clout of a few countries, excessive interest on loans, and the other elements in the unjust system of economic relations and exploitation that is imposed on the countries of the Third World, aren't eliminated once and for all — that is, if a new world economic order isn't firmly established — the situation would be the same as or worse than it is now.

DÍAZ: *How should this be handled? Could the pressure that the creditor banks bring to bear on the countries be somehow turned around, so that we can demand that they take a series of measures to avoid their own financial crisis?*

CASTRO: Because of their political importance, their political weight in the world, their enormous debts, their terrible economic and social crises and the dangers of a social upheaval of unforeseeable consequences, their deep community of interests, and their potential for joint action, the Latin American countries, in my opinion, are in a better position than those of any other region in the world to tackle this problem seriously. Many of their leaders have already set forth the premises concerning the foreign debt, which would be the first step in that struggle, clearly and precisely.

Yet, it is inconceivable at this stage that the first thing that is proclaimed and solemnly pledged is that the countries of this hemisphere that are affected by this situation will not form a debtors' club — even though the creditor countries are closely joined in the International Monetary Fund and the Paris Club. A club, a committee, a group, or whatever you want to call it is indispensable. Acting on their own, our countries cannot achieve any kind of lasting solution for our problems; all they can hope for are more palliative formulas that only mitigate their difficulties: a brief grace period on the payment of capital or a small reduction in the percentage of interest paid to the Libor [London inter-bank exchange] rate.

As I've already said, the problem no longer concerns just the payment of capital. Even if a four-, six-, eight-, or ten-year grace period and a similar — or longer — period after that for payment of the total debt are granted, the problem would still get worse and worse. The current renegotiations will solve absolutely nothing. The problem resides in the enormous amounts of interest that must be paid each year, religiously and punctually, accompanied by inapplicable political measures; exaggerated, unrealistic goals related to inflation; the reduction of the budgetary deficit; the limitation of social expenditures in countries riddled with problems in education, health care, nutrition, housing, unemployment, etc., and other measures demanded by the International Monetary Fund which become impossible to apply when the country is forced to make enormous disbursements simply to pay the unfair interest on its debt. The people don't understand this, nor can they understand it. There is no other message for them but the message of fruitless sacrifice: they've been promised a lot of things for a long time, and they see that things are getting worse and worse. They don't understand the technical aspects. Technical aspects mean nothing to them, for they offer them nothing when they get up in the morning to look for work or when they see their wages shrinking while products grow more and more expensive. Remember what Lincoln said: "You can't fool all of the people all of the time."

Membership in the Cartagena Group was limited to eleven countries. I met Enrique Iglesias, the director of ECLAC, who is now minister of foreign affairs of Uruguay. He is an economist who is highly esteemed in our hemisphere and has excellent relations with many heads of state. The prevailing view at that time was that the Group shouldn't be increased, because a larger number of countries would make negotiations and analyses more difficult. The principle wasn't at all democratic. No clear explanation was given of why some had the privilege of being members, while others didn't. This principle seemed more applicable to a social club than to the idea of how to face a serious, crucial situation involving each and every nation in Latin America. I believe that this criterion doesn't make any sense. All the Latin American countries should be included in the Group.

Even such countries as Guyana, Trinidad and Tobago, Jamaica, and others with a lot of weight and long standing as independent nations in the Caribbean could be included if they were ready and willing to cooperate loyally; their debts are also considerable. Probable disloyalties aren't to be feared. I don't believe that any self-respecting Latin American government would be capable of betraying the feelings and interests of the Latin American family in these critical circumstances. In any circumstances, the dissenters would never be anything more than individual cases or isolated groups. Cuba would be willing to exclude itself from those activities if this were advisable, if the other countries didn't want to displease the United States, as is already traditional. But I don't think it would be good tactics, in this situation, to display excessive caution or cowardice to the "Colossus of the North"—which must, of course, be persuaded to cooperate. Moreover, undignified, irresponsible attitudes (which not even the United States respects) shouldn't be adopted in order to achieve its cooperation.

I'm not saying this so Cuba will be included or to reflect some Cuban problem. Cuba is now the only Latin American or Caribbean country that is immune to the crisis. Its foreign debt in convertible currency is minimal, barely $300 per inhabitant. We don't have any problems in our financial relations or in our trade with the rest of the socialist community—with which, as I said, we have 85 percent of our foreign trade. Between 1981 and 1984 our gross social product (GSP) increased by 24.8 percent, and the per capita GSP grew by 22.6 percent; our economic and social development programs for the next fifteen years are guaranteed—something that is a privilege for any country at a time like this.

If it weren't for the principles of the new economic order which we have attained with the rest of the socialist community, as I explained, our annual sugar exports of over 7.5 million tons—at the current price of sugar on the so-called world market and supposing that there were markets for that volume of exports—wouldn't be enough to pay for even 25 percent of our fuel imports.

If the Latin American countries want to tackle the problems of their foreign debt they must reach a consensus in order to attain the goal of engaging in a political dialogue with the creditor countries, as many of their leaders have suggested, because, as has been correctly pointed out, the problem is political, not technical, and, at the rate things are developing, it's beginning to be a revolutionary problem.

I'd like to add something about the intermediate formulas that have been mentioned or similar ones that may crop up. From the mathematical calculations that I showed you, you can see that the payment formula involving only 20 percent of each country's annual exports, limiting those figures to $20 billion, solves nothing. Without considering new loans, they would have to pay $400 billion over twenty years and wind up, with interest at 10 percent, by owing $1.2 trillion. Even reducing the interest rate to 6 percent and having a ten-year moratorium, including interest, in line with the kindest formula, they would have to pay $857.5 billion in the next ten years. Such intermediate formulas as reducing payments to 20 percent of annual exports or simply reducing the interest rate without a moratorium of a least ten years wouldn't even give them a respite. Such intermediate formulas don't attract, don't rally, don't persuade, don't motivate, and they don't mobilize anyone, simply because they can't solve the problem.

One very important question would be what to do with those resources. I believe, on the basis of the austerity measures already established by many governments, that most of those resources would have to be used for economic development, to create a solid, essential base from which to attack unemployment, hunger, and many other social calamities. No matter how pressing the problems are, you can't just think of distributing and consuming those resources and of immediately raising the standard of living. Rather, a percent of them — 20 percent or at most 30 percent, depending on the circumstances — could be used to meet the most pressing health, education, and housing needs. You can do a lot with 20 percent of $400 billion to complement the resources being used for those purposes. All this would require great awareness and great national consensus equal to the challenge posed by the circumstances.

The solution of the debt would simply be a first step; we have to get at the real, root causes of this debt, of the economic crisis that has been unleashed, reaching the elements that gave rise to it. Solving the problem of the debt would be no more than the beginning. We would have to demand an end to unequal terms of trade; an end to protectionist policies; an end to the practice of dumping and to unjust, abusive monetary policies, excessive rates of interest, overvaluation of the dollar, and other diabolical procedures that make our countries' development impossible.

We should demand fair prices for our export commodities; we can't go on supplying coffee, cocoa, bananas, sugar, meat, minerals, and other essential raw materials, produced on the basis of starvation wages that often are less than $80 a month, to purchase merchandise, equipment, medicines, and other industrial articles that are processed in the industrialized nations on the basis of huge profits for the enterprises and wages of more than $1,000 a month — that is, twelve, fifteen, and sometimes twenty times as high as the wages that the workers and technicians in the Latin American countries receive. Our unemployed don't usually have any kind of subsidy, and a large part of the population doesn't even receive medical and educational services.

Paradoxically, this crisis is providing the Latin American and other Third World countries with the first real opportunity they've had of receiving due consideration of their demands. We have spent dozens of years in the United Nations, in the Movement of Non-Aligned Countries, and in all the other international agencies demanding a fairer economic order and requesting better prices for our products, loans, and resources for development. It wasn't long ago when, speaking on behalf of the Movement of Non-Aligned Countries, following the Sixth Summit Conference, I expressed the need for the Third World to have $300 billion in development assistance during this decade. Now, it isn't a matter of our getting on our knees and imploring the industrialized countries to supply us with funds or to assign a modest 0.7 percent of their gross national products to development — a commitment which only a few states have made. Now, when they are demanding that the Latin American and Caribbean countries turn over $400 billion in ten years, the decision making has passed to us. We have the power to simply declare that we won't accept this plunder and won't hand over the $400 billion. They couldn't even threaten us with suspending future loans. Well used, that $400 billion that they are demanding we produce from the sweat and sacrifices of the Latin American peoples could finance Latin America's development in the next ten years. Every country can lend itself what it's paying in interest.

If the industrialized countries are rational, not only will they benefit from our increased exports, but even their own banks will benefit through a formula such as the one suggested, which will guarantee them the availability of their credits, and they can make new loans — which, when you get right down to it, is their purpose in international finances and trade. If the new world economic order is really achieved, new loans can be received and paid on solid bases.

Since the OPEC countries managed to raise the price of oil from around $2.50 to $30 a barrel, the industrialized countries — the European ones, the United States, Japan, and others — have paid more than $1 trillion to cover these higher oil prices in just eleven years. This was much more than the entire accumulated foreign debt of the Third World, and it didn't ruin their economies or even affect their enormous military expenditures. Ninety percent of this money ended up in the banks of the same countries from which it started out. They also collected the money that the non-oil-producing Third World countries spent on oil imports. The prices of their exports soared. Many Western companies — including arms manufacturers — made fabulous deals, thanks to the new purchasing power of their oil-producing clients. Many technological innovations were made, and scores of measures were adopted to save fuel. New and old sources of energy were used. Waste decreased considerably. Only the non-oil-producing developing countries suffered from the catastrophe in all regards, and were subjected to new unequal terms of trade.

The cancellation of the Third World's foreign debt would be much fairer and economically more beneficial for all countries, much more vital and much less costly than was agreement to the oil exporters' demands in their day — demands that, with regard to most of the Third World countries, will only be fully justified and balanced when the branches of their basic exports are given the same treatment.

The new world economic order should mean fair trade relations for all the Third World countries, which will mean that the rich industrialized powers will have to stop wasting so many resources on arms. Nobody has the right to pay starvation wages for the cocoa, tea, coffee, cashew nuts, peanuts, coconuts, and fibers that are gathered leaf by leaf and grain by grain, the minerals, and other raw materials in order to manufacture aircraft carriers, battleships, strategic missiles, and nuclear submarines, and to pay for Star Wars weapons. Those resources should be invested in the war on hunger, here on earth.

If the Latin American and Third World countries take a firm, united stand, they will, for the first time, have a real opportunity to reach these goals, beginning with the question of the foreign debt. If total lack of understanding should force them to make a unilateral decision with regard to the debt, they cannot be threatened with a suspension of trade; since the other countries wouldn't be able to survive without trade with the Third World, they can't do without our fuel and other raw materials, and they wouldn't be happy without our coffee, tea, cocoa, shrimp, lobsters, and other tropical delights.

It is absolutely impossible for them to blockade the Third World economically or take over our countries because of the debt, as they did in Haiti, the Dominican Republic, and other countries in the first few decades of this century; they can't divide up the world again to assure their supplies of raw materials and markets, as they did in other eras.

The new Latin American leaders have an immense responsibility. I reiterate my conviction that, if the problem of the debt isn't solved, if efforts are made to pay it no matter what the cost, if the disastrous formulas of the International Monetary Fund are promoted, great social upheavals will be produced. I don't see any danger of a return to the wave of right-wing repressive, fascist coups—which may occur only in exceptional cases, in some countries, on an isolated basis. Rather, I think it is possible that, in the case of great social upheavals in some countries, leaders imbued with a patriotic spirit and a realistic sense of the situation who are ready to promote social changes along with the people will arise from among the military. In much less critical circumstances, figures who arose from the ranks of the military, such as Omar Torrijos in Panama and Velasco Alvarado in Peru, held high the banners of national demands and social reform.

The struggle for demands as rational as the solution of the problem of the foreign debt and fair economic relations between the Third World countries and the industrialized world is so essential for the survival and future of the Latin American peoples that it would doubtless be supported by all social strata and would generate great internal unity in all the countries. It would also strengthen the unity among all the Latin American countries and would receive the unhesitating, enthusiastic, determined support of all the developing countries in Asia and Africa.

I have no doubt that many industrialized countries would also support these demands. Nor do I doubt that the ideal, most constructive thing is for these problems to be solved by means of political dialogue and negotiation, which would promote essential solutions in an orderly manner. If this is not done, desperate situations will doubtless force a group of countries to take unilateral measures. This isn't desirable, but, if it occurs, I am sure that all the other countries in Latin America and the rest of the Third World will join them.

Translation by Editora Política, Havana, Cuba.

8

TWENTY-SIX YEARS OF CUBAN REVOLUTIONARY POLITICS: AN APPRAISAL

Max Azicri

After more than a quarter-century of revolutionary government, Cuba's institutionalized political system is the belated outcome of the radical transformation of the prerevolutionary socioeconomic and political structures which took place in the early sixties. A new constitution and new political, legal, and judicial institutions that mirror the revolution's chosen socialist model were finally established during the seventies. For a proper understanding of the regime's current political dynamics and institutions — the postinstitutionalization period of the eighties — it is valuable to keep the overall process in historical perspective, remembering how adopting a new, permanent institutional setting proved to be a necessary but demanding and complex experience for the revolution and its leadership. The magnitude of the problems confronted during that advanced stage of revolutionary state building was dramatized by the historical circumstances and events that surrounded it.[1]

The planning and implementation of the institutionalization of the revolution was to some degree encumbered by the dysfunctional effect of both affirmative and negative domestic and contextual pressures. More generally, it was affected by the systemic problems inherent in establishing a Marxist-Leninist developmental and state model, particularly in an underdeveloped Caribbean island-state. As a reminder of the geographical setting, there were the perennial hostile actions of an antagonistic imperial state in the vicinity. Since 1959, Washington has taken an adversarial stance, conspiring and acting against the revolutionary regime. It has been, and still is, very much opposed to the existence of a socialist polity in what once was a dependent, unevenly developed capitalist country, historically trapped within the immediate American sphere of influence.

There also was the internal problem of determining when, how, and to what extent the informal political mobilization modalities that came to characterize political life under the revolution in the 1960s were going to be modified or replaced by new, formal ones. The newly created structure would become a permanent feature of the system, providing clearly established avenues for regular citizens' participation in the political process.

It was necessary to improve the existing policy-making processes by replacing personalized and centralized decision-making practices with new, decentralized participatory channels, although questions were still being posed regarding the timeliness and advisability of this change. The leadership voiced certain skepticism: it wondered how sensible it would be in the middle (or even late) sixties to establish political structures that could have, by their very nature, a restrictive effect on the policy-making initiative and creativity so far exercised by the revolution. Even if not explicitly stated, there was uncertainty that replacing the practice of downward policy output, stemming mainly from the top leadership, with a broader upward input from the populace would translate into a qualitative policy improvement. Favoring one practice or another, especially as a long-term option, could have had both practical and philosophical implications for the present and future character of the revolution. While the latter process favors more open and participatory channels that the former neglects, or simply ignores, neither is ideologically more revolutionary in terms of its commitment to social reform and the principles it would represent. However, there is a potential and significant difference as far as the kind of public policy that each political modality would generate and support.[2]

Castro admitted candidly — and somewhat apologetically for having procrastinated the final institutionalization of the revolutionary political system — that it seemed only proper to allow the process of societal change to continue unhindered. He implicitly recognized that a premature formalization of the system would mean limiting the extent of social transformation achieved under the revolution, at least during the first ten-year period. If a new constitutional framework was imposed, ahead of the right time frame for social change, it would not represent the scope of social transformation intended by the regime.[3] Throughout the sixties, the primary objective of the revolutionary leadership was not to establish permanent political institutions as such, but to avoid cutting short, even if temporarily, the broadening scope of Cuba's overall social and economic revolutionary change.

THE SCIENTIFIC STUDY OF CUBAN POLITICS

In the United States and elsewhere, social scientists examining Cuban revolutionary politics have characteristically raised some probing questions. Many times, however, in both questions and answers, it appears that the purpose of this inquiry is not so much to grasp objectively the meaning of the facts and events under examination as to prove what had already been decided. A recurring question in the academic literature is whether or not the role played by President Fidel Castro is as central and domineering in the newly formalized political setting as was generally understood before. (This reads like a more sophisticated phrasing of the long-held symbiotic truism that characterized the charismatic leader, the revolution, and the nation as being essentially one: Fidel's Cuba and Cuba's Fidel, and not much more than that.)

The study of Cuban politics poses many questions. How truly democratic and participatory are the new political institutions? Do they permit or impede effective popular political expression? How stratified is the system of political participation today and is it limited, if not closed, to rank-and-file input? If upward participation of the populace is allowed, how significant is it, quantitatively and qualitatively? What is the extent of political control exercised by the Communist Party—especially its Central Committee, Political Bureau, and Secretariat—upon the National Assembly of Popular Power, the highest state political organ in the nation according to the 1976 socialist Constitution?[4]

This brand of scholarly inquiry and the ideological and methodological rationale behind it should not be accepted without critical analysis. Rather, it should be questioned to see how effective it actually is in attaining meaningful results, in terms of a heuristic analysis for social science. Is it really more than simply an inquiry conducted with the benefit of the alleged Western scholarly tradition of unrestrained criticism—in this case for the subject under examination—which is welcome among unsympathetic Cuba watchers? Are questions like these truly functional research tools, capable of producing valid and reliable findings by adroitly probing into the causes and nature of the political phenomenon under examination, as it is claimed? Or would it be more correct to assume that they mainly express liberal-democratic concerns (biases) which, even if legitimate and desirable to Western (bourgeois) politics, might nevertheless obscure rather than clarify the Cuban political experience? The Cuban Studies literature frequently implies or explicitly states that these issues are not solely the domain of bourgeois Western systems but represent universal political values and practices, and as such are relevant for studying both liberal-democratic and Marxist-Leninist systems, regardless of the implicit bias favoring the former.[5]

However, political structures and dynamics such as the division of power among the different branches of government, political pluralism and multiple-systems, the social and political autonomy of interest groups, and their open pursuit of political influence and participation in decision making, and the generalized acceptance of an individual's moral entitlement to political favors, and even major payoffs, in exchange for supporting a political party or candidate during election time—issues central to industrialized liberal-democratic systems—are not to be found in Marxist-Leninist systems. Among the latter, the political system usually functions with a single political party, the Communist Party (the one-party system as it became institutionalized in the Soviet model, especially after the New Economic Policy [NEP] was launched in 1921 and the death of Lenin in 1924). In other circumstances, the Communist Party functions with other, minor parties while exercising a dominant-hegemonic role, or within a united political (front) structure including other minor parties and mass organizations, while still retaining control.

In all of these possible variations within a well-established general model, the Communist party is situated at the center of an organically integrated social and political system. In a Leninist fashion, it would provide comprehensive leadership and guidance to the national polity and all its subsystems, performing as the country's most important political institution.[6] Moreover, Marxist-Leninist regimes function on the basis of the cardinal principle of democratic centralism. This principle justifies a double system of subordination between the party and the regime (the party always occupying a higher status and position), and between the party, the mass organizations, and the populace. Also, it bans factionalism within the party or within any other political institution of lesser status, such as the mass organizations. As prescribed by Lenin in 1921, the Central Committee had the right to exclude from the party those members accused of factionalism.[7] Understandably, widely accepted political practices of liberal-democratic systems such as interest group confrontational politics, sometimes in association with one or more political parties — through which some pressure groups are routinely rewarded, others are penalized, and all are kept vying for the government's attention and favors — are nonexistent under Marxist-Leninist regimes.[8]

CHOOSING A THEORETICAL FRAMEWORK

Like any other political phenomenon of such significance and complexity, the Cuban revolution has been examined following not one but several theoretical constructs. Besides being methodologically sound, this kind of research strategy recognizes the wisdom of conducting systematic empirical studies and analyses under the thoughtful guidance of theory, as it appears in the broader explanatory and conceptual literature. And yet, the issue still remains of deciding which of the different theoretical approaches available to the researcher is most suitable for the subject under examination. Hence, choosing a theoretical paradigm that would maximize the quality of the findings and therefore allow for a perceptive understanding of the probable relationship among the possible independent, intervening, and dependent variables under examination is always a paramount consideration for the researcher.[9]

The political institutions and dynamics of socialist democracy and the dictatorship of the proletariat (majority rule by the working class, under Marxist analysis) are not properly examined nor explained by applying to them the same conceptual and working rationale used for examining political regimes based on liberal democracy and the dictatorship of the bourgeoisie (minority rule by the propertied class, under Marxist analysis). Cuban revolutionary politics have been studied by a number of analysts using concepts and political standards associated with, or germane to, liberal-democratic systems. Many of these studies seek to demonstrate the revolutionary regime's "failure" to measure up to the standards assumed to be found among industrialized Western democracies. In reality, however, the revolution has not only avoided such bourgeois political practices and objectives but has committed itself to struggling for a substantively different kind of society: a socialist polity which is theoretically and practically in the initial phase of building a socialist society, to be developmentally followed by an eventual transition to communism.

Whatever latent and actual capacity there is in Cuba for effectively achieving the kind of political rule expected from socialist democracy, it must be measured by the institutional and behavioral standard of its own chosen system. Cuban society should not be evaluated using a yardstick which is inappropriate, if not irrelevant, to the societal objectives pursued by the revolution. Its socialist political system should not be held accountable for what is not intended to be; its commitment to political democracy and social equality is framed within a Marxist-Leninist doctrine. This should not be construed as a whitewash purposely obscuring any serious criticism of the revolutionary regime — quite the contrary. In addition to dealing factually with the regime's real, not imaginary, flaws, the nature and extent of its shortcomings would then be measured against the objectives avowedly pursued by the revolution. For this common-sense research purpose, nonprejudicial conceptual categories and empirical indicators must be used, so that the achievements and failures of the revolutionary system can be accurately examined and ascertained.

Dependency theory and, more recently, world systems theory are favored by some political analysts who aptly use concepts and generalizations germane to Third World countries' sociopolitical and economic phenomena. Notwithstanding past and present controversies among scholars — that is, the debate between dependency theory analysts and Marxist analysts and between those recognizing the merits of world systems theory and those alleging that there are serious limitations built into its core-periphery analysis — either one of these two approaches can be used to study Cuban politics with considerable methodological and theoretical consistency and sound applicability.[10] Therefore, empirical indicators measuring the context in which the revolution took place, and its development since — including internal and external social, economic, and political conditions, both opportunities and limitations — could be subsumed under some of the theoretical categories provided by either approach. This includes the pervasive influence exercised by American imperialism in Cuban life before the revolution and the inimical internal impact that Washington's campaigns against the revolution still have.

As the official ideology of the revolution, Marxism-Leninism represents, and is being utilized as, a political and cultural value system (the foundation of the revolution's political culture). By bringing together political theory and praxis, it represents the policy rationale for the reorganization of Cuban society under the revolution as well as the regime's short- and long-term internal and external politics. The recognition of the role played by ideology in the decision-making process does not preclude the realization that there is also a well-established pattern of nonideological but principled pragmatic decisions made by revolutionary leaders from the outset.

Moreover, Marxism-Leninism also represents, and is being utilized by social scientists in different quarters as, a conceptual framework compatible with sound scholarly methodology for sociopolitical research.[11] Hence, it is particularly appropriate to use Marxism-Leninism as the conceptual component of a research strategy dedicated to appraising the new political institutions established in the 1970s and the political dynamics that developed since. As a possible theoretical framework for studying the revolution's political system, it contains some normative concepts (discussed below) used in constructing the ideological rationale upon which the political system was institutionalized.

SUGGESTING A CONCEPTUAL FRAMEWORK

The need for a proper conceptualization of this political phenomenon is emphasized by a recent evaluation, by highly respected social scientists, of Cuba's potential and actual socialist performance during more than twenty-five years of revolutionary government. It was summarized as follows: "Cuba's size and geography partly account for the character of Cuban socialism as mobilized, participatory, and nondemocratic."[12] This insightful statement was provided as an unbiased and accurate assessment of the regime — even if it seems flawed by a conceptual inconsistency. Thus, while the political system is recognized as truly dedicated to political and other forms of popular mobilization, which provide the people with broad opportunities for participating in political life, it is still regarded as nondemocratic.

In support of this statement, it is precisely the Revolution's relentless mobilization of, and expected massive participation by, the populace in mass gatherings and all kinds of national campaigns and programs, that are regarded by some as nondemocratic political practices. For others, it is not the practice of officially planned or initiated mobilization and participation as such, but the methods used to gain compliance with them that are considered nondemocratic.

There is also the possibility that the assessment by Petras and Morley is imbued, even if remotely and unwittingly, with liberal-democratic biases that provoke objections against what appear to be nondemocratic practices. Their characterization of Cuba's socialism as nondemocratic could be a candid expression of their frustration with the revolution's failure to live up to their own expectation of what socialist democracy should be — possible rather than actual socialism, a notion that seems to guide their appraisal. It is important to note that their qualifier — "Cuba's size and geography" — is partly responsible for this situation. The former accounts for the island's limited internal resources, while the latter makes reference to the negative impact of the actions of a hostile neighbor. As long as these two long-term determinants are present, the likelihood of their continuing to affect the revolutionary process in one way or another is rather obvious. Nonetheless, whether this is significant enough to direct the regime into a nondemocratic path, and whether the revolution is politically nondemocratic for the reasons discussed here, are still controversial matters.

Evaluating "Totalitarian Democracy of the Left"

Tracing the origin of modern social engineering back to the eighteenth century, historian J. L. Talmon states in *The Origins of Totalitarian Democracy* that the secular rationale for "remaking society" branched into two democratic directions: liberal democracy and totalitarian democracy of the left.[13] The former made the values of "liberty" and "individual freedom" the foundation of its ideology and sociopolitical organizational scheme, while the latter stressed the democratic value of "collective" and "group" goals.

In keeping with his notion of the will of the majority (the general will), the nonliberal democratic connotations in Rousseau's philosophy and political theory find proper expression in the new political attitude that has been articulated by the political Left. Based upon the assumption of a nonpluralistic, single truth in politics, leftist movements and regimes seek a more perfect form of social organization. In this final stage of perfection the scope of politics would include the totality of human existence, with the pursuit of such an end itself taking the form of secular political messianism (that is, Weber's charismatic leadership and source of the regime's legitimacy). Politics would become the artful pursuit of particular (individual) human endeavors through group effort (social solidarity expressed in both means and ends). Society's faith in finally achieving its collectively defined and pursued ultimate ends under leftist movements and regimes, argues Talmon, is lacking under liberal democracy's individualized (atomized) values and organization.

Moreover, totalitarianism of the Left gains its democratic character by struggling to reach humanity's salvation through its own secular process and avowed goals (recognizing the individual's worth and self-realization, while working through the collectivity). By contrast, totalitarianism of the Right (nondemocratic) concerns itself not with human salvation, but with such collective abstractions as the state, the nation, or the race. The Left is always rationalist and individualist (if only through the group, class, or even party), while the Right operates with historic, social, and organic entities void of any sense of the individual person, and more importantly of rationalism. Hence the Left embraces creeds and goals of universal dimension (such as the intrinsic goodness and perfectibility of humankind) — values which are missing on the Right. The latter instead emphasizes the notion of human weakness and corruption, using this as a rationale for exercising tighter social controls.

Thus while the Left would reluctantly accept the notion that force might have to be used to bring about, and possibly hasten, human collective progress toward a more advanced stage of social harmony and justice, the Right would gladly accept the use of force as an ideal means for maintaining order and exercising strict control over society, which is seen to be made up of poor and unruly creatures. Therefore, Talmon would find it proper to apply the qualifier of democratic to totalitarianism of the Left (and the movements and regimes associated with it), while refusing to do so to totalitarianism of the Right (and the movements and regimes associated with it), which he considers to be nondemocratic.[14]

According to Talmon's conceptualization of those modern movements and regimes that are political heirs to the eighteenth century's nonliberal democratic traditions, the Cuban revolution has been democratic since it came to power in 1959, in the beneficial societal aims of its socioeconomic developmental policies and its avowed dedication, through its different phases, to redeeming the long-neglected Cuban masses. Under Talmon's dichotomous historical analysis, the institutional phase of the 1970s, the self-imposed legal restraints of the 1976 Constitution, and the postinstitutionalization phase of the 1980s simply add important elements of formalism and legalism to what was already democratic in substance and intent.

The Transitional Nature of Socialist Democracy

From the theoretical and ideological perspective of liberal democracy, it is difficult to comprehend that the cornerstone of socialist democracy is the dictatorship of the proletariat. (It is equally difficult to accept the socioeconomic class characterization of liberal democracy as the dictatorship of the bourgeoisie: the minority rule of the propertied class exercised over the majority of the population — the working class and the peasantry.)

Once it becomes a historical reality, the dictatorship of the proletariat — the political structure of workers' state power in a given locality and time — should be at work performing its initial developmental function: constructing socialism as an intervening period in the transition from capitalism to communism. In order to bring the dictatorship of the proletariat into actual existence, the workers must assume state power; historically, this has happened through an alliance with the peasantry and some sectors of the petit bourgeoisie associated with a Marxist revolutionary party.

The capitalist society would then be dismantled, turning the private ownership of the means of production into the public ownership. A phase of less-developed communism would be initiated: socialism. In a prolonged and complex process, the new political structures as well as the societal and economic system established under socialism would develop. Theoretically, and in practice, socialist-democratic institutions do not remain static; they must undergo long-term change and development in order to eventually reach a more advanced stage of systemic growth — such as the ultimate phase of "social self-government under communism."[15]

Historically, the 1871 Paris Commune became the first modern revolutionary expression (however brief) of the dictatorship of the proletariat in action. It was recognized as such by Engels in the introduction he wrote for a new German edition of Marx's *The Civil War in France.* With the benefit of twenty years of hindsight, Engels saw in it a concrete example of what was meant in Marxist theory. In his words, "Look at the Paris Commune. That was the Dictatorship of the Proletariat."

Although Marx did not define precisely the dictatorship of the proletariat, he discussed a developmental sequence, through social class struggle, that would ultimately bring it about:

1. the existence of social classes, determined by particular phases in the development of capitalist production;

2. the ensuing class struggle necessarily leading to the dictatorship of the proletariat; and

3. the new class dictatorship (state political power held by, and exercised for, the working class) constituting by itself a period of transition leading to the abolition of all social classes and, ultimately, to a classless society.[16]

In the *Critique of the Gotha Program*, Marx stated:

[B]etween capitalist and communist society lies a period of revolutionary transformation from one to the other. There is a corresponding period of transition in the political sphere, and in this period the state can only take the form of a revolutionary dictatorship of the proletariat.[17]

Furthermore, the intricate problems raised by the actual, concrete, application of state power under the dictatorship of the proletariat were anticipated and discussed by Lenin in *State and Revolution* – as he foresaw them in the fateful summer of 1917. In this work, Lenin addressed himself to some of the contradictions of the working class and the Marxist revolutionary leadership exercising political power over the state. He readily supported Marx's contention of the "propriety of [workers] seizing power and setting up a regime of 'proletarian dictatorship' which would rule by force and by the suppression of hostile class elements."[18]

Nonetheless, as one historical case after another seems to demonstrate, the different phases that a socialist polity has to go through are more than just problematic; many times they are outright conflictive, as in Lenin's New Economic Policy (NEP), Mao's Cultural Revolution, and Castro's campaign for a ten-million-ton sugar harvest. This is particularly true when socialism is built in a country like Cuba, under conditions of economic underdevelopment (or asymmetric and dependent economic growth as occurred during the period of American influence and control) and of limited natural and human resources. The much-publicized favorable trade relations, and economic, military, and other kinds of assistance Cuba receives from other socialist countries, particularly the Soviet Union, have so far guaranteed the survivability of Cuban socialism, especially economically. By no means, however, have these lopsided relations in Cuba's favor entirely removed the numerous pressures and challenges facing the revolutionary regime. The 1980 Mariel boatlift, after over two decades of Cuban socialism, is a case in point.[19]

From Bourgeois-Democratic to Socialist Revolution

The exercise of state power by the working class through the dictatorship of the proletariat was recognized and legitimized in the writings of Marx, Engels, Lenin, and others. In Cuba, however, when Fidel Castro and his fellow revolutionaries overthrew the dictatorship of Fulgencio Batista in 1959, revolutionary power was not held on behalf of the working class, nor on behalf of a workers' revolutionary party (not even on behalf of the Cuban Communist party, which at that time was known as the prerevolutionary Popular Socialist Party— Partido Socialista Popular, PSP).

The revolution was initially bourgeois-democratic in both its make-up and outlook. It had, however, a radical leadership headed by Castro, for whom there was unending and enthusiastic popular support, particularly from the middle, lower-middle, and lower-income sectors of the population, in short, the overwhelming majority of Cubans. From the outset the Revolution showed a rather progressive social orientation that was particularly important given the liberal-democratic ideology it was assumed to have. It also was profoundly nationalist and anti-imperialist. Its deep commitment to radical social change rapidly became the catalyst for the ensuing transformation from bourgeois-democratic to socialist revolution.

Nevertheless, the Cuban revolutionary government was not legitimized in terms of the Marxist-Leninist dictatorship of the proletariat; the socialist stage of the Revolution did not come to fruition until later. Among other factors, Castro's charismatic authority enriched the Revolution's legitimacy. The idiosyncratic national characteristics of Cuba departed significantly—much more so than in other cases—from the established theoretical patterns for setting up a socialist polity.[20]

Even though the revolution's transformation towards socialism took place in a relatively short period of time, the national bourgeoisie had an important initial role to play in what were less radical developmental plans. There was room for private ownership of the means of production, in combination with a built-in nationalist appeal to the native bourgeoisie that was expected to provoke a patriotic response from them. However, external and internal aggression combined with external and internal complicity to demonstrate the magnitude and ramifications of the economic class interests affected by the process of social change set in motion by the revolution.

The Revolution's social and economic policies were aimed at transforming such central institutions (both foreign and locally owned) as: the existent land tenure system; the banking, industrial, housing, and trade structures; education-al, public health, and utilities services; and employment opportunities for low-income groups. As never before seen in the country's history, the system became responsible to traditionally neglected social groups, and supported fairer distribution of national income. The response from the upper and upper-middle segments of the national bourgeoisie was along class lines: they became increasingly alienated from the Revolution and soon became openly hostile.

From January 1959 to October 1960, in only twenty-two months of revolution-ary government, Cuba had moved away from its initial "semicolonial" status towards "building socialism." All of this was accomplished contrary to the "proper" events and procedures laid out in Marxist-Leninist theory:

1. a revolutionary Communist party did not lead the process of social transformation;

2. real hegemony was not exercised by the working class as the leading social and political force conducting the revolution;

3. the nationalization of the industrial establishment, as well as the official attitude towards the small-industrial establishment, was different from what is customary in similar and previous cases; and

4. the transformation of agriculture took place under the so-called state property system (signifying ownership by the people at large), rather than by cooperative means—al-though a significant sector of agriculture is still in private hands.[21]

However, national and foreign bourgeois forces had been stripped of any actual power; as a country with a "semicolonial" status, Cuba severed it ties with its imperial neighbor, the United States. In this context, Cuba established new forms of ownership of the means of production and new production relations that were characteristic of an incipient socialist system. This was accomplished under revolutionary state power that was not as such representative of the dictatorship of the proletariat. There were theoretical and practical contradic-tions creating an awkward situation with serious long-term implications, par-ticularly regarding the nature and identity of revolutionary power and of the political system in general.[22]

Hence a transition period was initiated in which the socialist institutions already created were further developed, while a new political structure more in keeping with Marxist-Leninist theory and practice was being put in place. For this purpose the three revolutionary organizations sharing power initiated a difficult process of amalgamation leading to final integration. These organiza-tions were: first and foremost, Castro's July 26th Movement; second, the old Communist party, the PSP, especially the cadres and leaders who had been directly involved in the struggle against the Batista regime; and last, the Havana University-based student Revolutionary Directorate (DR), many of whose leaders had been slain by Batista's police in 1957. A succession of political parties followed: the Integrated Revolutionary Organizations (ORI), 1961–1963; the United Party of Socialist Revolution (PURS), 1963–1965; and finally, the Cuban Communist Party (PCC), which has been the revolution's leading political institution since its organization in 1965.

One approach to the analysis of Cuban history assumes that several transitional phases followed one another with parallel changes experienced at different societal levels — albeit with significant differences in formative content and import for the final direction of the revolution. The different societal levels involved include the following. First, at the level of the revolutionary leadership (the leading variable, as long as the revolutionary process was mainly conducted from above) there was an increasing awareness of the political-ideological and actual possibilities available to the revolution, given its national and international context, and decisions were being made accordingly. Second, at the level of the population at large, increasing political polarization pitted different social aggregates against one another: the popular sector was intensifying its identification, commitment, and support for the revolution, while upper-middle and upper class sectors of the population were rapidly becoming the revolution's antagonists.

A third level was the economic viability — even survivability — of the country itself, whose vulnerability was made painfully clear in 1961, when its traditional main export and import market was closed by the Washington-imposed economic blockade. A substitute trading partner and financier (a source of loans, grants, and credits) with sufficient economic and market capability and political clout to offset the country's loss had to be found; the Soviet Union and other socialist countries met this need. Last, at the level of the revolution's ideology and political institutions, after the short-lived phase of such liberal-democratic ideological constructs as "humanism" was over (having been mentioned in the spring of 1959 by Castro as a possible ideology for the revolution), Marxism-Leninism, as an ideological, political, and economic doctrine, fit a revolution that had already become socialist in deeds, if not in name. Castro proclaimed that Cuba's was a socialist revolution on April 16, 1961, the eve of the aborted invasion of the Bay of Pigs (Playa Girón) by Cuban exiles acting under the direction, training, and financing of the United States Central Intelligence Agency.

Therefore, what started as a national liberation revolutionary process, with patriotic, popular, and bourgeois-democratic components, rapidly turned into a socialist, and then a Marxist-Leninist system. This process can be summarized in three clearly defined historical stages:

1. January 1959 to the fall of 1960 (bourgeois-democratic stage, which lasted until the means of production were nationalized by the revolutionary government);

2. October 1960 (nationalization of the means of production) to April 16, 1961 (proclamation of the socialist nature of the revolution); and

3. April 16, 1961 to the present, recognizing the historical moment in which the revolution was further defined by Castro as Marxist-Leninist (December 2, 1961).[23]

From diverse and opposing ideological and scholarly perspectives, others have debated whether the Revolution would have been something other than what it finally became if the United States had restrained itself instead of pushing it to embrace the Soviet Union and join its sphere of influence. There is no question that these last twenty-six years of Cuban history would have been different, in more ways than one, had that been the case. However, regardless of the United States and its behavior towards the Revolution — even in the unlikely event that Washington had behaved as an understanding and supportive neighbor — Cuba would still have become a socialist nation. Once it moved into the kind of centralized, planned growth and state-directed development policy that followed the initial socioeconomic and political changes of the 1960s, it would have adopted, as it did, a socialist system.

In Havana, the adoption of a socialist system was seen as a logical step in the growth and development of the revolutionary process. Moreover, it provided a necessary response to the nation's economic underdevelopment, which demanded drastic measures to fully address the overall societal problem. The direction of this process in the first years of the revolution was evidenced, among other things, by the leading and increasingly comprehensive economic role played by the newly formed central planning board.

Nonetheless, whether Cuba would also have become a Marxist-Leninist state, the close ally of the Soviet Union and other socialist countries, and the antagonist of the United States, is another matter. Without the conditions that threatened the Revolution's survival and viability — that is, the danger posed by different pressures and insurgency operations against the country by overt and covert means, and the pressing needs and shortcomings faced by its weak and vulnerable economy, many of which were manufactured, supported, or promoted by Washington — the revolutionary leadership's behavior would most likely have had a different substance and meaning. Its decision-making apparatus would have turned out different kinds of policies, oriented in other directions than those that were pursued. In this sensitive area, Washington's myopic anti-Cuba policy failed to understand the Cuban Revolution from the beginning and still does today. Paradoxically, in its all-consuming desire to obliterate the Revolution and what it stands for, the United States has created an ever more formidable adversary.

Operationalizing Socialist Democracy

In today's world, the widespread desire of peoples to live under a democratic government is so strong that practically all rulers find it convenient, if not politically indispensable, to pay tribute to democracy. It has become customary for many heads of government to call themselves and their own political systems democratic, regardless of the real nature of their political practices. This led to the common "window dressing" pretense of abiding by well-known democratic rules and rituals, such as going through the motions of the electoral process, overseeing the existence of both government and opposition political parties, and other political modalities characteristic of liberal-democratic regimes, for appearance's sake. However, in spite of such democratic facades, these governments are not genuinely democratic, either in the substance or in the formality of their political life. In fact, they are frequently authoritarian or plainly dictatorial.

On the other hand, among defenders and officeholders of progressive regimes, including socialist governments, there can also be a mistaken assessment and understanding of what democracy really is. According to a Marxist Hungarian social scientist, Arthur Kiss, for some individuals the requirements of democratic rule seem (wrongly) satisfied if any of the following conditions are met:

1. "[If] power is concentrated in the hands of a clique [as long as it is done] in the name of the proletariat";

2. "[for some,] democracy means rule by a strong leader, provided he represents the people and not special interest groups"; and

3. "[for others democratic rule is] primarily a welfare system. [So] they equate democracy with social welfare, regardless of how it is achieved or maintained."[24]

The operational principles of socialist democracy, however, are more precise and demanding than those mentioned above. Power, it is true, should be exercised for the people's welfare and not for the benefit of special interest groups (power *for* the people), but it should also be exercised by the people or their representatives, allowing full means for the people's input in decision making (power *by* the people).

The proletarian class nature of socialist democracy (in alliance with the peasantry) should enhance rather than curtail its democratic tendencies. The exercise of state power by the working class under the dictatorship of the proletariat, covering the initial socialist stage discussed earlier, should mean just that (and not something else under the guise of what it is not). The result should be the progressive elimination of society's economic class differences among existing social aggregates. The majority of the population should finally have direct and effective access to the management of the affairs of the state (and of their own lives and those of future generations), while abolishing the private ownership of the means of production and the socially sanctioned practice of human exploitation, as exists under the bourgeois-democratic system. Thus the exercise of state power by a revolutionary Marxist party or movement (or one that adopted Marxism after coming into office), as a revolutionary government ruling on behalf of the people, is not enough in itself to qualify as the dictatorship of the proletariat according to Marxist-Leninist theory.

Exercising power under such conditions could still mean ruling for the welfare of the people, but only on their behalf, and not by the people themselves (power *for* the people, but not *by* the people in a direct and real sense). What, then, is the operational definition, and what are the observable and measurable empirical indicators, of socialist democracy? What, in practice, provides both the ideological rationale and the institutional setting whereby the democratic political practices properly expected from the dictatorship of the proletariat are actually achieved?

Some of the main theoretical and empirical components that together qualify a political system as a socialist democracy have already been discussed. By mentioning some of them again, along with others, we are able to construct an operational analytical framework that is germane and applicable to those political systems (such as Cuba's) which are presently engaged in constructing socialism, and whose performance is being examined here. Hence, socialist democracy constitutes a political system with the following characteristics:

1. an orientation toward mass political participation (proscribing any form of social or political elitism);

2. mutual subordination of the leaders and the governed (guaranteeing that no privileged status by either the leadership or any other group would be condoned);

3. assurance of a dialectical unity of direct and indirect democratic political representation (avoiding liberal democracy's indirect representation as the basis for a sole form of political representation);

4. the organization of power on the basis of democratic centralism, while different societal interests are expressed in a nonconfrontational fashion within the system's organic unity (avoiding liberal democracy's political pluralism both institutionally and behaviorally);

5. a central political role for the communist party, which includes providing leadership to the government, the mass organizations, the general population, and the nation at large, and offering a proper example to follow on most issues (this should be done, however, by enhancing rather than curtailing people's sovereignty, as long as the people—the working class and its allies—are recognized as the actual holders of state power);

6. continued development of its essential features, in order to facilitate the evolution of socialism towards communism;

7. anticipation of the eventual transition toward communism by the purposeful enhancement during the initial socialist democratic stage, of the features of self-government, which should continue unfolding by themselves and as part of the overall process of societal change.[25]

There seem to be built-in, latent, or manifest tensions (possibly contradictions), in practice if not in theory, within and between some of these analytical categories. Important questions come to mind in this regard. How can it be realistically guaranteed, for example, that the prominent role played by the political and administrative leadership will not be transformed into an institutionalized privileged (elitist) social and political standing? Such a dreadful possibility was acknowledged by the antibureaucratic sentiment shared, interestingly enough, by Lenin and Castro, both of whom had to launch anti-bureaucracy campaigns during the initial phases of their respective regimes.

How can it be assured that the central political function entrusted to and performed by the Communist party will not become a party dictatorship (or even one more personalized), instead of the workers democratically exercising power in pursuit of the dictatorship of the proletariat? How can it be assured that some upper- or middle-level political cadre or administrative official, who might be content with deriving substantive benefits from the system as it is, will not raise serious objections and obstacles which undermine present and future changes, therefore practically annulling whatever possibilities might exist for eventually accomplishing the transition from incipient socialism to developed communism?

Lacking a system of division of power within its organically unified structure of government, the Communist party, under socialist democracy, must police itself so that its functions and functionaries remain within its established boundaries and objectives. The political and legislative bodies represented in Cuba — at the national, provincial, and municipal levels — by the Organs of Popular Power must perform a similar self-supervisory function, as well as provide ample opportunities for the people to examine and criticize their performance. This is regularly done during the deputies' and delegates' *rendición de cuentas* (rendering of accounts). On such occasions, in public assemblies, they confront their inquiring constituents, reporting on what has been decided and acted upon regarding different public issues, both local and national. They also receive from the constituents new instructions for additional or future action on current issues of common concern.

And yet, are these and other systemic safeguards sufficient to keep the regime from overstepping itself? That is, are the Communist Party, the Organs of Popular Power, major and minor political cadres and administrative functionaries, and, more important, the revolutionary leadership, able to be properly responsible and responsive, so that Cuban socialist democracy functions according to its own established principles and objectives? Answering these questions with objectivity and accuracy is not simple. However, we will suggest some tentative answers.

Simply stated on a general level, the construction of socialism first, and of communism in a rather distant future, has proven to be a very difficult job. In the wake of the 1980 Mariel boatlift, Castro bitterly acknowledged that the sacrifices demanded and expected from those engaged in the historical task of constructing socialism had to be accepted and performed with free will; hence those already leaving, and others waiting in the wings, should go on with their attempted exodus and leave the country for good. When Castro finally closed the port of Mariel in September 1980, he was acceding to repeated requests from President Carter to stop the migration of Cubans to the United States. After over two decades of Cuban socialism, it became clear, internally and externally, that hardships and scarcity of consumer goods still characterized the daily life of the population, notwithstanding substantial advances achieved by the Revolution in many different fields.

Nevertheless, the fulfillment of the goals in the analytical categories listed above should be measured according to a continuum ranging from the present shortcomings and achievements (actual socialism) to the potential for future improvement and goals (possible socialism). Building socialism in a country like Cuba was, is, and will be, for years to come, a complex and demanding social engineering process that is further compounded by the island's historical, geographical, political, socioeconomic, and cultural idiosyncrasies.

EVALUATING CUBAN REVOLUTIONARY-SOCIALIST POLITICS

This brief discussion of the revolutionary political system will cover three consecutive time periods:

1. the 1960s, which primarily represent the foundation of revolutionary political modalities through intense political mobilization;

2. the 1970s or, more strictly, the period from the 1970 ten million-tons campaign to December 2, 1976, when the first elected deputies of the National Assembly of Popular Power were sworn in, completing the institution-building phase of the Revolution (the strengthening and expansion of the socialist legal system continued throughout the decade, and beyond, with new legislation and codification); and

3. the 1980s, which represents the third revolutionary decade. More exactly, the third period could be seen as starting in early 1977, once the newly established political and legal institutions were in force under an institutionalized revolution which continues today.

Perhaps more important than the division of the Revolution into chronological sequential stages would be an examination of the main and secondary issues that prevailed at the time and of the political dynamics that surrounded and influenced the evolution and direction of the political system. These issues and dynamics energized the system throughout its successive developmental periods. Hence, there appears to be a continuity in the internal logic of the change process, even if not in a unilinear direction. The interaction of internal and external forces affecting the overall transformation experience requires a multivariate type of analysis. This method should also investigate possible relationships among and effects of background variables in the institutional and behavioral direction of the revolution during its formative process. This analysis should be based on Marxist-Leninist theory, recognizing that in addition to being the ideological base and the contextual value system of the Revolution, it is also an analytical social science approach, as applied here.

The Foundation Stage, the 1960s

In retrospect, the 1960s is wrongly characterized by some political analysts as a chaotic and turbulent period; in these early years the Revolution was steered by what was then an inexperienced leadership determined to master the internal and external forces that had taken on a life of their own. The Revolution had to fight formidable opponents, and the odds were not on its side. And yet, the strength and dynamism of a popular and successful revolution defied common wisdom, and it was able to overcome the seemingly superior forces of its enemies (such as U.S.-supported counterrevolutionaries). The Revolution succeeded by galvanizing the people's support and turning it into a decisive force in defense of the regime. The aborted April 17, 1961 Bay of Pigs invasion by Cuban exiles under CIA sponsorship attested to that. (It took less than seventy-two hours to defeat the exile forces.)

At the same time, a massive exodus of nationals was under way. In fact, notwithstanding the depth of commitment shared by the majority of the population, a significant minority (numerically undetermined) never joined the ranks of supporters and most likely never will. Following its own internal dynamics and the changes in its own make-up and membership, this alienated social group alleviates the hardships of its own estrangement either by seeking alternative ways to leave the country (there is practically no legal access to the United States), by actually leaving against all odds, or by remaining on the island in isolation from the mainstream of revolutionary life, simply surviving within the country's social fabric.

The overwhelming majority of Cubans, however, remained and became actively involved in supporting and defending the Revolution. People's support for the Revolution was maximized by constant governmentally planned and initiated popular mobilization campaigns and programs. Revolutionary mobilization of the populace was open to, and expected by, all citizens. The people's compliance with the regime's requested mobilization campaigns was rather positive and enthusiastic, and widely shared by most social groups. However, compliance was also actively sought by different means available to the regime:

1. *participatory* (allowing the people to influence or refine the implementation of policies or programs);
2. *instrumental* (providing the incentive of gaining material benefits);
3. *normative* (allocating such symbolic rewards as esteem and prestige, and reinforcing them by the Revolution's political culture and value system; and
4. *coercive* (punishing or threatening to punish deviant behavior, mostly counterrevolutionary actions).[26]

However, while relentless mobilization energized the population, allowing it to become closely involved and part of the revolutionary process, the political and social system became, and remained for many years, institutionally weak.

Not only were the old regime's social and political institutions systematically eroded and eventually eliminated; in addition, even such revolutionary stalwarts as the trade union movement — the Cuban Confederation of Workers (CTC) —

were institutionally weakened to the point of near extinction during those years. The regime focused its attention instead on mobilizing workers in national campaigns, along with the rest of the population, or in more specifically labor-oriented goals such as increasing production (*emulación*), for which the CTC was utilized as a mobilization vehicle. Institutionally, the regime concentrated on the workers' vanguard movement, neglecting the trade unions as such. (This mistaken policy was reversed later in the 1970s, when the CTC's institutional strength and vitality were rebuilt.)[27] At that time the Communist Party was undergoing the initial pains of its founding. Even though it was finally organized in 1965, its first congress was not held until ten years later (December 1975); by then it was a necessary step that had to be taken prior to the overall institutionalization of the revolutionary political system.[28]

Revolutionary decision making was centralized at the top, with Castro playing the central and decisive role. This generally agreed-upon characterization of the system has led, however, to oversimplifications regarding the overall nature and dynamics of the political process, especially during its first decade, the period that led to the 1970 ten million-tons campaign. In addition to legislating policies that were by their very nature responsive to the needs of the popular sectors of the population — addressing needs and aspirations of prerevolutionary low-income groups traditionally been ignored by other regimes — the revolutionary government allowed a limited policy-making input from mass organizations at different levels of their political participation. Although this input may have been indirect in the process of original policy decision making it was at least possible during the subsequent policy implementation process of modification or alternation. By increasing political participation, this limited input encouraged people's compliance with the regime's policies and programs. Based on a systematic empirical study of the governing strategies pursued by the regime during the first ten year period, I stated elsewhere:

[T]he nature and significance of the role played by mass organizations. . . is something that has not been dealt with adequately by analysts of the revolution. . . .[T]he prevailing consensus. . . has been one whereby mass organizations have been downgraded. . . .They have been rated as non-initiators and non-creators of policies, even when, administratively speaking, the implementation of a policy implies a reinterpretation of the original policy a great deal of the time. [Regarding people's compliance and political participation], [t]he surprising element in such analysis is that they have never questioned how it is possible in a revolutionary process like Cuba's, where traditionally non-participant groups have become politically active in mobilization campaigns, that such participating individuals and institutions have nothing to do but to obey and follow directives without any creative effort on their part. If anything, that surely would have been a disastrous road for the revolution, alienating the masses from the revolutionary process.[29]

As discussed in this narrative, during the 1960s the revolutionary government was mainly engaged in the country's social transformation (the development of a new political culture) and economic development (the nationalization of the modes of production, which effectively limited the private sector to small farm holdings). In addition, it pursued people's political participation through all-inclusive mobilization. Practically the entire population (with the exception of children and senior citizens) and all social groups, men and women alike, were at one time or another involved in a mobilization campaign or program in some capacity.

The centralization of the decision-making structure and procedures led to the massive concentration of efforts and resources for the ill-conceived ten million-tons campaign. This policy blunder and its bitter aftermath (even though approximately 8.5 million tons were produced) provided the needed impetus for moving towards institutionalizing the revolution. In an apologetic speech given to the masses gathered for the 26th of July celebration immediately following that fateful sugar harvest, Castro offered his resignation for failing to meet the goal. The people responded by turning down his resignation and asking him to stay on. Nevertheless, it was then generally agreed that the system needed a major overhaul, decentralizing its decision-making process and establishing avenues for more systematic and broader input from different sources into all policy-making areas, as well as establishing more formalized political participation including elected representative organs.

The Institutionalization Stage, the 1970s

The period immediately following the 1970 ten million-tons campaign was characterized by contradictory elements, including both a sobering and a creative developmental phase for the revolution (institutionally the most creative so far). This was a time of reckoning with past and present realities, including the pressing demands for a clear definition of the regime's institutional and organizational identity. Cuba needed finally to formalize its state-building developmental process according to the institutional premises and political practices expected from a Marxist-Leninist state. Its search for formal avenues to decentralize decision making was meant to put an end to the subjective (arbitrary) practices of the 1960s — or at least to move decisively in that direction. Cuba wanted to limit and clearly define the boundaries separating state administrative tasks (government) from political leadership and guidance (Communist Party), and from the functions of elected representative organs (political representation of and participation by the people).

The revolutionary social transformation of the previous decade had to find its proper constitutional-institutional setting within a state political structure and legality that would permanently guarantee a socialist democracy. Henceforth, a citizen's revolutionary dedication and commitment, and any actions stemming from such values, would no longer be based mainly upon and reinforced by the established network of mass organizations and their mobilization campaigns, as was the case in the 1960s. Now such socialist values as social egalitarianism and political democracy would be safeguarded by a socialist constitution. This would provide, then, the bedrock upon which the state would be organized as a Marxist-Leninist polity.

In the early 1970s, the regime's main challenge was the belated task of constructing its own permanent socialist legality (constitutional and judicial state building) and formality (institutional and political state building). The people had to be able to exercise their political sovereignty and power through elected officials who would represent and pursue the aims of a socialist state. Meanwhile, the parallel spheres of administrative decision making and political decision making also had to be further clarified and defined. However, in an organically integrated state like a Marxist-Leninist polity there is considerable overlapping among the administrative and political organs discharging such functions. The Communist Party oversees both structures, in seeking to fulfill its function of political leadership and guidance, but without interfering with their work administratively.

After sixteen years of exercising legislative and executive powers (as well as exercising jurisdiction over the judiciary, the historical period of rule by the revolutionary government's Council of Ministers came to an end in 1976. This was preceded by the period of the Matanzas trial (1974–75), during which new political institutions were tested. Based on this experience, these institutions were later adopted as the revolutionary regime's new political system. The old period came to an end with the approval, in a national referendum, of the new socialist constitution on February 24, 1976. More exactly, it ended with the inauguration of the first National Assembly of the Organs of Popular Power on December 2, 1976. In anticipation of this event, the lower Organs of Popular Power, at municipal and provincial levels, had been inaugurated. Earlier, on October 11, 1976, the first national elections ever held under revolutionary rule had finally put in motion the political and electoral process institutionalizing the revolution: 10,725 elected municipal delegates proceeded to elect 1,084 provincial delegates and 481 national deputies. According to the 1976 Constitution, after the municipal delegates (representing 169 municipalities, and charged with politicoadministrative authority), have been elected by direct, secret, and universal vote, they must assemble and proceed to elect (by indirect vote) the provincial delegates (representing fourteen provinces and charged with political-administrative authority), and the national deputies (representing one National Assembly, and charged with legislative and political-administrative authority).

The Cuban state has been institutionalized on the basis of three major power pyramids: the Communist Party, the nation's main political institution and the only political party; the Council of Ministers, the government's administrative and bureaucratic center; and the Organs of Popular Power, the legislature's political and administrative center. The last two power pyramids share their administrative functions, communicating with each other through interlocking structures.

In this threefold political organization there are several major power centers: the Political Bureau and the Secretariat of the Communist Party (the highest policy-making echelon in the political party pyramid); the Executive Committee of the Council of Ministers (the highest decision-making echelon in the administrative-bureaucratic pyramid); and the Council of State of the National Assembly of the Organs of Popular Power, (the highest decision-making echelon in the politicoadministrative pyramid). Both the Council of State and the Executive Committee of the Council of Ministers are headed by the same person, who is elected for a five-year period by the National Assembly (which also elects the members of the Council of State), and who in practice becomes the country's president. Fidel Castro has been elected for this position in 1976, 1981, and 1986.

There are two legislative sessions every year, in July and December, which last from two to three days each. When the National Assembly is not in session, the Council of State discharges its functions, pending approval by the National Assembly when it convenes in the following legislative period. The Council of State functions as the National Assembly's administrative and planning (executive) center, thus providing the necessary continuity between its rather brief legislative sessions. During the rest of the year the standing committees, made of the different deputies assigned to them and their staff, work on drafting legislation in preparation for the legislative sessions of the National Assembly.[30]

The three major power pyramids are closely and systematically integrated, while still remaining functionally, operationally, and institutionally differentiated. Nonetheless, even though the National Assembly is constitutionally the highest state political organ, as representative of the people's sovereignty, its structural autonomy appears to overlap with the all-inclusive political leadership function exercised by the Communist Party. Under this system, even when the National Assembly is performing its assigned function as a forum for policy and legislative debate and as the nation's main law-making body, the Communist Party is so pervasive that it seems as though it would place the National Assembly under its political leadership, guiding the direction of its legislative decision making. This political dynamic is in keeping with the central political function entrusted to the party by the political system. Its leadership role, however, has to be performed not by demanding or dictating but by convincing others (nonparty members who are National Assembly deputies and Organs of Popular Power provincial and municipal delegates) of the wisdom of the party position. Legally, party decisions are not binding upon the Organs of Popular Power, but they are binding upon party members, according to party rules, under the principle of democratic centralism. All elected officials are constitutionally free to decide and vote independently from party policy, as are all citizens. This area of party influence and political guidance (and the viability of the Organs of Popular Power structural autonomy) is a source of potential political tension and stress within the system, if not properly handled.

Among other political leaders, Raúl Castro provided important guidance on this matter to both members and nonmembers of the Communist Party. Regarding the hierarchical standing and interrelationship among the three major power pyramids and the position occupied by the mass organizations in relation to them, he stated "that even if it is true that 'the Party *directs*, the state *directs*, and the mass organizations *direct*,' the level of importance in these directives is not always the same. . . .Therefore, the party directives stand above those from other political, governmental, and social institutions throughout the system. . . ."[31]

In spite of the growing pains and complex problems inherent in the process, the institutionalization movement of the 1970s placed the regime in a more advanced stage of socialist development. It could now properly exercise the dictatorship of the proletariat, both normatively and institutionally. Nonetheless, the real test for such a monumental state-building achievement still had to come. This included the regime's effectiveness in overcoming political tensions arising from the newly established institutions, as well as in bridging the gap between expectation and reality. It would be possible to empirically determine its level of success, that is, to determine how much of a gap might still remain between what was promised (implicitly and explicitly) and what has been and is being delivered. By purposely building the new political and judicial institutions, however, the regime had moved forward into a new state-building stage. It made itself face the even tougher test coming in the years ahead: the demands and expectations built into the postinstitutionalization period. This is the time when socialist democracy should be exercised on a daily basis and in all walks of life.

The Postinstitutionalization Period, the 1980s

Critics of the revolution, in the academic world and elsewhere, were not highly appreciative of Cuba's institutionalization. The "sovietization of Cuba" thesis became their common conceptual and critical framework. The arguments raised against Cuba were varied, but their objective seemed to be the same: to delegitimize whatever external gain the revolution could accrue from its state-building stage, especially in the United States. This delegitimizing argument was based upon the following points: first, that for reasons too well known by then, Cuba had to embrace a Soviet "look-alike" political and economic structure (especially after the "New System of Economic Management and Planning," SDPE, had been adopted in 1975); second, that Moscow's virtually complete control over Havana had been sealed with the newly established institutions, which were characteristically copied from the Soviet Union and to a lesser degree from other socialist countries. From this perspective, the Castro regime had simply publicly recognized its dependency on the Soviet Union, and this helped explain Cuba's new Soviet look-alike status.[32]

Moreover, as I stated elsewhere in regard to this brand of scholarly pursuit:

What characterizes this thesis—analytically and ideologically—is its interpretation. . . that. . . asserts that the revolutionary leadership adopted as its own a Soviet bureaucratic decision-making model that defines power relations within the political system according to its pyramidal and hierarchical structure. Hence the institutionalizing process has allowed the power-holding elite—Castro and his close associates—to position itself at the top and control the Communist Party, even much more so than before. [According to the sovietization of Cuba thesis, decentralization tendencies are not present in the institutionalization of the revolution; on the contrary.] Rather than decentralizing the regime's decision-making practices and bringing a more meaningful political participation by the populace, this political change allegedly brought Cuba closer to the Soviet bureaucratic model. [Thus, t]he newly created socioeconomic, political, and. . . legal and judicial institutions amount to not much more than a Cuban version of the main features of the Soviet model, copied and applied with some adjustments. Finally, [it]. . . increased the Soviet Union's grip on Cuba. . . .[33]

According to this kind of analytical reasoning, the Organs of Popular Power are equivalent to the U.S.S.R.'s soviets. The comparison continues, then, with other features of the system, in order to draw conclusions similar to those mentioned above. At least two important concepts are ignored by this kind of criticism. First, that as the first Marxist-Leninist state in existence, the Soviet Union not only built its own system, but also provided a model for others. This, however, is not new: for over a century, especially in Latin America, the United States has provided a liberal-democratic political model (and a capitalist economic model) for others to copy, imitate, and adapt as their own. According to John M. Merriman, "The constitutions of the Latin American nations that achieved independence in the 19th century. . . frequently used the U.S. Constitution as a model. . . ."[34]

Following previous historical experiences regarding the transference and assimilation of a sociopolitical and economic model developed elsewhere, the countries adapting such a model would normally select those features that are relevant and applicable to their own milieu, while still developing modalities that would be congruent with their own system as a whole. Throughout this dissemination process, the original model has been both adopted and modified, therefore expanding the scope and number of states involved in a similar state-building experience. Thus the twentieth century is witnessing the establishment of socialist states organized along lines drawn by Marxist-Leninist politics, not unlike what liberal democracy has done since the nineteenth century.

Second, socialist legality, including its constitutional and public law features, is recognized today by jurists all over the world as a new legal family, along with civil (Roman) law and common law. A Marxist-Leninist state model, which includes operational features of the dictatorship of the proletariat, has been adapted and modified by several socialist states. This experience enriches the growth of the socialist legal family, and of its state model. Cuba has been both a recipient of and a contributor to this process. Using a readily available model, it still had to select, adjust, and especially add, indigenous features to its own final system. Such features all have to come together, fitting neatly into a new whole. The people's compliance with and support for the new legal and political institutions are dependent, to some extent, upon their realization that the new system is a natural and logical outgrowth of its own national development. Today, the majority of the Cuban population sees socialism as the natural, for many even the ideal, culmination of over 100 years of struggle for the country's independence. That this opinion may not be universally shared by the entire population and that it still lacks legitimacy among most Cuban exiles and in the United States at large do not detract from its truth and historical reality.

The political dynamics and formalities of the postinstitutionalization period, from 1977 to today, have changed the political system from its earlier stages. Both the Communist Party congresses and the electoral process have basically continued as expected. The first party congress was held in December 1975, the second in December 1980, and the third, initially planned for December 1985, was postponed until February 1986. The substantial resources and time-consuming efforts involved in organizing the international conference on Latin America's external debt (held in Havana in August 1985) seems to be the reason for briefly postponing the third party congress.

Elections have followed the two-and-one-half year cycle established in the 1976 Constitution. In addition to the first elections held in October 1976, there have been four others: April 1979, October 1981, April 1974, and October 1986. While municipal delegates and their provincial counterparts are elected for two-and-one-half year terms, the deputies of the National Assembly are elected by the municipal delegates for a five-year term. Consequently, there have been only three elections for National Assembly deputies, in 1976, 1981, and 1986.

Almost ten years after the beginning of the postinstitutionalization period, some of the most pressing problems confronted during the Matanzas experiment — as discussed at the first congress of the Communist Party in 1975 — have subsided. This was made possible by appeals made by the regime and the people's positive response while facing the challenges and opportunities provided by the newly established political structure. Such a generalized demonstration of popular support was particularly significant in the light of the Matanzas experiment, when it became obvious that "the absence of administrative expertise and know-how on the part of the OPP [Organs of Popular Power] cadres, . . . in some way accounts for the ensuing backlash when people failed to participate in the new decision-making opportunities available. . . ."[35]

However, other problems confront the political system today. Some of them seem to originate in the structural characteristics of the new political institutions themselves. A central question is preserving the structural autonomy (in an organically integrated system) of the Organs of Popular Power while exercising its institutionally differentiated legislative and political-administrative functions. This entails avoiding any possible dominance of its constitutional domain by the Communist Party. This structural problem is compounded by the high percentage of party members elected to the three different levels of the Organs of Popular Power, particularly the National Assembly. In 1979, party members and aspirants increased their percentage from the municipal to the national level. At the municipal level, party members constituted 64.7 percent of the delegates in assemblies and 99.2 percent in executive committees; at the provincial level, 90.6 percent in assemblies and 99.2 percent in executive committees; and, finally, at the national level, 91.7 percent of all deputies in the National Assembly and 100 percent in the Council of State. If the members of the Young Communist League represented in the Organs of Popular Power (municipal, 11.1 percent in assembly, and 5.2 percent in executive committees; provincial, 3.3 percent in assemblies and 0.4 percent in executive committees; and national, 5.0 percent in the Assembly and none in the Council of State) are added to party members, it leaves those nonaffiliated as follows: municipal, 24.2 percent in assemblies and 4.4 percent in executive committees; provincial, 6.1 percent in assemblies and 0.4 percent in executive committees; and national, 3.3 percent in the Assembly and none in the Council of State.[36]

In reality, even with such a high representation of party members (or perhaps because of it) the Organs of Popular Power have so far demonstrated that they do make a difference, seriously addressing their legislative and politicoadministrative functions at all levels. There seems to be agreement among most Cuba watchers regarding the important and beneficial work performed by delegates at the local level, and regarding the existence of broad and intense grassroots input. At the national level, where major policy questions are discussed and legislation is decided upon, it appears that there is an increasing trend toward spending more and more time debating the different issues before the deputies and expressing in these discussions a wide range of arguments that frequently conflict. Most of the criticism seems to be focused at the national level, because of the overwhelming presence of party members at that level. Consequently, questions are raised concerning the true nature of the National Assembly, and whether or not it is simply a politically elected front dedicated to validating or confirming policies previously approved by the party.[37] To pose the question along these lines is, again, another way of obscuring rather than clarifying the real nature of the system under examination. Pitting the Communist Party against the Organs of Popular Power is not a sound approach to the examination of Cuban politics.

Unquestionably, there are merits in having a large and varied group of unaffiliated delegates, and particularly deputies (given their legislative function) elected to the Organs of Popular Power — so that a broader spectrum of opinions and perspectives is represented to match those put forth by the party after its own lengthy discussions and decisions. However, it is not necessarily true that a lower proportion of party representatives among delegates and deputies would increase the effectiveness, or even the representativeness, of the Organs of Popular Power. To argue this position is to overlook the real nature of the Marxist-Leninist model adopted by Cuba.

The effectiveness of the Organs of Popular Power as a democratically elected and functionally differentiated legislative and political-administrative institution rests on having, above all, genuinely open discussions of national policies and legislation. These discussions include such areas as the operation of schools, stores, movie theaters, cultural houses, transportation, hospitals and clinics, and other services (and the collection and provision of the necessary information for the allocation of funds to their jurisdictions) at the provincial and municipal levels. They also involve the deputies and delegates bringing their grassroots representation and concerns to bear upon the decision-making process, and on their reporting at length in the official press regarding the discussions held — particularly the discussions in the National Assembly.

Furthermore, the system has provided, through the *rendición de cuentas*, a way in which elected representatives remain responsible to those who elected them. The power to recall delegates and deputies who do not perform to the satisfaction of those that they represent has been in effect since the beginning of the system, and remains so.

The institutionalization of the state in the 1970s also meant the strengthening and institutionalization of the Communist Party. In order to operate satisfactorily, the party needed substantive improvement, both institutionally (defining and delimiting its functions clearly so it would not intrude into other institutions' domain) and in the make-up of its membership (increasing not only its membership, but also its representativeness, especially of production workers).

In 1965 the party had 45,000 members and 5,000 aspirants (applicants for party membership); this increased to 211,642 members and aspirants by 1975 (almost a 423 percent growth in a ten-year period, for an annual 42.3 percent rate of growth) and reached a total of 434,143 by 1980 (an almost 105 percent increment in a five-year period, for an annual 21 percent average growth, which is slightly less than half of the first decade's annual rate of growth). If the party membership continues growing in the 1980s at the same annual rate of growth as it did from 1975 to 1980, it could reach a total of 1,345,843 members and aspirants by 1990.

Party nuclei grew from 20,344 in 1975 to over 26,500 by 1980 (almost a 30.25 percent increase in a five-year period, for an annual 5.5 percent rate of growth). The party membership rate of workers engaged in production (industry, agriculture, and construction) and services grew from 36.3 percent in 1975 to 47.3 percent in 1980 (from more than a third of total party membership to almost half in a five-year period). The level of education also improved noticeably: from approximately 60.3 percent (almost two-thirds of all party members) having completed an elementary education (or more) in 1975, to 80.7 percent (slightly over four-fifths of all members) by the early 1980s. At the secondary level, there was an increase from only 16 percent (less than a fifth) having completed this level in 1975 to 75.5 percent (over three-fourths) having done so by 1980.

Furthermore, between 1975 and 1980 24,512 party members graduated from party schools, receiving social science degrees, while 81,324 members and aspirants took courses on Marxist-Leninist theory.[38] The party has an assigned central function to perform in the political system, and for that purpose it increases its overall membership, its ratio of production workers to total membership, and the level of education of members and aspirants. Given the pervasiveness of the Communist Party's political function in a Marxist-Leninist regime similar to Cuba's, the effectiveness of the system, politically and otherwise, rests on the quality of party leadership and on its efficacy in responding to and representing the people's needs and aspirations.

Another significant problem confronted by the regime is that of women's political participation, especially their poor representation at the different levels of the Organs of Popular Power, as a result of the low number of those elected in the various elections held so far. In reality this is a broader problem reflecting traditional values still present in Cuban society. There are still segments of the population, particularly in isolated rural areas, that while supportive of the revolution, have not yet been able to sufficiently develop their *conciencia* (political consciousness) to the level of revolutionary modernization expected in today's Cuba. Despite substantive strides made by women in all fields since 1959, there is still resistance by some men and women to the election of women to major political positions. In the mid-1980s women are approximately half of the population and constitute almost a third of the labor force (in all kinds of occupational categories); their educational achievements can be measured not only quantitatively, but also qualitatively: if only grades rather than quotas were used in the selection process for such an elite group as the Finlay contingent of medical students, two out of three selected would be women.[39]

In the famous thesis discussed at the first congress of the Communist Party in 1975, "On the Full Exercise of Women's Equality," it was indicated that, while women constituted only 13.23 percent of party members, their equally meager representation in leadership positions was distributed from lower to higher levels, with 2.9 percent, municipal; 4.1 percent, regional; 6.3 percent, provincial; and 5.5 percent, national. In comparison with mass organizations, women had the highest level of national leadership in the CDRs (Committees for the Defense of the Revolution), with 19 percent, followed by the Young Communist League, with 10 percent. At the municipal level, the Cuban Confederation of Workers (CTC) had the highest percentage of women exercising leadership positions, with 24 percent, followed by the Young Communist League, with 22 percent.[40]

In the first national elections held in 1976, with a turnout of 95.2 percent of all electors, the 520 women elected represented only 6.6 percent of all electors (it improved slightly in 1979, to 7.2 percent). Urban areas elected more women in 1976 than rural areas: the highest number was in Havana province, 13.1 percent; followed by City of Havana, 12.6 percent; and Matanzas, 9.9 percent. In contrast to this, in the remote special municipality of the Island of Youth (formerly Island of Pines), no women were elected.[41] Almost ten years later, the improvements in this area have not been substantial.

The question of women's low level of representation in the Organs of Popular Power was an important subject of discussion at the Fourth Congress of the Federation of Cuban Women (FMC), held in Havana in March 1985. In the closing speech President Castro discussed the problem openly, and insisted on the need for improving women's political representation in the Organs of Popular Power, and the need to work purposefully to have more women elected in the future. According to him, presently only 11 percent of local delegates are women, while at the national level the picture is only somewhat better, with women constituting 22 percent of all National Assembly deputies.

In Castro's estimation, the problem with women's political representation is the result of subjective and objective factors which demand further socioeconomic and cultural changes (including freeing women from housework, which sometimes constitutes a "double shift" if they work outside the home, and modifying traditional values and perspectives towards women performing political roles). Castro proposed to the *federadas* in attendance that, "it is the duty of our society, our Revolution, our Party, and our state to wage a resolute struggle in order to gradually overcome such difficulties."[42]

Almost ten years into the postinstitutionalization period, the revolutionary government still faces many challenges to its socialist-democratic system. Some problems are more complex than others; some may prove more resistant and difficult to solve. The system, however, seems capable of not only identifying them, but also trying new solutions, which is often more than half the battle.

CONCLUSIONS

The twenty-six years of Cuban revolutionary politics examined here cover a broad and rather complex political and socioeconomic process of national change. What began as a bourgeois-democratic revolution turned rapidly into a socialist one, and soon became identified as Marxist-Leninist. In over two decades, in which it underwent a long and at times agonizing process, the revolution's political system experienced successive developmental phases, culminating in final institutionalization as a Marxist-Leninist state; that is, the state political organization of a nation engaged in building a socialist system, the initial phase of less-developed communism.

This chapter has examined the proposition that there is considerable heuristic social science value in applying a conceptual framework based on Marxist-Leninist theory to the study of Cuban revolutionary politics. It also discussed an operational conceptual paradigm which included variables measuring the actual exercise of the dictatorship of the proletariat (the stage of building socialism), and empirically evaluated the performance of the Cuban revolutionary system. The methodological approach discussed in this paper, then, is that in pursuing the analysis of Cuban politics through a relevant and coherent conceptual framework, the system can (and should) be evaluated according to its own avowed political and societal goals and cultural and ideological premises. This approach measures what Cuba intends to do by its own aspirations, instead of determining possible achievements or failures by superimposing values that the regime avoids in the first place – that is, liberal-democratic political practices. The purpose of this research strategy is not to deflect criticism, but to examine and apply with rigor and consistency those conceptual and empirical categories that are meaningful to the political phenomenon under examination, and, therefore, to avoid using ethnocentric and ideologically biased conceptual categories. Both the developmental direction pursued by the regime and its achievements and shortcomings have been discussed here using a research strategy based on Marxism-Leninism as a conceptual approach.

The Cuban regime currently confronts political problems that, in some instances, are institutional and structural in character. Other problems seem to be the product of its own societal developmental shortcomings, including those remnants of the prerevolutionary society's cultural system that linger on among some groups in the population. All in all, however, the prognosis for the future is positive. In addition to the objective reasons for this assessment – as evidenced throughout this paper – this positive prognosis is also based on the self-confidence demonstrated by Cubans in their remarkable record of revolutionary achievements. The revolution has demonstrated an extraordinary capacity to overcome what initially seemed to be insurmountable obstacles and difficulties; to plan and direct its future action; and, altogether, to successfully achieve collective goals. That is not to deny that the remaining years of this decade will demand as much dedication as was needed before. It is, rather, an expression of a Cuba watcher who believes in Cuba's determination and capacity to succeed.

NOTES

An original version of this chapter was presented at the XII International Congress of the Latin American Studies Association, Albuquerque, New Mexico, April 18–20, 1985.

1. For a discussion of the institutionalization period of the 1970s and the historical events that led to it, see "Forum on Institutionalization," *Cuban Studies/Estudios Cubanos* 9 (July 1979): 63–90. For a critical evaluation of the alleged impact that the ten million-tons campaign had upon the regime, forcing it to accept the institutionalization movement, see Max Azicri, "The Institutionalization of the Cuban State: A Political Perspective." *Journal of Interamerican Studies and World Affairs* 22 (August 1980): 315–44.

2. The question discussed here seems central to an operational definition and analysis of Cuban socialist democracy as it is practiced today. Regarding the historical course pursued by the revolution, it is a controversial issue whether its centralized decision-making structure (especially during the preinstitutionalization years, which allowed the top leadership to set the course to be followed by the revolution as it saw fit) was responsible, and to what degree, for promoting a more radical revolution (as it became after the 1960s) than would have developed under a noncentralized (and possibly more moderate) decision-making structure (in which the populace would have participated

from the outset with a substantial input in the decision-making process, determining to a significant extent the content and goals of revolutionary policy). Also, assuming that the latter was more democratic in that it allowed a broader policy input in the decision-making process, it is still questionable that its policy output would have been as responsive to the populace's needs and to national developmental goals, while still charting a successful revolutionary path for the country, as was the case under the centralized decision-making structure.

3. As far back as 1966, Castro said, "We have not rushed into setting them up [the new legal and political institutions] because we would like them to conform to [social] reality, and not the other way around." He also said, "There are many things. . . which demand definitions, concepts, and ideas, which should come from our revolutionary ideology and our Marxist view of society." Fernando Diego Cañizares, *Teoría del Estado* (La Habana: Editorial Pueblo y Educación), p. 303.

4. These issues have been discussed, from different ideological and scholarly perspectives, in the literature of Cuban studies. See for example: Arthur MacEwan, "Incentives, Equality, and Power in Revolutionary Cuba," in Ronald Radosh, ed., *The New Cuba: Paradoxes and Potentials* (New York: William Morrow, 1976); Jorge I. Domínguez, "Revolutionary Politics: The New Demands for Orderliness," in Jorge I. Domínguez, ed., *Cuba—Internal and International Affairs* (Beverly Hills: Sage, 1982); William M. Leo-Grande, "The Communist Party of Cuba Since the First Congress," *Journal of Latin American Studies* 12 (1980): 397–419; Eldon Kenworth, "Institutionalizing Community Politics in Cuba: Cultural Proclivities and Revolutionary Dilemmas," paper presented at the Latin American Studies Association annual meeting, Atlanta, 1984; B.E. Aguirre, "The Conventionalization of Collective Behavior in Cuba," *American Journal of Sociology* 90 (1984): 541–66; Rhoda Pearl Rabkin, "Cuban Political Structure: Vanguard Party and the Masses," and Archibald R. M. Ritter, "The Organs of People's Power and the Communist Party: The Nature of Cuban Democracy," in Sandor Halebsky and John M. Kirk, eds., *Cuba: Twenty-Five Years of Revolution, 1959–1984* (New York: Praeger, 1985).

5. For an insightful and up-to-date bibliographical summarization of Cuban studies literature, see Louis A. Perez, Jr., "The Cuban Revolution Twenty-five Years Later: A Survey of Sources, Scholarship, and State of the Literature," in Halebsky and Kirk, eds., *Cuba: Twenty-Five Years of Revolution, 1959–1984.*

6. Y. Turscheve, *El Partido de Lenin: Estructura y Dinamismo del Desarrollo* (Moscú: Editorial Progreso, 1975); Fidel Castro and Raúl Castro, *Selección de Discursos Acerca del Partido* (La Habana: Editorial de Ciencias Sociales, 1975).

7. Moshe Lewin, *Lenin's Last Struggle* (New York: Monthly Review Press, 1968); Jesús Díaz, "El Marxismo De Lenin," *Pensamiento Crítico* 30 (March 1970): 6–59.

8. The Brazilian social scientist Helio Jaguaribe coined the term "Cartorial State" to signify the utilization of state political power as a means of guaranteeing the socioeconomic status quo. "In the Cartorial State, the government tends to subsidize various middle-class interest groups in exchange for their political support. Most state revenues are provided through taxes on the middle class, which subsequently are returned to the middle class through favorable clientele policies. . . .The basic model for the Cartorial State is the United States with its emphasis on the role of interest groups, its government policies that often exchange subsidy programs for electoral support. . . , and its strong emphasis on maintaining the status quo." Ernest E. Rossi and Jack C. Plano, *The Latin American Political Dictionary* (Santa Barbara, Calif.: ABC-Clio, 1980),

p. 165. Since 1981, the assault by the extremely conservative policies of the Reagan administration on the traditional vision (à la Cartorial State) of the U.S. polity has substantively altered the ideological and socioeconomic balance of the American political system, which has been characterized, validly or not, as pursuing a middle road and traditionally rejecting "left-wing and right-wing extremism in politics."

9. "The theory thus encompasses a dual relationship between theory and praxis. On the one hand, it investigates the constitutive historical complex of the constellation of self-interests, to which the theory still belongs across and beyond its acts of insight. On the other hand, it studies the historical interconnections of action, in which the theory, as action-oriented, can intervene. In the one case, we have a social praxis, which, as societal synthesis, makes insight possible; in the other case, a political praxis which consciously aims at overthrowing the existing system of institutions." Jürgen Habermas, *Theory and Practice* (Boston: Beacon Press, 1975), p. 2. Also, see Richard J. Bernstein, *Praxis and Action* (Philadelphia: University of Pennsylvania Press, 1971).

10. For the dependency-Marxism theoretical debate, see Ronald H. Chilcote, "Issues of Theory in Dependency and Marxism"; Joel C. Edelstein, "Dependency: A Special Theory Within Marxian Analysis"; and John Weeks, "The Differences Between Materialist Theory and Dependency Theory and Why They Matter," in Ronald H. Chilcote, ed., *Dependency and Marxism, Toward a Resolution of the Debate* (Boulder, Col.: Westview Press, 1982). A critical evaluation of world-systems theory and a scholarly application of this theory to the Cuban case are included in Vincente Navarro, "The Limits of World-Systems Theory," and Susan Eckstein, "Cuba and the Capitalist World-Economy," respectively, in Christopher K. Chase-Dunn, ed., *Socialist States in the World-System* (Beverly Hills, Calif.: Sage, 1982). Combining an evaluation of Cuba's international trade problem with a criticism of world-system's core-periphery relations as an analytical concept, Petras and Morley state: "Clearly, the effects of Cuba's participation in the world market are decisively shaped by the island's organization of production and its internal class relations—a fact that should be highlighted in view of the monumental oversimplification that so-called center-periphery theorists of development make in subsuming all primary-product export countries under the same 'peripheral' 'dependency' category." James F. Petras and Morris H. Morley, "The Cuban Revolution: An Historical Perspective," in Halebsky and Kirk, eds., *Cuba: Twenty-Five Years of Revolution, 1959–1984*, p. 435.

11. A good discussion of the validity of the function performed by normative philosophy, and the place that it had historically occupied in empirical social science research, is included in Stefan Nowak, "Philosophical Schools and Scientific Working Methods in Social Science," *International Social Science Journal*, XXXVI, 4 (1984), pp. 587–601. According to Nowak, "These concepts [philosophical 'visions' of social reality, such as Marxism-Leninism's and others] constitute the verbalizations of the structure of such aspects of social reality as are in the focus of interest of the approach; they constitute a classificatory pattern or frame of reference in which phenomena are located and from which they derive their more or less theoretical meaning."

12. Petras and Morley, "The Cuban Revolution: An Historical Perspective," p. 413.

13. This section draws on J. L. Talmon, *The Origins of Totalitarian Democracy* (New York: Praeger, 1961), pp. 1–13, 17–65.

14. Ibid., pp. 6–8.

15. The theoretical discussion included in this and following sections draws on original and secondary sources included in the following: Tom Bottomore et al., eds. *A Dictionary*

of Marxist Thought (Cambridge, Mass.: Harvard University Press, 1983); Arthur Kiss, *Marxism and Democracy* (Budapest, Hungary: Akademiai Kiado, 1982); Marta Harnecker, *Los Conceptos Elementales del Materialism Histórico* (México, D. F.:Siglo Veintiuno, 1981); Carlos Rafael Rodríguez, *Cuba en el Tránsito al Socialismo*, 1959–1963 (La Habana: Editorial Política, 1979); Robert C. Tucker, ed., *The Marx-Engels Reader*, Second Edition (New York: W.W. Norton, 1978); and Robert C. Tucker, ed., *The Lenin Anthology* (New York: W.W. Norton, 1975).

16. Bottomore, *A Dictionary of Marxist Thought*, pp. 129–30.

17. Ibid., p. 129; Tucker, *The Marx-Engels Reader*, pp. 538, 525–41.

18. Tucker, *The Lenin Anthology*, pp. 311–98.

19. For a discussion of Cuba's assistance from, and trade with, the U.S.S.R. and other socialist countries, see Cole Blasier, "COMECON in Cuban Development," and Jorge Pérez-López, "Sugar and Petroleum in Cuban-Soviet Terms of Trade," in Cole Blasier and Carmelo Mesa-Lago, eds., *Cuba in the World* (Pittsburgh: University of Pittsburgh Press, 1979). Regarding the internal problems that led to the 1980 Mariel boatlift, as seen from a perspective critical of the Cuban regime, see Gastón A. Fernández, "The Freedom Flotilla: A Legitimacy Crisis of Cuban Socialism?" *Journal of Interamerican Studies and World Affairs* 24, 2 (May 1982):183–209.

20. Fabio Grobart, member of the Central Committee of the Cuban Communist Party and President of the Institute of the History of the Communist Movement and Socialist Revolution, takes issue with the argument proposed by some historians and political analysts that "[Cuba's]. . . socialist revolution [is]. . . an example denying a basic Marxist-Leninist tenet: the need for a vanguard working class party, because [the revolution] was not accomplished under the guidance of such a party. . . ." According to him, this type of analysis ignores the important fact that "Fidel Castro, as well as the leading nucleus that was with him during the revolutionary struggle—Raúl Castro, Abel Santamaria, Ñico López, Che Guevara, Camilo Cienfuegos, Ramiro Valdes, Jesús Montané, and others—even though they were not formally leaders or members of a Marxist-Leninist party, had studied and assimilated the essential elements of Marx's, Engels' and Lenin's thought and had become believers and supporters of their doctrine even before the attack on [the] Moncada [barracks] [July 26, 1953]" (my translation). Fabio Grobart, "El Proceso de Formación del Partido Comunista de Cuba," *Cuba Socialista* I, 1 (Diciembre, 1981), pp. 57, 56–86. For a discussion of the historical development of Marxism and the Communist party in Cuba, as well as the contributions made by leaders of the revolution to Cuban Marxist thought, see Sheldon B. Liss, *Marxist Thought in Latin America* (Berkeley, Calif.: University of California Press, 1984), pp. 238–70.

21. Rodríguez, *Cuba en el Tránsito al Socialismo*, pp. 10–11.

22. Regarding the publicly assumed identity and ideology of the revolution before 1959, Castro went on record explaining the complex motivations behind his actions during the insurrectionary war, and after coming to power in 1959. In his own words, "I can say the following—and this comes from a very profound conviction—that we could not have done it [winning the war against Batista] if we did not operate based on Marxist-Leninist principles. . . without such a theoretical base we could not have conceived a successful and proper revolutionary strategy. . . we could not have freed ourselves from imperialist domination. . . ." Castro also stated: "I was a passionate communist, but formally I did not belong to the party. And I did not belong to it because I was [already] elaborating my own revolutionary strategy for Cuba. Why did I take such a decision? Because anticommunism reigned in the country, the people were confused, and the Communist party was highly isolated. That is, objectively the Communist party did not have any possibility of

leading the revolution in Cuba. I figured that if it was possible to lead the masses, then without speaking of communism, it would be possible to come to power." Castro explained further this course of action on the basis of the critical danger posed by the U.S.: "During the insurrectionary war we could not propagandize socialism or Marxism-Leninism because of the international situation; the Americans would have destroyed the revolution" (my own translation). Grobart, "El Proceso de Formación del Partido Comunista de Cuba," pp. 58–59.

23. Fernando D. Cañizares, *Teoría del Estado* (La Habana: Editorial Pueblo y Educación, 1979), pp. 298–304.

24. Kiss, *Marxism and Democracy*, pp. 7–8.

25. Ibid., pp. 206, 206–315.

26. Max Azicri, "The Governing Strategies of Mass Mobilization: The Foundations of Cuban Revolutionary Politics," *Latin American Monograph Series 2* Erie: Northwestern Pennsylvania Institute for Latin American Studies, 1977, pp. 5–8, *passim.*

27. Marifeli Pérez-Stable, "Whither the Cuban Working Class?" *Latin American Perspectives*, 2 (Supplement, 1975), and "Class, Organization, and Conciencia: The Cuban Working Class After 1970," in Halebsky and Kirk, eds., *Cuba: Twenty-Five Years of Revolution, 1959–1984*, pp. 291–306.

28. William M. LeoGrande, "The Development of the Party System in Revolutionary Cuba," *Latin American Monograph Series 6* Erie: Northwestern Pennsylvania Institute for Latin American Studies, 1978, and his "The Communist Party of Cuba Since the First Congress," *Journal of Latin American Studies* 12, 2 (1980), pp. 397–419.

29. Azicri, "The Governing Strategies of Mass Mobilization," p. 25.

30. For a discussion of the new charter and state political institutions built during the 1970s, and their interrelated functions, see Azicri, "The Institutionalization of the Cuban State: A Political Perspective." For a detailed analysis of the parallel legal and judicial state-building processes, see Azicri, "Socialist Legality and Practice: The Cuban Experience," in Halebsky and Kirk, eds., *Cuba: Twenty-Five Years of Revolution, 1959–1984*, pp. 307–29, and his "Crime, Penal Law, and the Cuban Revolutionary Process," *Crime and Social Justice* 23 (1985), pp. 51–79.

31. Azicri, "The Institutionalization of the Cuban State," pp. 328, 325–29. Fidel Castro and Raúl Castro, *Selección de Discursos Acerca del Partido* (La Habana: Editorial de Ciencias Sociales, 1976), pp. 84–85, 55–93.

32. For a discussion of the sovietization of Cuba thesis, see Azicri, "Socialist Legality and Practice: The Cuban Experience," pp. 315–18; and Frank T. Fitzgerald, "A Critique of the 'Sovietization of Cuba' Thesis," *Science and Society* 42 (1978), pp. 1–32.

33. Azicri, "Socialist Legality and Practice: The Cuban Experience," pp. 315–16.

34. John H. Merriman, "Comparative Law and Social Change: On the Origins, Style, Decline and Revival of the Law and Development Movement," *The American Journal of Comparative Law* 25 (1977), p. 463.

35. Azicri, "The Institutionalization of the Cuban State," p. 330; *Sobre los Organos del Poder Popular* (La Habana: Departamento de Orientación Revolucionaria del Comité Central del Partido Comunista de Cuba, 1976), pp. 9–10.

36. Ritter, "The Organs of People's Power and the Communist Party: The Nature of Cuban Democracy," p. 279.

37. Ibid., pp. 270–90; Domínguez, "Revolutionary Politics: The New Demands for Orderliness"; and Rabkin, "Cuban Political Structure: Vanguard Party and the Masses."

38. Grobart, "El Proceso de Formación del Partido Comunista de Cuba," pp. 84–86; José R. Machado Ventura, "La Composición Social de las Filas del Partido," *Cuba Socialista* 2 (*marzo* 1982), pp. 3–27.

39. Fidel Castro, "Speech Given at the Fourth Congress of the Federation of Cuban Women," *Granma Weekly Review*, March 24, 1985, p. 4.

40. *Tesis y Resoluciones. Primer Congreso del Partido Comunista de Cuba* (La Habana: Departamento de Orientación Revolucionaria del Comité Central del Partido Comunista de Cuba, 1976), pp. 585, 563–603.

41. *Granma Weekly Review*, October 24, 1976, p. 11; Azicri, "The Institutionalization of the Cuban State," p. 333.

42. Castro, "Speech Given at the Fourth Congress of the Federation of Cuban Women," pp. 4, 2–11.

9

HAITI: A COMPLEX SITUATION AND AN UNKNOWN STRUGGLE

Gérard Pierre-Charles

In the long history of Latin America, the struggle for freedom has rarely confronted more difficulty than it has in Haiti over the past quarter century. The real circumstances are not well understood, even by those sectors of international public opinion that sympathize with the Haitian cause and express unlimited solidarity with the struggle for national liberation. Although the oppressive situation in Haiti is a secret to no one, few people understand the complexity of this sociopolitical phenomenon within its own context. The Haitian people's long and difficult struggle for liberation is unknown and unrecognized; although it has continued for many years it has been unable to counteract the dominant tendencies which favor the forces of darkness. This popular struggle has been commonly known only for the blows it receives, not for those it strikes.

Even now [in 1985] the news from Port-au-Prince describes many arrests. Youth leaders, engineers, agronomists, and members of the resistance throughout the country have disappeared, been repressed, tortured, or jailed.

The dictatorship imposes its violent domination with the complicity of powerful international forces, while the people's struggle has to be waged under unfavorable conditions. A genuine "curtain of silence" has been drawn over the scene by joint action of the U.S. government and Duvalierism. This means that Haiti goes unmentioned by international press agencies and by official organizations that speak so much of human rights and routinely cite neighboring socialist Cuba and revolutionary Nicaragua as countries where fundamental liberties are not respected.

STATE TERRORISM AND THE INTERNATIONAL CONTEXT

In order to understand the situation in Haiti, we must emphasize that the dictatorship of the Duvaliers has been much more violent and consolidated than that of Pinochet in Chile or the regimes which arose in Uruguay and Argentina during the 1960s. From its inception the Haitian dictatorship has been as deadly and destructive of human life as its Southern Cone counterparts with widespread use of torture, disappearances, murder, and forced exile. But its impact has been more brutal for two reasons:

1. In the Southern Cone the structure of civil society was more solidly established with a highly advanced tradition of trade union and political party organization. This tradition was reflected in civic, social, and political consciousness, and therefore the people had more domestic resources at hand to use in their resistance.
2. International solidarity with the struggles in the Southern Cone existed from the very beginning. Strong pressure by foreign governments, parties, and public opinion neutralized the excesses of repression.

In Haiti, during the bloodiest moments of the dictatorship of François "Papa Doc" Duvalier, which lasted from 1957 to 1971, international solidarity had not yet attained the level of effectiveness it would later manifest. There were few worldwide institutions struggling for human rights in Haiti, and those that did exist then could not exert the degree of pressure that they can now.

Furthermore, during the 1960s the most politically conscious forces in Latin America, Europe, and the United States were expressing solidarity with the Cuban Revolution in its gigantic struggle against imperialism. The struggle for the survival of democratic sectors in Haiti attracted little attention because of its limited strength. The international press, if it made any mention at all of "the situation in Haiti," represented the dictatorship as a rather natural product of backwardness, and identified Papa Doc and his Tontons Macoutes [members of a paramilitary group loyal to the Duvaliers whose name derived from the creole term for bogeymen who kidnap bad children — M.R.] as one more expression of voodoo and illiteracy — implicitly, merely "a black people's problem." This attitude erroneously implied that the roots of the unbridled fascism which swept this Antillean island were cultural, racial, or mystical, when in fact fascism came into being with the systematic support of U.S. counterinsurgency policy in its efforts to avoid another Cuba in the hemisphere.

In Haiti, as in Somoza's Nicaragua or Stroessner's Paraguay (and as demonstrated in the literate "model republics" of Chile, Uruguay, and Argentina), a fascist-like dictatorship actually constituted a new system which was inspired, as Duvalier himself often proudly stated, by Hitler. With instruments provided by the United States, a new formulation of the state was created. The Haitian people still suffer under this fascist-like state, which makes the attainment of democracy so complex.

We must also remember that state terrorism in Haiti is of a nature and at a level unknown in any other country in the hemisphere, with the exception of Guatemala and Paraguay. These countries have in common the fact that political prisoners generally do not face trial, but rather are summarily executed in cold blood. With regard to repression, Haiti and Guatemala share the sad honor of being the countries in which disappearance as a method reached massive proportions at the end of the 1950s, when thousands of families wept for at least one of their members who had been vaporized during the unending reign of terror. In Guatemala, however, as distinct from Haiti or Paraguay, the popular forces organized, structured a violent response to official violence, and created mechanisms for evoking international condemnation.

State terrorism in Haiti reached maximum intensity during the presidency of François Duvalier, with a systematic attempt to strike terror in the hearts of the people by the murder of entire families and the display in the streets of the bodies of opponents. The supreme expression of political terror was the paramilitary force of some 40,000 members, the Tontons Macoutes, which covered the country with a layer of blood and a "Himalaya of corpses," as described by one of Papa Doc's closest supporters. This one-way violence was institutionalized and internalized through a combination of counterinsurgency techniques taught by Washington and the full force of class violence in a country where the socioeconomic contradictions are very profound. Thus the dictatorship maximized its oppressive power.

A LONG-TERM FASCIST DICTATORSHIP

Another set of characteristics that should be mentioned is made up of the social, political, and psychological consequences of a long-term dictatorship. These effects have been noted in innumerable testimonies and studies of the Nazi occupation in European countries. But the Nazi occupation was short-lived — five years, and in Germany a few years longer. Also, it was foreign troops that liberated Germans and Italians from their nightmare. If we consider that repressive forces in the new type of dictatorship mentioned above behave unmercifully, like "fascist armies of occupation," we can understand the deep sociological implications of terrorist regimes, which over an extended period of time unite the physical power of annihilation with the ideological weapons proffered by modern means of communication.

Pinochet's dictatorship has entered its twelfth year. In Haiti and Paraguay today, as yesterday in Nicaragua, fascist violence has employed the most sophisticated instruments provided by imperialism, in conjunction with the most barbaric methods. It has been in action for some three decades, with long-lasting effects. In a recent conversation with a Paraguayan colleague about the unique situation of our two countries, we began to think about the need to organize a conference to analyze the psychosocial and sociopolitical effects of such long-term dictatorships as those suffered by our peoples.

In effect, regimes such as that of Franco in Spain, Trujillo in the Dominican Republic, or Salazar in Portugal set out to destroy all previous models of political and social organization, civic education and politicization, under a prolonged reign of terror. They clearly contribute to the ensuing inertia, depoliticization, and lack of dynamism in the political processes. The results of ideological bombardment and of twenty or thirty years of systematic brainwashing are catastrophic in terms of dissuasive power. This dissuasion is made more effective by the lack of alternative value and educational systems to counteract the state monopoly of the mass media and the ideological apparatus in general. Furthermore, the people suffer genuine solitude and isolation, given the information blockade on world events, and the ideological manipulations and institutional barriers against change and progress. These regimes also utilize international relations to their advantage, brandishing the aid received from foreign governments and organizations as proof of their legitimacy.

With the passing years, changes in demographic composition have had objective political implications for some two generations. Sixty percent or more of the population of Haiti and Paraguay has been born under a dictatorship, and therefore the majority of the population see dictatorship as a natural phenomenon. Such a phenomenon is even more useful in maintaining the status quo when the installation of fascism has not occurred after a great mass struggle marked by victories of the popular sectors, as in the case of Franco's Spain or of Chile. Popular victories would have prompted the conservation of democratic or revolutionary values at the level of social consciousness or at least of collective memory.

In Nicaragua, *Sandinismo* was a ray of light that pierced the long night of *Somocismo*. The FSLN rekindled that flame by providing popular discontent with a banner and the means to move the mountain.

In Haiti, contemporary history and especially the struggle against Duvalier is filled with heroes, sacrifices, and battles. Yet we have never known how to use these precedents as a mobilizing force, or as the basis of a sense of continuity for new generations. The heroism that is so present in our national life has not been transformed into revolutionary energy. We have been unable to create banners and symbols that would activate the people out of the historical popular struggles against repression: the epic struggle from 1916 to 1918 of Charlemagne Péralte against the U.S. Marines during the long period (1915–1934) of U.S. occupation; the popular battles of the Worker-Peasant Movement (Mouvement Ouvrier-Paysan) from 1946 to 1957; the democratic struggles against the dictatorship during the period of its consolidation (1960–1961 student strike, 1963 movements by the Haitian Association of Labor Unions [L'Union Intersyndicale d'Haïti], and mobilizations of various democratic forces); and the heroic struggle of the communists, 1966–1969, based on strict clandestinity and armed action.

These popular movements have failed to fully nurture today's struggles for several reasons — the lack of continuity, the murder of so many revolutionary leaders and cadres, objective difficulties in the development of new revolutionary cadres, the strength of censorship, the weakness of written culture in our country, the impossibility of legally writing the history of this resistance as a vehicle for the transmission of popular experiences – in short, the inability demonstrated up to now by revolutionary parties or leaders to adapt our struggle to the difficult, concrete conditions of our country.

On the other hand, during this long period of Duvalierism an important split has occurred between Haitian society and the state. After more than a quarter century, the Duvalier clan in its diverse components still controls the state apparatus. It has learned, if not the art of government, the art of repression and domination. Terror and corruption have given it the instruments of control and political authority. To this end, a two-pronged technique has been employed:

1. destroying natural or potential popular leaders through murder, repression, and exile, or coopting them through corruption and intimidation; and
2. taking control of various power mechanisms (vassalizing the army by enthroning the paramilitary Tontons Macoutes, manipulating the legislative body into a permanent masquerade, and using the Tontons Macoutes as an effective force).

To complete this picture we must add the change in the social composition of support for the regime, whose class base has been expanded to include the bourgeoisie. During the first years of his reign, Duvalier I, with his Negrist demagogy and attacks on mulattoes, alienated and even repressed certain sectors of the bourgeoisie. Duvalier II, however, enjoys the full support of this class. As a result of his presence in the palace from childhood, he became an integral part of the old oligarchy, and the bourgeoisie benefitted greatly from the "Pax Duvalier" (including prohibition of unions, extreme exploitation of workers, corruption) and eventually allied itself with the regime.

This convergence of objective interests was concretized by the marriage of the young dictator to a woman from the mulatto bourgeoisie, which has become more comfortable and more compliant under a regime that it considers its own. In the latter years, however, the tendency of the dictator's father-in-law, Ernest Bennett, to monopolize all the privileges has won him the resentment of some sectors of his own class. Today more than ever, Duvalierism is at the service of the bourgeoisie and of the centers of transnational capital, in particular the assembly shops (*maquiladoras*) installed in the country to take advantage of the cheapest labor force in the hemisphere, which is also, of course, the most exploited.

Under these conditions, the privileges enjoyed by businessmen, together with U.S. economic support, have served to strengthen the bourgeois class, linking it with financial centers in Miami and New York and with capitalists of the Dominican Republic. This dependent internationalization of the bourgeoisie greatly favors the ruling class, which has assumed responsibility for the stability and defense of the regime. It has created a center for the promotion of development in Haiti, sponsored by André Apaid, president of the Association of Haitian Industrialists, which participates in economic policy within the framework of Reagan's Caribbean Basin Plan. This alliance between the dictatorship and the bourgeoisie, under the banner of development and U.S. economic aid, constitutes yet another element in the prolongation of the dictatorship.

THE CONSEQUENCES OF U.S. SUPPORT

In the process of subjugation, the dictatorship has counted in a fundamental way on important technological elements supplied by its international masters and allies. Since 1957, the Duvalier governments have received unlimited aid from the United States in terms of military and police technology. With this support, the ruling apparat has become rather effective and now includes modern weapons, armored helicopters, machine guns, artillery, and M-16 rifles. Its police and military cadres go to specialized U.S. training centers at Ft. Bragg and in the Panama Canal Zone – even to Israel – to perfect their counterinsurgency and security techniques. The different repressive groups within the country – the army, Volunteers for National Security (paramilitary internal security forces), Tontons Macoutes, militia, Leopard Corps (elite presidential military unit for internal security and counterinsurgency), Presidential Guard, Commission of Military Investigation (popularly known as the Detective Service), and Interior Ministry police – have military equipment disproportionate to the country's need. These forces have unlimited access to financial resources as well as computerized means of communications linked up with security forces in the Dominican Republic and the FBI, so they can exercise rather effective control within the country and over emigrants.

Thus the technological gap is broadened between the power apparatus and the society, which remains archaic in the areas of production, consumption, daily life, and political mentality. Even in terms of the preparation of civilian professionals, Haitian society is at a technical and cultural level more backward, in many aspects, than twenty-eight years ago, when the Duvaliers took power. While the public school system has deteriorated due to the forced exile of thousands of teachers (engineers, doctors, and all sorts of technicians), government officials and the bourgeoisie have sent their children and protégés to be educated elsewhere. After completing their studies in Europe or the United States, many return to Haiti and place themselves at the service of the dictatorship. They join the legion of experts and officials of foreign governments and international organizations who offer their services, for extraordinarily high fees, in grandiose development projects throughout the national territory.

As demonstrated by the administrative ineptitude and failures of the regime, these influxes of "human resources" have not signified any real administrative modernization or ability to promote development. During Jean-Claude Duvalier's fourteen years in power, Haiti has received more than $1.5 billion in aid of very diverse sorts, principally from the United States. This aid has been in the form of loans and official gifts by governments and development agencies (USAID in particular), food subsidies, contributions from nongovernment organizations, financial support from the IMF and others. These millions of dollars have gone to fatten the Swiss bank accounts of the Duvalier dynasty and to pay for such extravagances as the collection of race cars and luxurious yachts bought in July 1984 with a price tag of $3.5 million.

Haiti's economic situation has never been so disastrous. The World Bank acknowledged in 1979 that 70 percent of the Haitian population lives in absolute poverty. Sixty percent of the population in Port-au-Prince, 83 percent in provincial cities, and 94 percent of the rural population eat no more than three meals per week. This is a very bleak situation after so many years of developmentalist policy, promoted by the government with the advice and guidance of USAID, the World Bank, and various "experts." The original plan included a project to transform Haiti into the "Taiwan of the Caribbean," by trampling on workers and offering all sorts of incentives and privileges to foreign capital. In fourteen years, this approach has created only 30,000 jobs. Meanwhile, 40 percent of the labor force is unemployed. Thousands of farmers have been stripped of their land and, facing death by starvation, have had to seek their way to Florida. This is one of the most dramatic demonstrations of the failure of the long regime of the Duvaliers and U.S. tutelage.

The real effect of foreign aid is linked to the creation of the Junior Tontons Macoutes and has been evident in the past few years in a refinement of terror, a use of selective repression, and a clever management of public relations and state diplomacy in order to disarm criticism in the foreign press and protest from some liberal sectors in the United States. This latter policy was evidenced when the Haitian government contracted the illustrious Alejandro Orfila as its public relations agent in the United States while he was still serving his term as general secretary of the Organization of American States.

The power to buy international representatives is considerable when a dictatorship has millions of dollars at its disposal. In April 1971, U.S. Ambassador Clinton Knox charged $1.5 million to guarantee personally the transmission of power from Papa Doc to his son. In January 1981, a State Department official arrived in Port-au-Prince to sign an agreement under which U.S. ships could operate in Haitian territorial waters to prevent boat people from reaching Florida. A high Haitian government official offered him $250,000 if the United States, in a "gesture of reciprocity," would intercept opponents linked to Bernard Sansaricq who were carrying out armed actions against the regime from Florida. This type of maneuver is old hat to Roger Lafontant, currently [in 1985] minister of the Interior. In 1960, while a medical student, he became an agent of the regime and betrayed the student strike. Today, after serving as consul in New York and Montreal and climbing all sorts of repressive staircases to power, he is the official who wields the real power.

The most consistent factor in the development of this complex situation has been Washington's support for the dictatorship. It should be remembered that this aid began in the context of the Cuban Revolution and as part of the implementation of U.S. counterinsurgency policies in the Caribbean and Latin America. Also in that context, the popular uprising against Trujillo took place in the Dominican Republic, which brought an end to the thirty-year dictatorship and began a slow process of democratization in that country, culminating in the popular insurrection of April 1965 and the subsequent intervention by 25,000 U.S. troops in Santo Domingo.

The Haitian dictatorship was consolidated over two decades, and challenges to it have not been strong enough to constitute a threat. It has enjoyed the unlimited support of U.S. administrations from Eisenhower to Reagan. There were some reservations during the Kennedy and Carter administrations, but they brought no significant change in Washington's policy. This relationship has had its moments of glory, as in April 1969, when Governor Nelson Rockefeller visited Papa Doc and embraced him in continental, democratic brotherhood. And in 1971, Ambassador Clinton Knox became the artisan of the smooth transmission of power from François to Jean-Claude Duvalier by requesting the presence of U.S. warships along Haiti's coasts (to prevent any action by exiles) and by later spreading the myth that the regime had been democratized in the passage from one Duvalier to another.

U.S. policy is always validated by the subterfuge of the communist threat. During the 1960 student general strike, François Duvalier accused Archbishop Msgr. François Poirier, who was French, of providing funds to communist students attempting to overthrow his government and expelled him. This was at the time of a general strike by the students. Shortly afterward, Msgr. Remy Augustin, the first Haitian-born bishop, was removed from the country under similar charges. Ever since, the communist threat has become the supreme argument to justify, in Washington's eyes, a systematic trampling on human rights. In November 1984 Roger Lafontant announced "a communist plot to assassinate Jean-Claude Duvalier." On this occasion the victims were agronomy students from the Institute of Agricultural Technology, which promotes cooperative development in the farmlands, and members of a patriotic movement which had called on the people to observe a national day of protest, as had been done in Chile against the Pinochet dictatorship.

And so the ruse of a communist threat allows the government to destroy any opposition. Under an infamous decree of April 1969, capital punishment is authorized for "any communist, communist sympathizer, or person suspected of maintaining any relationship with communist elements."

THE STRUGGLE OF THE PEOPLE

The struggle of the Haitian people to free themselves from the dictatorship has not ceased during these years and has taken on various forms, from the early antidictatorial movements organized by sectors representing a broad range of politics to attempted military actions and landings by exiles, the armed struggle of the left at the end of the 1960s, and the struggles of the democratic journalists at the end of the 1970s. The battle continues today, promoted by diverse groups of Christian, socialist, communist, or simply democratic inspiration. The difficulty of the struggle must be emphasized, because only through a clear awareness of it can a path be opened, as in Nicaragua, to overcome a regime so strongly supported by U.S. imperialism.

From 1957 to 1976 any expression of resistance, dissidence, or opposition to Duvalierism constituted a direct confrontation. The prison at Fort Dimanche, the death house, was the government's sole response to any citizen who dared defy or merely criticize any official, even as an individual. The dictatorship allowed no legal space for any other independent institutions or sectors of the population.

With the advent of Carter's human rights policy, the State Department put timid pressures on the Haitian government and even conditioned certain aspects of U.S. aid upon that government's respect for human rights. This was in fact a two-faced policy, since the Carter administration never cut off aid to the dictatorship, even with full knowledge that Duvalierism implied the negation of all the rights of the people.

In any event, because it was totally in the pay of the United States, the dictatorship tried, at the beginning, to appear sensitive to such pressures. Prodemocratic sectors attempted to take advantage of this apparent discord between master and lackey, and social and political contradictions began to surface. An independent press emerged (*Le Petit Samedi Soir*, "Radio Haiti-Inter," "Radio Metropole") as a voice for demands which had been silenced for two decades; it initiated a valiant attempt at denunciation and consciousness raising. With great reserve at the beginning, the democratic clamor began little by little to extend to include the popular sectors and the petite bourgeoisie. Under the banner of human rights, workers began to raise their demands against the cynical exploitation that victimized them. The Human Rights League was organized and two parties emerged, the Social Christian and Christian Democratic.

As soon as these efforts seemed to crystallize organizationally, the government signaled very clearly its decision to constrict the movement. On November 14, 1979, a meeting called by the Human Rights League and its president, Prof. Gérard Gourgue, was broken up amid gunfire and clubbings by the Tontons Macoutes. Even a senior official from the U.S. Embassy and diplomats from Canada and France attending the meeting were beaten, which resulted in pro forma protests by their governments.

The events of November 14 put human rights fighters on notice that the regime, knowing itself to be well backed, was unwilling to accept any criticism or recognize any rights, much less to yield space to the opposition. This situation was confirmed a few days after Reagan's victory when, on November 28, 1980, the government exiled all the visible leaders of the emerging democratic move-ment – a dozen public figures including journalists, trade unionists, and such political leaders as Jean Dominique, Director of Radio Haiti-Inter, Grégoire Eugène, leader and founder of the Social Christian Party, and Jean-Jacques Honorat, well-known economist, all of whom ended up in the United States or Venezuela.

Meanwhile, economic aid continued to pour in from the Western powers, especially from the United States. Between 1980 and 1984, the United States provided more than $500 million in various forms of aid (direct investments, gifts, loans, subsidies). This did nothing at all to reduce the level of misery and hunger that, along with unlimited political oppression, caused the greatest exodus ever of Haitians and the phenomenon of the boat people.

Official Haitian government policy legally prohibited public activities by any other political grouping. After three and a half years of negotiations with the government, Grégoire Eugène, exiled leader of the Social Christian Party, was able to return to his country in February 1984 through the support of some sectors of the U.S. Congress, particularly the Black Caucus. He sought to carry out a political struggle within the legal framework imposed by the regime. He was followed and arrested, and the office and presses of his newspaper, *Fraternité*, were destroyed. Likewise Sylvio Claude, founder of the Christian Democratic Party and a symbol of domestic resistance, has been systematically persecuted, and it is a miracle that he is still alive. This figure, a small businessman in a local marketplace who was unknown until a few years ago, has affirmed his stand and has gained international attention by defying the dictatorship almost alone, with truly admirable consisten-cy and courage. Arrested, tortured, persecuted along with his family, he continues to support the opposition from underground, often at the risk of his life.

The Catholic religious sector, in the name of human dignity, has maintained a strong resistance to totalitarianism. However, it has been restricted in this good effort by intimidating pressure from the government and by the conduct of the Church hierarchy and the Vatican. Pope John Paul II visited Haiti in March 1983 and gave his support to Msgr. François Wolf Ligondé, archbishop of Port-au-Prince and a known accomplice of the regime. Social action and protest by progressive elements of the clergy have therefore been limited. Nevertheless, pressure from the base, for example from priests and from the Conference of the Religious, continued to manifest itself, with increasingly strong positions taken in favor of human rights. This led the Episcopal Con-ference, under the direction of Msgr. François Gayot, bishop of Cap Haitien, to join the struggle for human rights.

The socialist movement, which can be found in grassroots organizations and intellectual sectors, cannot operate legally due to the anticommunist fury of the government. The Unified Communist Party carries out a rigorously clandestine, systematic program. This organization was the only organized force within the country during the early 1960s and carried considerable political weight. It was severely beaten down by the 1965 repression, at the end of which some 400 leaders, cadres, and members had been massacred. Ex-Maoist sectors grouped in the IFOPADA (from the Creole for Union of Patriotic and Democratic Forces) are attempting to gain ground in the petite bourgeoisie under the banner of Social Democracy.

Those democratic sectors born between 1976 and 1980 that survived have been systematically persecuted. The Human Rights League cannot function because of the constant intimidation to which its members are subjected. Independent cultural activity has been silenced. In the last months of 1984 renewed repression against domestic resistance struck at popular and intellectual sectors. Poet-filmmaker Rassoul Labuchin and his wife, Michaele Lafontant, were exiled from the country. Poet and writer Michel Soukar, as well as Victor Benoit, director of a secondary school, had to seek asylum in foreign embassies. Engineer Jean Paul Duperval, agronomist Fred Joseph, and dozens of other patriots are still incarcerated, tortured, and held incommunicado. The reelection of Reagan in 1984 guaranteed that the government would have renewed support.

For twenty-eight years the Duvalier dynasty has wielded a violent monopoly on power and shown total disregard for the law, the constitution, elections, and human rights. At this point in its long reign, it offers a net balance of failures that no other government in the world has to show, that no other nation in the world has had to experience so dramatically, and that no people can endure eternally. The forces of oppression keep tightening the screws, but social, economic, and political contradictions are mounting. The middle sectors, the city and farm workers, the mass of unemployed and underemployed – in a word, the majorities – are so discontented and have had to muffle so many legitimate demands that even a small spark will ignite the explosive force of their anger.

In May and June 1984 this quiet resistance suddenly and almost spontaneously exploded in Gonaives, Cap Haitien, and a dozen other cities and towns, when multitudes took to the streets to repudiate the dictatorship. These and many other incidents of resistance and popular struggle – the assimilated errors and experiences of so many years, the recapturing of a sense of history that has not been excised from the collective, popular memory, the sacrifices and conscious efforts of many women and men – these lessons in resistance are weaving and forging the organization of the people for their own liberation.

Only a great popular revolution along the lines of a war for national independence can free the land of Haiti from the many sufferings and humiliations that we have endured during this long and infamous period. Only a great popular revolution can resolve the immense problems of underdevelopment and bring about progress for Haitian society.

EDITORS' POSTSCRIPT

Gérard Pierre-Charles's chapter, presented here, was written in 1985, prior to the wave of massive popular mobilizations in Haiti leading to the fall of the

Duvalier dictatorship in February 1986. Since that time, the struggle in Haiti has entered a new phase, dominated by the daily contradictions of the struggle between two competing conceptions and realities of democracy—that of the Haitian people versus that of the Reagan administration.

What emerges from observation of subsequent developments in Haiti, and from a reading of the more recent writings of Pierre-Charles, is the complexity of the present situation in that country. On the one hand, the United States and its Haitian allies are doing their utmost to keep the situation in that country "under control"; indeed, in some respects, this was the U.S. objective in facilitating the ouster and instituting a "controlled transition," once the handwriting was on the wall. The United States hoped in this case to take action "in time"—that is, to avoid repeating the error made in Nicaragua in 1978–1979 of supporting Somoza until the very last minute, by which time the Sandinistas were dominant among the anti-Somoza forces. On the other hand, the impetus for this democratic uprising came not from "the top down," nor from abroad, but from the very heart of the Haitian people. In this regard, we are seeing something genuinely new in Haiti.

Among the new elements of democracy which must be understood in regard to Haiti are the following, as summarized by Gérard Pierre-Charles in a March 1986 essay, "A Difficult Road: The Construction of Democracy in Haiti":

1. The advances of the collective consciousness with regard to the repudiation of torture and the disappearance of fascism and its terrorizing attributes, and in terms of the priority given to human rights;

2. the posing of a new debate with regard to democracy, its real content versus its formal presentation, its necessary characteristics of participation and pluralism, and the importance of the effective exercise of popular sovereignty;

3. the recognition of the intimate relation between democracy and sovereignty, which brings governments arising out of these processes to take a stance of disobedience toward the imperial center of financial and political power.

Based on these considerations, in the face of the situation which has arisen in Haiti, a number of questions arise: What are the roots of the popular movement which, in a surprisingly short time, broke up so brutal and compact a dictatorship, and which also enjoyed U.S. support? What have been and are the motor forces of this democratic revolution? What are the objectives and the possibilities of success of a popular movement so broad, in a nation marked by the mortgage of so many years of oppression, and whose evolution is conditioned by geopolitical factors so obvious, now that the Reagan administration, more than ever before in U.S. policy, is calling into question the right of peoples to self-determination?

Concretely, among the issues which emerge from a reading of the international press, as well as of Pierre-Charles's writings on Haiti, are the following:

— The extent to which the army will be forced to share power with the opposition political forces (parties, church, etc.) and the extent to which these forces will be transformed by the new situation;

— The ability of popular opposition forces to maintain pressure to oust Duvalierista forces remaining in power;

— The degree of pluralism and participation which, in the space opened up by the ouster of Duvalier, will challenge the "controlled" democracy;

— The level of real development, structural change, and challenge to continuing domination by the oligarchy—a domination which is maintaining the same level of misery that has always plagued the Haitian people, and which today is compounded by a growing foreign debt and restrictions imposed by the IMF;

— The question of national and popular sovereignty versus open control by the United States through programs of U.S. aid, including extensive police and military aid and training.

In short, the dialectic between a popular, even potentially revolutionary, democracy and a new version of U.S.-imposed and controlled "redemocratization" is likely to characterize the Haitian scene in the coming years. In his March 1986 essay, Pierre-Charles sees the potential for radical change emerging from the present uncertain situation:

In Haiti we are seeing a process of change with a popular and democratic content which could be channeled toward a true revolution in the measure to which the revolutionary sectors play a leading role. All this within the framework of a situation in which the peoples of the Caribbean and Central America have erupted onto the international scene, in which the correlation of forces at the Latin American level is influenced by the presence of governments and political forces dedicated to the increasing exercise of sovereignty in a world context—leading to a situation in which the progressive forces are broadening their perspectives, in spite of the aggressivity of empire.

Translation by Maria Roof, Allegheny College.

10

ECONOMIC CRISIS AND DEPENDENCY: THE CASE OF THE DOMINICAN REPUBLIC

José A. Moreno

The purpose of this chapter is to present considerations and reflections that might help in analyzing how the present world economic crisis affects small developing countries, especially the countries of the Caribbean region. The basic hypothesis underlying this chapter is taken from an analogy between the poor under-developed countries and the poor or marginal classes of the industrialized countries. Just as in the industrialized countries the present economic crisis has taken a social and economic toll principally among the less privileged classes, so have the poor, small countries in the world economic system been more harshly affected by the consequences of the international crisis.[1] Furthermore, since the poorer and smaller countries are affected more profoundly by the economic crisis, and also lack adequate means of recovery, the crisis will be more lasting there, and will hinder the development process for a longer period.

The empirical basis of this research is supported by recent studies (on the Caribbean countries) undertaken by the U.N. Economic Commission on Latin America (CEPAL).[2] I will use the case of the Dominican Republic as an illustration of the different aspects of the crisis that I wish to analyze. I am not attempting to generalize my analysis to other countries of the Caribbean since, given the great diversity of political and economic systems, such a broader scope would require a more systematic study than the present effort.[3]

POVERTY OF NATURAL RESOURCES

The islands of the Caribbean (excluding Trinidad and Tobago), although fertile for tropical agriculture, are generally poor in natural resources. The existence of bauxite and nickel on some of the islands or the recent discovery of gold in the Dominican Republic do not radically change the general scarcity of natural resources. Furthermore, the fact that the majority of the islands are small means that their physical geography and climate are homogeneous, thus limiting diversified agricultural production and hindering self-sufficiency. The result is that almost all the islands produce the same agricultural products. This forces them to compete among themselves for nontropical markets for their crops and to depend on those external markets for agricultural or manufactured goods that they do not produce.[4]

To the poverty of natural resources one must add social poverty and poverty of human resources, historically created and maintained by internal and external political and economic forces which imposed slavery, colonialism, imperialism, and dependency. It would not be hazardous to maintain that throughout the region's history such systems of exploitation have affected the levels of education, health, survival, and mortality there.

In contrast to the poverty of natural resources, above all of minerals and hydrocarbons, one must counterpose the richness of the soil, which favored the cultivation of certain products that were in great demand in the metropolitan centers during the colonial period. That demand in the colonial and industrial centers induced and structured the development of a dependent export economy in the Caribbean. From the beginning of the seventeenth century, the Caribbean islands produced not the goods needed by the indigenous inhabitants, but those needed in Spain, France, and England.

CLASSICAL DEPENDENCY: YESTERDAY AND TODAY

The theory of dependency maintains that dependency exists when there are asymmetrical relations between two countries: one country holds a dominant position in respect to the other that permits it to expand and maintain its development, while the dependent country can develop only as a consequence or reflection of the expansion of the dominant country.[5] In other words, relations between the two countries are unequal. In general, one can note three principal consequences of dependency. First, the dependent country does not have control of its own development since it is dependent on economic and political factors that are determined in the industrialized countries. Second, dependency produces long-term decapitalization of the dependent country, which explains its incapacity to generate its own sustained development. Third, the benefits of dependent development accrue to a privileged group in the dependent country. This impedes the distribution of beneficial income to broad sectors of the population, which could otherwise contribute to the expansion of demand in the internal market and support continued development of economic and social productivity.[6]

If we apply the classical dependency theory to the system of production in the Caribbean countries, it can be amply confirmed that the commercial relations existing between those countries and the industrial centers of Europe and North America are asymmetrical, that is, they are clearly unequal and unfavorable for the small Caribbean countries. The economy of each of the Caribbean countries is dominated by the production of one or two goods, generally agricultural, which are produced at very low cost (using cheap manual labor) and also exported at a low price (in order to be able to compete with other exporters) to one or two industrial centers. At the same time, manufactured goods are imported from those centers at higher prices. The deficit in the commercial balance of goods and services has been traditionally used as an indicator of the disadvantageous and asymmetrical relations that exist for the developing countries.

It must be noted that the asymmetry of relations is caused not only by the deficit or surplus in the balance of trade but also by the forces that generate the exchange and by the factors that determine the process. It is the demand in the industrial centers that determines what must be produced by the dependent country, and in what quantity. Continued demand for certain products has historically created the structural conditioning of the dependent economies to such a degree that a short-term, quasi-irreversible economic process has been created in the dependent country. The structural dependence of the Cuban economy on sugar can be cited as an example. During the 1960s, Cuba made an effort to free its economy from an exaggerated dependence on the export of sugar and tried to diversify agricultural and manufacturing production. Partly for external reasons related to the U.S. blockade and partly for internal structural reasons, the attempt at accelerated industrialization failed, and Cuba continued to depend on sugar production. In 1976, sugar represented the same percentage of Cuba's total exports (88 percent) as it had represented in 1951.[7]

There are other problems inherent in the economic dependence of a country on one or two products. In the first place, the economy of such a country is extremely vulnerable to factors outside its control. These include climatic factors (hurricanes, droughts, blights) as well as internal politics and international economics (such as domestic strikes, fluctuations of the world market, external blockades). One need only cite the example of the fluctuation in the price of sugar on the world market, which climbed from 3.68¢ a pound in 1970 to 29.66¢ in 1974, only to fall to 8.38¢ in 1982 and down to 5.0¢ in 1984.

Such fluctuations are not limited to agricultural products. Recently, in the Dominican Republic, the production of ferrous nickel had to be halted for six months and the production of bauxite halted until 1986 because, according to Alcoa, the production costs of bauxite in the Dominican Republic make it noncompetitive in the world market.[8] The decision to suspend or resume bauxite and ferrous nickel production was made by Alcoa and Falconbridge without consulting the Dominican government and without taking into account the effects such a decision could have on the economy, which greatly depends on those exports.

Since the beginning of the 1970s, the majority of the Latin American countries have experienced a deficit in their trade balance. In the 1980s, partly because of increase in exports by some countries and partly because of restrictive import policies implemented by various countries, there has been a movement toward recovery in the balance of trade for the larger and richer countries, above all for those exporting hydrocarbons. These export surpluses brought the trade balance for the entire region from a deficit of $694 million in 1980 to a surplus of $3,470 million in 1981, and to $6,575 million in 1982. We must add that this favorable increase in the balance of trade in no way affected the poor and small Caribbean countries, which continue to experience a deficit in their trade balance.

Another indicator of the degree of dependency of the Caribbean countries is the percentage of the gross national product represented by exports and imports. Whereas for Latin America as a whole exports represent less than 15 percent of the total GNP and imports oscillate between 18 percent and 20 percent of the GNP, in the Caribbean countries exports represent between 27.7 percent (Dominican Republic) and 78.4 percent (Bahamas) of the GNP, and imports represent 33 percent and 82 percent, respectively. These differences suggest to us that there are different levels of dependency even among the underdeveloped countries. In 1982, the exports of Brazil and Argentina represented 7 percent and 13 percent of their respective GNPs; exports of goods and services that same year represented 48.2 percent of the GNP of Jamaica and 59.1 percent of the GNP of Barbados. This means that variations in foreign trade, although important, are much less significant for the economies of the big countries than for those of the small countries. For in the large countries, economic activity is principally oriented toward the satisfaction of domestic demand, while economic activity in the small countries is ultimately conditioned by external demand.

Latin America drastically reduced its imports from $98 billion in 1981 to $56 billion in 1983, that is, by 20 percent in 1982 and an additional 29 percent in 1983.[9] This decline was principally due to the drastic reduction of imports by the oil-exporting countries, the countries of the Southern Cone, and Brazil. During the same period the Caribbean countries experienced a very moderate reduction in imports, which, in the majority of those countries, still constitute more than 50 percent of their respective GNPs. Various reasons for this seemingly counterproductive phenomenon have been suggested to explain why the poor and small countries continue importing goods and services in quantities and values out of proportion to their present economic possibilities.

First of all, it has been shown that the main economic activities of those countries, such as the production of sugar, tobacco, and bauxite, are not functionally integrated with the rest of the production process. Moreover, a disproportionate percentage of available natural, human, and technological resources is committed to these activities, impeding the use of those resources in other production that would be more functional in relation to the rest of the economy. On the other hand, domestic demand in those countries is so limited that it imposes serious restrictions on the production of many consumer goods, including food products, clothes, and construction materials. Many of those consumer goods cannot be produced in the country because of the lack of natural resources or conditions (raw materials, beneficial climate), or of the capital necessary to produce them, or of the necessary technology. In other cases, the manufacture of a product has become so costly that it is not economical despite protectionist policies.

If we study the composition of imported goods in the Dominican Republic, it can be seen that in 1970 49.1 percent of imports were consumer goods, including food, and 17.3 percent represented capital goods. The remaining 33.6 percent were what are called intermediate goods, which include combustibles, fuels, and other raw materials used in agriculture and manufacturing. In the 1970s, during the second administration of Joaquín Balaguer (1970–74), the Dominican government implemented a domestic development program with an aggressive policy of import substitution. All kinds of economic incentives were offered to multinational firms so that they would invest in the country.[10] The government negotiated all types of loans, which were partly used to defray government expenses and partly used for sumptuous construction, mostly in the capital. When Balaguer took power in 1966, the foreign debt of the country was approaching a little more than $100 million. By the end of his third term (1978) the external debt was over $1.3 billion.[11]

The protectionist policy of the Dominican government succeeded in reducing the import of consumer goods: by 1980 those goods represented only 22.6 percent of all imports. The import of capital goods was also reduced in this period, from 17.3 percent to 16.1 percent of total imports, while so-called intermediate goods jumped from 33.6 percent of total imports in 1970 to 61.3 percent in 1980. One must note, however, that in this period the value of imported hydrocarbons rose from 6.7 percent to 30 percent of total imports. The negative trade balance of the country doubled between 1978 ($322 million) and 1980 ($673 million) despite the fact that consumer goods represented only 22 percent, and capital goods only 16.1 percent, of the total of $1,514 million in imports.[12] Intermediate goods, excluding hydrocarbons, represented the remaining 31.3 percent. Those intermediate goods and raw materials were utilized in the import substitution program.

The model of domestic development based on import substitution has been used with varying results by various Latin American countries since the 1940s and 1950s. The late application of this model to small countries generates problems different from those experienced by Argentina and Brazil in the 1950s. While large countries such as Mexico and Argentina were able to implement this model using their own natural resources and their domestic markets, countries like Jamaica and the Dominican Republic have to import raw materials or intermediate products for their manufacturing, and soon saturate the domestic market with products that are not very competitive with foreign imports from Mexico or Puerto Rico.

It is possible that in the Dominican Republic import substitution has produced benefits for the country, although the distribution of those benefits has been very unequal. In the first place some new jobs have been created, but their number has been clearly insufficient to absorb more than a small fraction of the unemployed (estimated at 24 percent) or underemployed (estimated at an additional 30 percent) work force.[13] This is due to the fact that some of the substitution industries which have been introduced are capital-intensive. Other industries, principally of an assembly nature, like many industries in the so-called free zones, are labor-intensive but pay minimum wages varying between $2.00 and $3.50 per day. On the other hand, the Balaguer government implemented a two-pronged policy of price decontrol in the market and wage freezing for workers in an effort to encourage national and foreign investment. According to Law 91, in force from 1974 to 1978, the established minimum wages were 95 pesos (officially equal to $95 US) a month in the capital, 85 in the interior, 75 in the free zones and from 2.50 a day in agriculture.[14]

This dual policy of incentives for capital and austerity for labor generally favored foreign investors, as well as the emerging Dominican national bourgeoisie. President Balaguer recognized this fact when he presented the balance sheet of his government's economic policy on February 27, 1975:

If we focus specifically on the public sector, it must be taken into account that today we probably have more than a hundred millionaires who have justly earned their fortunes as a result of the development achieved by the Dominican economy in recent years. At least fifty contractors, principally engineers and builders, have signed contracts with the state for projects of up to several million pesos, some of them up to ten, fifteen and up to fifty million. . . .This group of new wealthy people is steadily increasing. . . .Industry and commerce have expanded extraordinarily and a sizable group from the entrepreneurial sector has become rich overnight.

An immediate consequence of the high concentration of income in the hands of the new entrepreneurial and commercial class is that a large sector of the productive population continues to be practically marginalized from the consumer market.[15] When this domestic market for substitution industries did not expand, it soon reached the saturation point; the domestic demand for its products was depleted. Nor could the producer compete in the international market, because the limited volume of his productivity increased the price of his product. On the other hand, since the substitution industry in the Dominican Republic uses imported raw materials, every increase in the cost of foreign exchange, decrease in the value or volume of exports, or increase in the price of imports has a negative effect on industry's capacity to increase or even sustain a profitable productivity.

Thus, the aggregate value of manufacturing production almost quadrupled between 1960 and 1979, but stagnated or grew very slowly after 1980. The manufacturing industry is concentrated principally in consumer goods (85 percent), with only 15 percent in the production of intermediate and capital goods such as construction materials and equipment. Among consumer goods, food, drink, and tobacco represent 57 percent of total production. If foodstuffs are excluded, the percentage of raw materials imported by the Dominican manufacturing industry rises to 60 percent of the total utilized. But it must be stressed that external dependency in the substitution process is even greater if one takes into account that the totality of goods used in the process includes machinery, electrical energy, fuels, lubricants, and imported containers.

Furthermore, the fact that the manufacturing industry uses very few intermediate goods produced in the country (such as leather, textiles, glass, rubber) reveals the limited interrelationship of the domestic productive sectors. The country produces raw materials for export, but imports other raw materials for its manufacturing. The world-market value of exported raw materials (which is not controlled by the exporting country, but by the importer) will determine the volume of imported raw materials (the value of which is not controlled by the importing country, but by the exporter). In other words, the industrialized countries establish both the price of their imports from dependent countries and their exports to them. Thus, the model of import substitution which was presented in the 1950s as a solution to the problem of traditional dependency (the problem of unequal exchange between raw materials and manufactured products) is now recognized as a new type of dependency.

As early as 1981, a Dominican economist believed that an economic policy based on the import substitution model had exhausted its possibilities and had become a heavy burden for the country, since it did not generate, but rather consumed, foreign exchange, and had to be subsidized by the government.[16] As a burden to the economy, substitution industries have to compete with traditional agroindustrial exports, which have been the primary source of government revenue, for privileges and favors from the government. Therefore, since 1980 the Dominican government has reduced the subsidies and privileges that it had previously offered to substitution industries.

Moreover, we can see a change of policy which puts emphasis on externally oriented development, through the export agroindustry, rather than internally oriented development. In its 1984 bulletin on the Dominican Republic, CEPAL already underlined this change in development policy: "In 1983, emphasis was placed on a policy of incentives for the export of nontraditional products, especially those of agroindustrial origin. This policy grants exemption from duties and taxes to temporary imports, and total or partial freedom from the obligation to surrender to the central bank foreign exchange generated by exports."[17] According to the same document, in 1983 the obligation to hand over foreign exchange earnings to the central bank ceased to apply to some eighty-six nonprocessed agricultural products.

These considerations seem to suggest that dependency based on import substitution is no longer viable in the Dominican Republic, and that there is a new tendency toward reversion to traditional dependency based on an unequal exchange of raw materials and semiprocessed products for manufactured goods – but with a greater diversification of agroindustrial export products produced in the dependent country.

THE NEW DEPENDENCY: PRESENT AND FUTURE

In this section I would like to make some comments on the new modalities of dependency which have sometimes emerged in support of, and sometimes as a consequence or complement of, traditional dependency. I do not intend to discuss all of them, nor all aspects of each of the new forms; I only wish to analyze some of the modalities that particularly affect the countries of the Caribbean. These new forms of dependency need to be studied in the context of traditional dependency, which they do not replace but rather complement. It is possible, above all, that one of these new modalities will be the most strategic component of asymmetrical relations in the future, and that traditional dependency based on the export of raw materials will move to second place. It is also possible that some of these new modalities of dependency, just like import substitution, will be exhausted, and traditional dependency based on exports will again become the key factor in the asymmetrical relations.

Dependent Tourism

At the beginning of this chapter I emphasized that the Caribbean countries are poor in natural resources. It must be added that these countries possess climatic and ecological characteristics that make them potentially very rich in tourist resources, which are highly valued by the inhabitants of the Northern zones. It is also worth noting that some of those resources have an inexhaustible capacity and durability, if the ecology is not upset. It is my opinion that these are the most valuable resources of the Caribbean countries and that their development and exploitation should be considered a priority in the economic development of those countries.

Until 1960 Cuba was the most important tourist center of the Caribbean. Cuban tourism was a typical example of dependent tourism. Transportation, hotels, casinos, and other tourist attractions were controlled by North American companies.[18] The flow of tourism brought the international mafia, gambling, and drugs to Cuba, and prostitution had become widespread.[19] It is not strange that, with the triumph of the revolution of 1959, a series of laws was passed which drastically restricted the tourist trade between Cuba and the United States. When Cuba closed its doors to North American tourism, the tourist traffic rapidly shifted toward other centers of the Caribbean, primarily Puerto Rico, Jamaica, and the Bahamas. By the middle of the 1970s the Caribbean countries had an influx of foreign exchange through tourism greater than that of all the countries of South and Central America, with the exception of Mexico.

Tourism is basically a service industry and should leave a positive balance in the recipient country. The tourist pays an elevated price for transportation, accommodations, food, and recreational services while enjoying the sun, and beaches, and other amenities. With a basic infrastructure of hotels, highways, transportation, and beaches, the services required by the tourist are relatively low-cost, so the visit of the tourist is highly profitable for the recipient country. In places like Puerto Rico, Jamaica, and the Bahamas, where adequate tourist infrastructures were constructed during the 1960s, tourism developed as one of the principal economic activities. In other Caribbean countries like the Dominican Republic, Trinidad and Tobago, and Haiti, development of the tourist industry has been much slower.[20]

Still, the tourist industry that has developed in the Caribbean is a dependent industry, since most of the air and sea transportation facilities and the great majority of the tourist hotels belong to foreign companies. Moreover, much of the food consumed in those hotels consists of imported products which have been purchased with foreign exchange obtained by national exports. As in the case of the free zones, the governments have granted all kinds of fiscal and import privileges to the hotel enterprises in order to encourage tourist investment.

It is true that the tourist industry supplies work in the service sector and, in general, has a positive effect on other branches of the economy (such as transportation, hotel and food services, handicrafts). However, the majority of workers employed in this branch of service work are unskilled and generally earn minimal salaries in kitchen, cleaning, and laundry jobs.

As happens with traditional dependence on exports, whereby the dependent country generally exports or imports the majority of its products to or from a single other country, dependent tourism becomes increasingly vulnerable when the great majority of tourists come from a single industrialized country, since all economic changes in the industrial country (such as recessions and depressions) will be reflected in the flow and extent of tourist expenditure. It is well known that in times of economic recession the first expenditures to be limited are those directed toward recreational activity. This has been the case with the recent economic recession in the industrialized countries, which has affected the flow of tourists to almost all of the countries of the Caribbean.[21]

The development of tourism in the Dominican Republic offers a typical example of what I have called "dependent tourism." Until 1965 there was hardly any tourism in the country since an adequate infrastructure did not exist. The government of Balaguer gave priority to the development of this industry, and public and private funds were invested to create the material infrastructure. So-called tourist zones were created, and the government granted all kinds of fiscal incentives and tax relief and forgiveness to both national and foreign investors for the development of these zones. Hotel capacity grew, and air services and internal communications were improved.[22]

Statistics submitted by the Inter-American Development Bank (IADB) indicate that until 1977 the monetary benefits of tourism in the Dominican Republic were very modest in comparison to the earnings from tourism in Jamaica, Barbados, and Panama. Moreover, the Dominican Republic presents a very peculiar case: up to 1980 it was the only Caribbean country in which nationals consistently spent more on trips abroad than the country received from tourism. Only large, rich countries like Venezuela and Brazil or countries with little tourist potential like El Salvador and Bolivia had the same kind of negative balance. In the case of the Dominican Republic, it is only in the 1980s that expenditure by foreign tourists has come to exceed expenditure by Dominicans abroad. This was due, in part, to the economic recovery in the United States, the source of 75 percent of the tourism in the Dominican Republic, which permitted an increase in the number of tourists and their expenditures.

But the principal factors in the change were severe government restrictions on the exchange of foreign currency and the rise of the dollar with respect to the peso on the parallel market, which drastically limited Dominicans' ability to travel abroad.[23] Expenditures by Dominicans traveling abroad were reduced from $166 million in 1980 to $87 million in 1982, to only $77 million in 1983, while expenditures by foreign tourists climbed from $173 million in 1980 to $326 million in 1983.[24] It should be noted that in 1983 the influx of foreign exchange by way of tourism was far greater ($326 million) than the influx from sales of raw sugar ($263 million) and that the tourism-based influx nearly equalled the revenue from all nontraditional exports of gold, silver, ferrous nickel, and other products ($332 million).

These figures allow us to suggest that by 1983 the tourist industry already represented a very important factor in the Dominican economy, one that could replace sugar as the country's most important export. However, we are not able to determine what percentage of tourism-based earnings directly benefits the country and what percentage is repatriated by foreign companies which totally own or hold majority interests in transportation facilities, hotels, or travel agencies. As I indicated above, tourism can represent the most productive natural resource and service network for the economies of the Caribbean. On the other hand, if the benefits of tourism are mostly repatriated by foreign companies while the costs of the material infrastructure are borne by the country, it would be appropriate to claim that tourism is already a new form of dependency.

Migratory Dependency

In the countries of the Caribbean, where the number of unemployed can oscillate between 24 percent and 40 percent of the work force according to the country and time of year, it is not strange to encounter high rates of internal migration and emigration abroad also. The landless peasants migrate from the countryside to the villages and cities, and the urban unemployed emigrate to the industrialized countries of Europe and North America. The migrants from the countryside and villages constantly increase the percentage of unemployed in the cities and form a reserve of cheap manual labor ready to work for minimum wages in the periphery as well as in the industrial centers.[25]

The new modality of dependency which I have called migratory is an adaptation of traditional dependency based on the export of raw materials: it does not export products per se, but rather cheap labor.[26] I would like to mention three illustrations of "migratory dependency" in the Dominican Republic.

The first illustration focuses on the so-called free zones created by the Balaguer government to attract foreign capital. The free zones exist in various parts of the country and are dedicated to light industry, primarily the assembly of simple equipment, the manufacture of clothes and footwear, and the packaging of certain products like cosmetics and toys. This type of industry imports semifinished products, finishes or assembles them in the country, and exports them to the world's industrial centers. The technical or skill level needed to assemble these products is minimal, and therefore the labor utilized is compensated with minimum wages. As stated above, Law 91 of 1974 set the minimum salary in the free zones at $75.00 per month, that is, approximately $3.50 per day for eight hours of work.[27] Moreover, foreign enterprises in the free zones leave very few benefits for the country since they receive all kinds of incentives in terms of tax relief. One of the few benefits for the country is that these enterprises employ a number of people who would otherwise be unemployed. When the products of these firms are re-exported to the industrialized countries, the only thing that has been added to them is the surplus value of cheap manual labor at minimal cost to the producer.

The second illustration of migratory dependency is the massive migration of workers from the Caribbean to Europe and the United States. The number of immigrants from the Caribbean to the United States in the last twenty years may already exceed 5 million.[28] The majority of these immigrants (many of them illegal) are swelling a reserve of cheap manual labor; they compete among themselves and with other minorities (in the host countries) for less desirable, worst-paid jobs — jobs which other, more established groups in the social system refuse to accept, preferring to take refuge in welfare benefits offered by the state.[29] This new migratory labor force (legal or illegal) undermines the bargaining power and capacity of the established labor force to demand better wages.

In spite of the development of technology, there are still jobs in the industrialized countries that no one wants to take because they are unpleasant, of a low status, and poorly paid. In general, these jobs offer little security and do not include additional benefits or protection by labor unions; many of them fall outside the system of pensions and social security. These are the jobs which the immigrants of the Caribbean — above all the illegal ones who find themselves under the constant threat of deportation, forcing them to accept wages and working conditions very inferior to those prescribed by law — are recruited to fill.

As in all situations of dependency, there is an asymmetrical power relation-ship here between the class that imports migratory labor and the immigrant reserve which offers its imported work at a price and under working conditions determined by the importer. What the immigrant worker offers is not a product (sugar or bauxite) whose value embodies a quantity of accumulated labor, but the labor itself, to be incorporated in a product or service. The importing class determines the value and imposes the conditions of that labor. The imported reserve accepts the value offered and the conditions under which it is offered, since the threat of unemployment or deportation is less acceptable than the offer of poorly paid work. Under traditional dependency, the exporter of sugar accepts the established world market price of 5¢ a pound because this low price, although less than the cost of production, is preferable to being left with the entire harvest unsold.

It is necessary to mention here a less obvious function of emigration abroad: the remittance of convertible foreign exchange highly beneficial to the economy. Between 1978 and 1983 these remittances from Dominicans in the United States totaled $1,074 million. In 1983, remittances approached $200 million, which was more than the foreign exchange obtained in the export of all agricultural products with the exception of sugar.[30] These remittances from Dominicans abroad are changed in the Exchange Houses of the parallel market, and the dollars exchanged are used to buy necessary imports for the substitution in-dustry.[31] In this way, migratory labor becomes a strategic element in the cycle of traditional dependency based on the export and import of goods. Confronted with a negative balance of trade, the dependent country sends part of its work force to the industrial centers and uses the remittances of those workers to help pay the elevated cost of imports. Under traditional dependency, cheap labor is exported in the product or in raw materials produced at low cost; under migratory dependency, cheap labor is exported in the migrant worker himself. The industrial country exploits the productive capacity of the immigrant without providing him, particularly if he is an illegal alien, with the benefits usually granted to its own workers.

The third illustration of migratory dependency is that of Haitian immigration to the Dominican Republic.[32] Migratory dependency exports Dominicans to the United States and imports Haitians into the Dominican Republic to work the sugar harvest. In a seeming paradox, a country which exports cheap manual labor and has more than 350,000 unemployed imports about 30,000 workers a year for the sugar harvest. Around 15,000 Haitians are officially recruited by state enterprises; the other half are the "undocumented" who cross the border looking for work and better living conditions. It is estimated that of those 30,000 annual immigrants, more than half remain in the country every year. A Dominican economist estimates that around 230,000 Haitians emigrated to Dominican territory between 1967 and 1981.[33] Undoubtedly, this population increase tends to aggravate the country's demographic and occupational problems and begins to have repercussions in its cultural and political life.

This double migratory process can be attributed to the backward technology and inefficiency in the agricultural phase of Dominican sugar production. The Dominican sugar industry absorbs about 60 percent of the work force in the industrial sector. The production cycle utilizes less than half of this work force during the "dead season." In 1977, the State Sugar Council (CEA) employed some 50,000 workers during the harvest, but gave employment to only 20,000 during the dead season.

Some 90 percent of the workers in the agricultural phase of sugar production are Haitians who have displaced Dominican workers.[34] The reason for this displacement lies in the salary structure of the sugar industry, which does nothing about mechanization since it can count on having a reserve of unemployed that far outstrips its productive capacity. Agricultural jobs are paid by contract or by piecework, and according to production. For cutting and gathering, the worker earns 2.50 pesos a day or 65 pesos a month. For weeding, the worker earns between .90 centavos and 1.50 pesos a day. That rate is clearly below the subsistence level. These are salaries paid in 1980, when the price of sugar experienced a relative "boom" of 28¢ per pound; in 1982 the price fell to 8¢ per pound and in 1984 to less than 5¢ per pound. It is not strange that the Dominican peasant prefers to emigrate from the countryside to the cities, and from there to New York or Miami.[35]

Salaries are better in other agricultural sectors such as rice and coffee, where a day's wage can be 4.00 pesos. Many Haitians who stay in the country after the sugar harvest have begun to invade these sectors and to displace Dominican workers. Plantation owners sometimes prefer to contract Haitians since, being "undocumented," the Haitian workers accept lower salaries and do not belong to trade unions or peasant leagues.[36] A recent survey indicates that farm owners consider Haitian manual labor indispensable and are opposed to any change in legislation that would try to limit its use in agriculture.

Financial Dependency

The last modality I want to consider is that of financial dependency. This new form of economic dependency is derived, in part, from traditional dependency based on the asymmetrical exchange between the developing countries and the industrial core. As we have already seen, the dependent countries have accumulated, over the years, a deficit in the balance of trade of goods and services that results in a negative balance of current accounts. In the past, large injections of foreign capital (in the various forms of investments or short- or long-term loans) solved the deficit in the balance of the current account for the time being, but began to increase the foreign debt. With the implementation of austerity policies in Latin America, which drastically limited salaries and imports while maintaining the value of exports, the region in general succeeded in reversing the commercial balance, from a deficit of $1,601 million in 1981 to a surplus of $31,170 million in 1983. This gain—spectacular in the history of Latin

America—was hardly sufficient to pay the $34 billion in interest, repayments, and repatriation of capital to foreign creditors. Taking into account the fact that the net capital inflow for the whole region in 1983 amounted to a little more than $4.4 billion, we find that in 1983 Latin America transferred a sum of $29.5 billion in real resources to the industrialized countries, an increase of 42 percent over the amount transferred in 1982. Even CEPAL, in its neutral and moderate tone, criticized this transfer of resources as "a perverse situation."[37]

It was estimated that the external debt of Latin America amounted to $310 billion in 1983, and that the service charges on the debt already amounted to 35 percent of the region's total income from exports of goods and services. There is no doubt that the large countries of the continent carry the bulk of the debt. The foreign debt of Mexico, Venezuela, Argentina, Brazil, and Chile amounts to $257 billion. What we have to realize, nevertheless, is that those are precisely the countries that had a positive trade balance. In reality, the trade balance of those five countries is greater than the balance of the entire region ($32.73 billion against $31.17 billion), since many of the poor, small countries had a negative balance. All of the countries of the Caribbean, with the exception of Trinidad and Tobago, had a negative balance of trade.

I believe that financial dependency is the modality that has most deeply affected the large developing countries. For reasons of distance, physical size, natural resources, these countries have felt the impact of other forms of traditional dependency less than the Caribbean countries. However, I will limit my comments here to the impact of financial dependency on the Caribbean countries, rather than on the other countries of the hemisphere that I have called "big" or "rich."

Most commonly, Latin American countries make use of their surplus earnings in the balance of trade to pay various charges and services on their foreign debt. When there is a negative balance of trade, a country must obtain new loans, renegotiate the terms of its debt, and possibly make use of some of its own international reserves. In 1983, this was the case in all the Caribbean countries, since all (with the exception of Trinidad and Tobago) had a negative commercial balance, and had to renegotiate for new loans and credits on various terms, and make use of their meager international reserves. Such solutions to the economic and political crisis affecting the small countries are only temporary in nature, since the increase in the foreign debt will impose new financial obligations that cannot be met by countries that have exhausted their internal markets and cannot expand their foreign trade.

In the case of the Dominican Republic, the total external debt has been growing to the point that in 1983 it represented about 30 percent of the GNP. At the same time, the service charge on the external debt has come to represent a value equivalent to 50–60 percent of the total exports of goods and services, including earnings from tourism. Since the foreign exchange obtained by exports was insufficient to cover the cost of importing food, petroleum, and other raw materials necessary for industry and manufacturing, the country had no other solution but to renegotiate the debt, obtain new loans, and use its own reserves. The external debt grew about 30 percent between 1982 and 1983.

The Balaguer government (1966–1978), in order to implement its development policy, increased the external debt from $100 million in 1966 to $1,346.6 million in 1978.[38] As already indicated, the policy of internally oriented development following the model of import substitution produced mixed results for the economy. By 1978 this policy was already being replaced by a new policy that represented a return to traditional agroindustrial exports. The social-democratic PRD government of Antonio Guzmán assumed power with popular support and promised to curb the escalation of the foreign debt; in 1982, at the end of his administration, the external debt had increased by almost 50 percent. The government of Salvador Jorge Blanco renegotiated part of the debt and secured new commercial bank loans and new credits from the IMF; these measures produced an increase in the debt of 32 percent in 1983.

In 1984 President Blanco entered into new negotiations with the IMF, which called for measures to restrict the import of consumer goods, freeze salaries, devalue the currency, and limit government expenditure. Although Blanco refused to accept all of these conditions, his attempt to implement some of them was met by street demonstrations and riots that left more than fifty dead.[39]

It is possible that the conditions imposed by the IMF for extending credits could produce a lower deficit in the current account balance. It is my opinion that the conditions of the IMF have less applicability in the Dominican Republic (and other countries of the Caribbean) than in Brazil, Mexico, or Argentina. First of all, the Dominican Republic cannot, at this time, appreciably increase the volume or value of its exports. The value of exports has been falling since 1981. With the price of sugar around 5¢ a pound, it can be expected that the value of exports will fall still further in the future. As for imports, we also saw that after a reduction of 13.4 percent in 1982 there was an increase of 3.3 percent in 1983, which above all reflected increased imports of oil and food, since the imports of capital goods and "intermediate goods" for manufacturing decreased. The decline in imports of materials for manufacturing and in capital goods is particularly noteworthy, since these are precisely the areas where productivity and industrial development should be stimulated.

As for other austerity measures exacted by the IMF, we must realize that during the last fifteen years the Dominican Republic has had a policy of freezing salaries and decontrolling prices. Over the years, this has created a considerable erosion of the purchasing power of the peso. Using the 1969 purchasing power of the peso as a base, a Dominican economist estimates that the value of the peso was reduced to 0.30 centavos in 1980. Therefore, we can understand that the recommendations of the IMF are not realistic when applied to a country where 24 percent of the work force is unemployed and another 30 percent is underemployed, and where the minimum wage remains between 65 and 95 pesos a month.

The weight of the austerity measures demanded by the IMF could also fall on the emerging industrial bourgeoisie, which already feels overly burdened by taxes and excise duties. The IMF has demanded greater control of the fiscal structure and government expenditure. This also seems to put the burden of austerity on the entrepreneurial class and the state bureaucracy. At the same time, the government has begun to eliminate the import privileges previously granted to the import substitution industries. All of these measures would tend to put part of the burden of the austerity program on the still-small national bourgeoisie, which prospered under the Balaguer government. It is doubtful that the social-democratic government of Jorge Blanco would want to have a confrontation with this bourgeoisie, from which it has elicited support up to the present.[40]

Financial dependency affects poor countries with a negative commercial balance in a special way, since despite their austerity policies they are unable to meet service charges on the debt without obtaining new concessions and loans. Such renegotiations sometimes do not bring new capital into the country but rather capitalize the overdue repayments and interest on new terms and at new interest rates higher than the original ones. Thus, in 1983, the Dominican Republic renegotiated (among others) loans for $565 million with private banks; 82 percent of these consisted of short-term loans at interest rates 2.125 percent above the prime, with an origination fee of 1.25 percent at a time.[41] It is evident that this type of renegotiation postpones the crisis for a short time, but increases its seriousness in the immediate future.[42]

In 1983 the Dominican Republic had a negative balance of the current account of $454 million, even though tourism brought $249 million to the country and emigrant Dominicans sent remittances of about $200 million. With the loans obtained in 1983 to cover the debt service charge and other obligations, the country ended with a favorable balance of $276 million in its capital account, which it used to pay for part of the deficit in the balance of the current account. The country thereby ended 1983 with a negative global balance of $178 million, which it had to renegotiate with the IMF or cover with its own reserves.

CONCLUSION

This chapter has discussed some factors that contribute to the serious economic crisis presently affecting the small and poor countries of the Caribbean. My analysis of the current situation suggests that the present world financial crisis impinges on the Caribbean countries in a special way, because of their lack of natural resources and because of limitations to development imposed by their small size and scarce resources. Using a theoretical paradigm of dependency, the essay explores the scope and the depth of the crisis in the Caribbean. The paper suggests that classical dependency, with its two modalities of traditional import-export trade and of import substitution, should be distinguished from modern dependency. Three different modalities of modern dependency are discussed: tourist, migratory, and financial. The article does not attempt to demonstrate that these three modalities of modern dependency are substitutes for the traditional ones. Rather, the article seeks to show that tourism, migration and foreign indebtedness represent new modalities of the asymmetric economic relations that bind the developing countries to the industrial core. It suggests that these new modalities of dependency coexist with the traditional modalities of the past, and that in the future they could gain primacy over more traditional forms of dependency and become the structural links of dependency that bind the less-developed countries to the industrial core.

Translation by Jerry Dekker.

NOTES

An earlier version of this chapter was presented at the Ninth Conference on the Political Economy of the World System held at Tulane University, New Orleans, March 28–30, 1985. Detailed statistical tables to accompany this chapter, omitted for editorial reasons, are available from the author.

1. CIES, "Problems of Small States: The English-Speaking Caribbean Countries and the Role of Inter-American Cooperation," OEA/Ser. H/X 39, Washington, D.C., 1981.

2. CEPAL, *Preliminary Balance of the Latin American Economy* in 1983, ECLA Information Service, No. 387/388, January 1984. Consejo Económico y Social, *Notas para el estudio económico de América Latina, 1983: República Dominicana*, May 1984; CEPAL, *Notas para el Estudio Económico de América Latina 1983: Haití*; April 1984; CEPAL, *Estudio Económico de América Latina 1982: Cuba*, November 1983. Other documents consulted were: CEPAL, *Economic Survey of Latin America*, 1980; CEPAL, *Statistical Yearbook for Latin America, 1980*, Santiago, 1982; Centro de Estudios Monetarios Latinoamericanos, *Boletín*, Vol. XXIX, No. 3, suplemento, May–June 1983; *International Financial Statistics: Yearbook 1980*; International Monetary Fund; *World Development Report 1983*; Inter-American Development Bank (IADB), *Progreso Económico y Social en América Latina: Informe 1983*; IADB, *Economic and Social Progress in Latin America, 1985*, Washington D.C., 1986; World Bank, *World Debt Tables: External Debt in Developing Countries*.

3. See, for example, Paget Henry and Carl Stone, *The Newer Caribbean* (Philadelphia: ISHI Publications, 1983).

4. George C. Beckford, ed., *Caribbean Economy: Dependence and Backwardness* (Kingston, Jamaica: Institute of Social and Economic Research, 1975).

5. Theotonio dos Santos, "The Structure of Dependence," *American Economic Review* 60, 1970, pp. 231–36. See also, R. H. Chilcote and J. C. Edelstein, eds., *Latin America: the Struggle with Dependency and Beyond* (New York: Wiley, 1974); Frank Bonilla and R. Girling, eds., *Structures of Dependency* (Stanford: Institute of Political Studies, 1973).

6. William LeoGrande, "Cuban Dependency: A Comparison of Prerevolutionary and Postrevolutionary International Economic Relations," *Cuban Studies/Estudios Cubanos* 9(2).

7. William LeoGrande argues convincingly that although Cuba continues to depend on sugar production, its dependency on the Soviet Union is significantly less than its dependency on the U.S. before the revolution. For a different point of view, see Carmelo Mesa-Lago, *La economía en Cuba socialista* (Madrid: Editorial Playor, 1983), pp. 117–62.

8. CEPAL, *Notas para el estudio de América Latina, 1983: República Dominicana*, p. 14.

9. CEPAL, *Preliminary Balance of the Latin American Economy in 1983* (Santiago, Chile, 1984), p. 1.

10. José A. Moreno, "Intervention and Economic Penetration: The Case of the Dominican Republic," *Summation* 5(1–2).

11. To situate the Balaguer governments in recent Dominican history: the Dominican Republic was run by the Trujillo dictatorship from 1930 to 1961. In 1961, Trujillo's assassination was arranged by the CIA, to prevent "another Cuba" in the Dominican Republic and to assure a stable, pro-U.S. government there. The 1962 election was won by Juan Bosch of the social-democratic Partido Revolucionario Dominicano (PRD), but he was in office less than a year before being ousted by a 1963 military coup. Two years of right-wing military rule were disrupted by the 1965 popular uprising aimed at restoring constitutional rule and returning Bosch to power. The uprising had all but succeeded when it was stopped by the intervention of 22,000 U.S. marines. In the wake of the U.S. invasion, the 1966 election (held while the island was still occupied by U.S. marines) brought to power Joaquín Balaguer, who had been in Trujillo's cabinet, and in fact had been legally president when Trujillo was assassinated. Balaguer was elected three times, in 1966, 1970, and 1974. The 1978 and 1982 elections brought in the PRD governments of Antonio Guzmán and Salvador Jorge Blanco, which faced the most massive economic crises in the country's history. In 1986, Balaguer, seventy-eight years old and blind, defeated the PRD and Bosch (this time running against each other) to become, once again, head of the Dominican government.

12. CEPAL, *Economic Survey of Latin America, 1980* (Santiago, Chile, 1982).

13. Lucas Vicens, *Crisis económica: 1978–1982* (Santo Domingo, República Dominicana: Editorial Alfa y Omega, 1982), p. 339.

14. Ibid., p. 320–28.

15. Vicens cites a poll on the cost of living in Santo Domingo, published by *El Nuevo Diario* on June 5, 1981, according to which 65 percent of the families polled earned incomes of less than 200 pesos a month. Ibid., p. 322.

16. Ibid., p. 139.

17. CEPAL, *Notas: República Dominicana 1983*, pp. 28–29.

18. *Granma Weekly Review*, "When the Mafia tried to make Cuba a Caribbean Monte Carlo," July 15, 1984.

19. C. Wright Mills, *Listen Yankee, The Revolution in Cuba* (New York: McGraw-Hill, 1960).

20. Vincent A. Richards, "Decolonization in Antigua: Its Impact on Agriculture and Tourism," in P. Henry and C. Stone, eds., *The Newer Caribbean* (Philadelphia: ISHI Publications, 1983), pp. 15–39.

21. CEPAL, *Notas: República Dominicana, 1983*, p. 33.

22. Organización de Estados Americanos, *El Desarrollo del Turismo en República Dominicana*, Serie de Informes y Estadísticas, no. 14, Washington D.C., 1974.

23. The *Notas* of CEPAL indicates that due to the recession in the United States, the number of tourists arriving in the Dominican Republic on cruise ships fell by 35 percent in the period 1981–83.

24. CEPAL, *Notas: República Dominicana, 1983*, p. 35.

25. Alejandro Portes, "Migration and Underdevelopment," *Politics and Society* 8(1)(48), 1978.

26. Alejandro Portes, "Toward a Structural Analysis of Illegal (Undocumented) Immigrations," *International Migration Review* 12(4): 469–84. Portes briefly discusses the double immigration, i.e., industry which emigrates in search of cheap labor and the worker who emigrates in search of work. Portes also points out how the immigrant weakens the established bargaining capacity of workers in the industrialized countries.

27. *The New York Times* has published several special supplements with paid advertisements by Gulf & Western and other companies aimed at attracting new industry to the Dominican Republic. In these ads it is emphasized that the companies which set themselves up in the "free zones" enjoy tax exemption for ten years and that workers' salaries are $2.00 a day (sic). See *The New York Times*, Oct. 3, 1971, Section 14, and Jan. 28, 1973, Section 11.

28. Roy Simon Bryce-Laporte, "New York City and the Caribbean Immigration: A Contextual Statement." *International Migration Review* 13(2):214–34. See also Vivian Garrison, "Dominican Family Network and U.S. Immigration Policy: A Case Study," *International Migration Review* 13(2): 264–83.

29. Portes, "Toward a Structural Analysis," p. 474.

30. CEPAL, *Notas: República Dominicana*, pp. 29 and 35.

31. Patricia R. Passar, "The Role of Households in International Migration from the Dominican Republic," *International Migration Review* 16(2): 342–64.

32. See ONAPLAN (National Planning Office), "Participación de la mano de obra haitiana en el mercado laboral: el caso de la caña y el café" (Santo Domingo: ONAPLAN, 1980).

33. Vicens, pp. 310–14.

34. Sherri Grasmueck, "Migration Within the Periphery: Haitian Labor in the Dominican Sugar and Coffee Industries," *International Migration Review* 16(2): 365–77.

35. Antonio Ugalde et al., "International Migration from the Dominican Republic: Findings from a National Survey," *International Migration Review* 13(2): 235–54.

36. Vicens, p. 314.

37. CEPAL, *Preliminary Balance*, p. 9. Fidel Castro, discussing the transfer of capital from the Third World to the industrialized countries, characterizes it as "an irrational, nonviable expression of an obsolete international economic system." See Fidel Castro, *The World Economic and Social Crisis* (Havana: Publishing Office of the Council of State, 1983), p. 37.

38. Vicens, p. 250.

39. *The New York Times* April 30 and May 1, 1984. Juan Bosch estimates the number of deaths during the crisis at more than 100. See D. de Pérez, "Entrevista a Juan Bosch," *Areito* 10(38):14–15.

40. Before this chapter went to press, elections were held in the Dominican Republic, and Joaquín Balaguer was again elected president. The result of this election could be interpreted as a rejection of Jorge Blanco's policies by both the small bourgeoisie and the popular masses upon which the PRD had relied for support in the past.

41. CEPAL, *Notas: República Dominicana*, p. 38. According to information from the *World Development Report*, 1983, published by the World Bank, the international reserves of the Dominican Republic in 1981 were $282 million.

42. On monetary aspects of the crisis, see Andres S. Dauhaire, "The Dominican Republic: Eighteen Years of Economic Policy," in A. Jorge, J. Salazar Carillo, and F. Díaz-Pou, eds., *External Debt and Development Strategy in Latin America* (New York: Pergamon Press, 1985), pp. 129–43.

INDEX

CONTRIBUTORS

MAX AZICRI is professor of political science at Edinboro University of Pennsylvania. He has written numerous studies on contemporary Cuba. His book, *Cuba: Politics, Economics, and Society*, was recently published in England and the United States.

REGINO DÍAZ, as editor of the Mexican daily newspaper *Excelsior*, interviewed Fidel Castro in March 1985.

EDUARDO GALEANO, a writer and editor of various weekly and daily publications in his native country, including the internationally known weekly, *Marcha*, was exiled from Uruguay in 1973. He spent the next twelve years in Argentina and Spain, where he wrote prolifically and on two occasions won the "Casa de las Americas" prize. A number of his books have been published in English and are widely known in the United States, including *The Open Veins of Latin America* and the *Memory of Fire* trilogy. He currently lives in Uruguay, where he edits the weekly, *Brecha*.

PABLO GONZÁLEZ CASANOVA is the former rector of the Universidad Nacional Autónoma de México (UNAM) and one of Latin America's most eminent sociologists. He is currently at the Instituto de Investigaciones Sociales of UNAM. In recent years he has written extensively about Mexico and Central America, as well as about broader theoretical issues concerning democracy and power in Latin America.

SUSANNE JONAS teaches Latin American studies at the University of California at Santa Cruz and is on the research staff of Global Options in San Francisco. She has written extensively on Central America for twenty years and is currently working on a new book on Guatemala, as well as analytical articles concerning recent developments in Central America.

JOSÉ A. MORENO is a professor of sociology at the University of Pittsburgh. He has done extensive research in Latin America, focusing in particular on political movements and development in the Caribbean. Among his writings are two previous books on the Dominican Republic: *Sociological Aspects of the Dominican Revolution* and *Barrios in Arms: Revolution in Santo Domingo*.

JAMES PETRAS is professor of sociology at the State University of New York, Binghamton. He is among the best-known and most influential progressive North American writers on Latin America and international affairs. His most recent book is *Latin America: Bankers, Generals, and the Struggle for Social Justice*.

GÉRARD PIERRE-CHARLES is a Haitian social scientist, specializing in the Caribbean; he has taught at the Instituto de Investigaciones Sociales at the Universidad Nacional Autónoma de México (UNAM). Among his numerous books are two on Haiti, one on the Cuban Revolution, and two on the contemporary situation in the Caribbean. Having lived for years in exile in Mexico, Dr. Pierre-Charles was able to return to Haiti in the spring of 1986, following the overthrow of Duvalier.

NANCY STEIN has researched and written extensively on U.S. policy toward Latin America for twenty years, with a focus on Central America and U.S. military policy. She is a former president and current board member of Global Options, a San Francisco-based research and education organization.

EDELBERTO TORRES-RIVAS, a Guatemalan, is secretary-general of the Facultad Latinoamericana de Ciencias Sociales (FLACSO) in Costa Rica. He is one of the leading social scientists of Central America, having written numerous books and articles on a wide variety of topics regarding Central America. A collection of his essays, in English, is published under the title *Repression and Resistance: The Struggle for Democracy in Central America*.